PRAISE FOR *WALK IN MY SHOES*:

"A motivating history and personal story about family, courage, and faith. *Walk in My Shoes* is filled with the wisdom, insight, and candor only experience could harness."
—*Newt Gingrich, former Speaker of the House*

"This book reaffirms what all of Andrew Young's friends and colleagues have always known. Andy is a preacher. Every story, episode, illustration is in fact a sermon. And every reader will be instructed and inspired by Andy's wisdom and experience."
—*Vernon E. Jordan Jr., senior managing director of Lazard*

"Andrew Young witnessed the depths of modern times—he saw us at our very worst, and yet he has written an intensely personal love letter to America. This is a love story—love of country—it's also a story about loss and regret, good and evil. Andrew Young was present at the creation of the movement that changed our country forever."
—*Brian Williams, anchor and managing editor,*
NBC Nightly News with Brian Williams

"Andrew Young and Kabir Sehgal have produced a valuable book, one that offers timeless lessons of faith, love, and leadership. The book illuminates the civil rights revolution of the 1960s and calls upon its readers—each in our own way—to carry on the work of building a more perfect America with courage and vision and humility."
—*Senator Joe Lieberman*

"Working with Ambassador Young has taught me that we share more similarities than differences between our generations. The conversations with his godson should remind us how important it is to combine what we have in common with our unique perspectives in order to change the community and the world."
—*Clifford "T.I." Harris Jr., entertainer and actor*

"This is a great gift to America's children—now and in the future. Andy Young has perfect pitch when it comes to telling the great story of a civil rights crusade that is a hymn to courage, nonviolence, and rule of law. He was there, every step of the way, and his reflections are deeply personal and historic. I am personally grateful for this important work."
—*Tom Brokaw*

"Ambassador Young wears many hats, and in this book he takes on the role of godfather speaking to his godson. As I read it I can picture many of the conversations he and I had on the many trips I've taken with him to Africa. And having just an opportunity to walk with him on the continent of Africa showed me a different Africa and a different Andrew Young. For that I am eternally grateful. He is my friend, he is the world's friend and I hope that every emerging leader picks up this book as a reference for what it takes to change the world."
—*Chris Tucker, actor, comedian, and activist*

"Engaging, raw, and impactful, this book should be a required reading for us all. Ambassador Young imparts wisdom on his God son with an organic humor and sensibility that can make you laugh and cry at the same time."
—*Jamie Foxx, Oscar-winning actor and Grammy-winning performer*

WALK IN MY SHOES

CONVERSATIONS BETWEEN A CIVIL RIGHTS LEGEND AND HIS GODSON ON THE JOURNEY AHEAD

ANDREW YOUNG AND KABIR SEHGAL

palgrave
macmillan

First published in hardcover in 2010 by PALGRAVE MACMILLAN® in the
US—a division of St. Martin's Press LLC, 175 Fifth Avenue, New York, NY
10010.

Where this book is distributed in the UK, Europe and the rest of the world,
this is by Palgrave Macmillan, a division of Macmillan Publishers Limited,
registered in England, company number 785998, of Houndmills,
Basingstoke, Hampshire RG21 6XS.

Palgrave Macmillan is the global academic imprint of the above companies
and has companies and representatives throughout the world.

Palgrave® and Macmillan® are registered trademarks in the United States,
the United Kingdom, Europe and other countries.

ISBN: 978-0-230-11429-6

Library of Congress Cataloging-in-Publication Data
Young, Andrew, 1932–
    Walk in my shoes : conversations between a civil rights legend and his
godson on the journey ahead / Andrew Young and Kabir Sehgal.
        p.   cm.
    ISBN 978-0-230-62360-6 (hardback)
    (paperback ISBN 978-0-230-11429-6)
    1. Young, Andrew, 1932——Interviews.   2. African American civil rights
workers—Interviews.   3. Young, Andrew, 1932——Political and social views.
4. African Americans—Civil rights.   5. United States—Race relations.
6. Racism—United States.   7. African Americans—Conduct of life.
8. Conduct of life.   I. Sehgal, Kabir.   II. Title.
E840.8.Y64A3   2010
323.092—dc22

                                                                    2010000242

A catalogue record of the book is available from the British Library.

Design by Letra Libre, Inc.

First PALGRAVE MACMILLAN paperback edition: December 2011.

10 9 8 7 6 5 4 3 2 1

Printed in the United States of America.

FOR
UNCLE ANDY'S GRANDCHILDREN,
TAYLOR MARIE, KEMET, LENA, CALEB,
JOSHUA, NOAH AND ABIGAIL

FOR
MY TEACHER, FRIEND AND MOTHER,
SURISHTHA GILL SEHGAL

"FOR WHOEVER DESIRES TO SAVE HIS LIFE WILL LOSE IT, BUT WHOEVER LOSES HIS LIFE FOR MY SAKE WILL FIND IT. FOR WHAT PROFIT IS IT TO A MAN IF HE GAINS THE WHOLE WORLD, AND LOSES HIS OWN SOUL? OR WHAT WILL A MAN GIVE IN EXCHANGE FOR HIS SOUL? FOR THE SON OF MAN WILL COME IN THE GLORY OF HIS FATHER WITH HIS ANGELS, AND THEN HE WILL REWARD EACH ACCORDING TO HIS WORKS."
—MATTHEW 16:25–27

"A GENIUS IS THE ONE MOST LIKE HIMSELF."
—THELONIOUS MONK

"THERE CAN BE NO DEMOCRACY WITHOUT TRUTH. THERE CAN BE NO TRUTH WITHOUT CONTROVERSY, AND THERE CAN BE NO CHANGE WITHOUT FREEDOM. AND WITHOUT FREEDOM, THERE CAN BE NO PROGRESS."
—ANDREW YOUNG, *A WAY OUT OF NO WAY*

CONTENTS

SECTION III
LEADERSHIP

FOREWORD

BY PRESIDENT BILL CLINTON

The people of America owe a great debt to Andrew Young. For nearly half a century, this remarkable man has been a fixture in our nation's political life. Whether as an activist or public servant, teacher or preacher, he has dedicated his life to strengthening our human community, through equality and economic opportunity, justice and social progress.

Beginning with his days as a leader in the civil rights movement in the 1960s, Young has always made an impact. As a congressman from Georgia, he was an advocate for the poor and underserved populations. In the 1980s, as our Ambassador to the United Nations, he helped to shape both U.S. foreign policy and U.N. consensus for greater emphasis on economic empowerment in developing nations around the globe. Later, through his leadership as Atlanta's mayor, Andy advanced interracial cooperation to improve education and increase prosperity, to encourage Atlanta's growing diversity and make it the headquarters for many international companies, and to pave the way for the next generation of African American leaders. For almost twenty years now, as a private citizen, he has continued to advance all the causes he championed as a public servant, bringing to a wide variety of endeavors the passion and energy of a man half his age.

One of Andrew Young's most meaningful contributions is the power of his example to young people, because of the nobility of his ideals, the strength of his convictions, and the determination and effectiveness with which he has acted on them. As a mentor and professor, he demonstrates the relationship of education and guidance to success, changing the lives of many young people.

I've known Andrew Young for more than thirty years, though he was a hero to me before we met because of his civil rights work. We have been friends for more than twenty-five years now; and knowing him has been a real blessing. Andy's life is a model for responsible and successful service, and future leaders can learn much from his example. Through *Walk in My Shoes,* Andrew Young and Kabir Sehgal offer a unique perspective on Andy's amazing life. This book is also the story of a very good mentorship, and all readers can benefit from the lessons Young has shared with his mentee and godson, Kabir.

INTRODUCTION

"Don't open it until you are back home and alone." Uncle Andy pushed the envelope into my hands and grinned. I tried to feel through the envelope. "Too thin to be a wad of money," I thought to myself. "Maybe it's a traveler's check." I folded the envelope and put it in the empty part of my wallet, the part meant for cash. "Thank you," I said to him, not knowing what I was thanking him for.

It was an oppressively muggy June day in 2005 in Hanover, New Hampshire. It was the day the Lord and my father's bank account had made happen. My family and my godfather Andrew Young and his radiant wife, Carolyn, made the trek from Atlanta to join me on my college graduation day. I don't remember much about my graduation, but I remember Andy received an honorary degree and spoke at the baccalaureate service. I remember Tom Brokaw was our commencement speaker. I also remember Uncle Andy dozing off while on the dais during the speech. I teased him afterward. "I was tired, and Tom gave the same speech at the last commencement address we were both at," he laughed. "When you get past seventy with my schedule, you might doze on anyone."

"Didn't I tell you to check your pockets before you put your pants in the hamper?" my mom said a week later, at home in Atlanta. I dashed to collect my wallet. I didn't know what was in it and didn't want her to look. I went to my room and opened it. I had forgotten about Andy's envelope. Inside was a letter. "You have a wonderful life ahead of you, but it is a marathon not a sprint. . . . Don't burn out. Don't be anxious or even ambitious. You have all the talent, energy and vision that the world needs. There's time to truly relax and enjoy each phase of your life and let 'life' lead you." I'll always remember what he wrote at the end of the letter: "Persons as brilliant and energetic as you will always generate envy, jealousy and other challenges. You relate well to people. Help them to share the credit." It was better than money.

Andrew Young, or Andy as his friends call him, is a profoundly intellectual, curious and contrarian thinker, who has witnessed history firsthand. When Dr. Martin Luther King Jr. marched in the Deep South, Andy was at his side. When intense negotiations among member states occurred at the United Nations concerning peace in the Middle East in 1979, he was deeply involved. When a group of Atlanta residents wanted to host the 1996 Centennial Olympic Games, Andy encouraged and led them. An ordained minister, top friend and aide to Dr. King, executive director of the Southern Christian Leadership Conference, congressman, ambassador to the United Nations, mayor of Atlanta, and cochairman of the Olympic Games in Atlanta—he hasn't just witnessed history, he's made much of his own. He has held many titles, and I am blessed to call him my godfather and mentor.

My father, R.K. Sehgal, and Andy were introduced in 1978 by the Indian ambassador to the United Nations, Rikhi Jaipal, while Andy was the United States ambassador to the United Nations. Jaipal took an early interest in the civil rights activist-turned-diplomat because of their mutual interest in the teachings of Mahatma Gandhi. Jaipal understood the importance of mentorship, so he took Andy under his wing and helped him garner allies at the UN. Jaipal had served at the UN for many years and was always willing to answer Andy's questions. He took Andy aside when he felt the well-known US ambassador needed guidance. Like Dr. King, Jaipal helped Andy to realize the importance and value of mentors in a young person's life. After he resigned under pressure from the UN because of his controversial meeting with a representative of the Palestinian Liberation Organization, he ran for mayor of Atlanta and won.

I first met Andy when I was a five-year-old boy and he was still mayor. In fact, in second grade I interviewed him for my elementary school newspaper. After his second term as mayor of Atlanta, my father hired Andy to work at Law Companies, a fast-growing engineering firm with offices around the world that had its headquarters in Atlanta. My father likes to tell the story that Andy once came into his office distraught that he couldn't make significant money for the company. His skill, my father realized, was not in sales but in the currency of inspiration. Andy would become the conscience of the company. He became its vice chairman and traveled to distant lands like Mauritius and Uzbekistan to build relationships with government officials and inspire employees.

Our families grew very close. We traveled together on family trips. One of my fondest memories is of me as a peach-fuzzed youth walking down a trail with Uncle Andy toward Victoria Falls in Zimbabwe. In Atlanta, his son Bo and I shot hoops in my driveway. He is a few years older than I am and usually won our scrimmages because of his height advantage. Bo turned to my father for advice and counsel. I turned to Uncle Andy.

My most treasured memories of Uncle Andy are of our talks on lazy, southern Sunday afternoons in Atlanta. When I was a teenager, I visited his house to give him computer lessons. I was your typical geeky Indian American computer jock. Andy, of course, thought I was a whiz kid because I could open his CD drive. An avid photographer, he wanted to print photos, and he often called me to change the printer toner or reconnect a wire. It was always a convenient excuse and a magnificent opportunity for me to learn from him and spend time with him. I would spend eleven minutes fixing his ThinkPad laptop and two hours discussing with him the readings of Walter Russell Mead, Kahlil Gibran, Thomas Friedman, Reinhold Niebuhr and Deepak Chopra, and municipal financing, welfare reform and the deaths of his first wife and my grandfather, among other things. Heavy stuff. I asked questions. He answered. Our conversations continued through my college years and to this day.

I am very aware of Andy's contribution to America and my unusual proximity to this living legend. Andy, I believe, is responsible for many things that have impacted our society—many of which historians may never know. He admits as much, calling himself a "behind-the-scene catalyst." His conversations with Dr. King helped to influence the strategy and tactics of the boycotts and marches in the 1960s. His intense lobbying of the International Olympic Committee helped to inspire and glamorize a once-sleepy southern town. Uncle Andy has always urged me to act behind the scenes. One should evaluate the merit of an idea, not the ownership of it: "You can get anything you want done, as long as you give others credit." A mentor of Dr. King and Andy and the first African American to win the Nobel Peace Prize, Ralph Bunche told Dr. King and Andy that they were taking on too much (civil rights, the Vietnam War and poverty), were too public about their activities and should acquire the shield of silence.

I wanted to transcribe my lessons with Uncle Andy because his wisdom has always served as a compass for me. Some of these lessons, I suspect, I have yet to realize. Like when rereading Ralph Waldo Emerson or Henry David Thoreau, I think I'll learn more from our conversations when I return to them years from now. He is and always will be a shaping influence on my life.

These conversations were also a way for Andy to formalize his thoughts and meditations, to inspire and provoke discussion for the next generation. "My fire might be dwindling, but before it's out, I wanted to get my thoughts out. I have found in dealing with younger Americans like you, the last thing that you want to hear is the conventional wisdom and the status quo viewpoints. You seek new insights and ideas, and I have always tried to oblige you by sharing my ideas. I want to provoke you to have an active mind and to think for yourself."

"It sounds like you want to teach us how to change the world with these new insights," I commented to him.

"I don't believe that the world changes, nor do people," he replied. "But they grow toward that which they believe in the deepest recesses of their hearts and minds. It is my hope that I will stir those growth enzymes in you so that you and your generation can avoid some of my mistakes and see beyond our hopes to new possibilities toward which you may help the planet and its people grow."

This book was created over many years, yet while we traded notes and recorded our telephone conversations, it didn't occur to us that our communications would one day be turned into a book. Our exchanges were raw and unedited, what he likes to call "no bullshit." When I gathered all of our transcripts, I asked him whether he wanted to strip the many expletives in this book as parishioners might shy away from such language. He pointed out that Jesus was a young minister who didn't speak in Hebrew and certainly not King James English, but the "street language of Aramaic." He then responded, "No, keep it. The churches I speak at won't mind. They value honesty and authenticity." And so we kept the expletives.

Andy is as honest as a mirror. "Obama has not been tested enough to become president. And I fear he won't survive the election. Too may crazies out there, not to mention the character assassination he will face." In one of our many dustups on Gandhi, he referred to the patron saint of India as "an arrogant prick who was overcome with piety" because of Gandhi's call for renunciation of material things. He pulled no punches. He named names. He offered a blunt and authentic diagnosis of the world. I pushed back where I could, questioning his bald assertions, but I mostly listened to this wise man. "This book should be a natural outgrowth of an organic conversation between godfather and godson. Hell, I've known you for twenty years. I've seen you grow up. Got to be honest with each other." If some of the conversations and vocabulary make you uncomfortable, I understand. I was uncomfortable and confused at times too. Uncle Andy likes to push me out of my comfort zone.

Our conversations are actually a continuation of a promise Andy made to Ethel Kennedy in 1968: "Robert Kennedy never turned down an opportunity to visit schools and talk to young people. At Senator Kennedy's funeral, I gave my commitment to Senator Kennedy's wife, Ethel, that I

would honor and carry on this tradition. I've tried to live up to that promise and have talked to as many schoolchildren as I possibly could because I
know from my own life how important words of wisdom can be at the
right time. And that one word very seldom comes from parents," he said.

Andy didn't shy away from publishing our talks, for he is fully aware
of the greater role he wants to play not only in my life but in the lives of
many young Americans. "One of the things that I learned from Dr. King,
Dr. Benjamin Mays and all of my mentors," he said, "is that it's important to pass along as much of your knowledge and experience as you possibly can to future generations. It's difficult to pass along wisdom to your
own children because they are rightly in rebellion, and they must find
and determine their own destiny and opinions. Their struggle is not to be
overly influenced by their parents."

Andy and his late first wife, Jean, had three daughters—Andrea, Lisa
and Paula—and one son, Bo. He has seven grandchildren. "You usually
can't pass on your own dreams to your own family because they appropri-
ately resist you. I've offered $1,000 to any one of my grandkids who reads
my first two books. I'm still waiting." I can relate to his grandchildren. I
didn't read my grandfather's autobiography *Up Against Odds* until he
passed away. It wasn't until he was gone that I felt compelled to learn
more about him.

Andy ardently believes that the best way to pass down knowledge
from one generation to the next is by conversation and dialogue, continuing the oral tradition from which he learned. He believes the next generation can learn from his vivid oral history. "How boring are those many
books written by senior statesmen for young Americans? They are pabu-
lum." He smiled. I didn't know where he was going. "Whenever there is a
controversy or heated issue, you and I seem to talk," he said. "I like when
you challenge me or stretch my imagination. You're twenty-six, and I am
seventy-six. That gives us a fifty-year understanding gap that not only we
must bridge, but our society must also bridge to survive. So much has
happened in the past fifty years. The better your generation understands

and has an opinion on those events, the better you will be able to shape the future of our planet."

Andy promised that he would reflect upon his life throughout our conversations: "I want to share the very clearest understanding of my life and the events that I have been a part of over the past half century. I'm compelled to humbly pass along a few anecdotes and life lessons to prepare you for the long journey ahead. While these are intergenerational discussions, I don't want you to feel obligated to agree with me. Nor do I wish anyone else to agree with me. But I hope that by answering your questions and giving my most stimulating responses, I can help you and your generation to face a brave new world with a compassionate and sensitive worldview, to understand that an active mind is necessary for self-discovery. I hope that our conversations highlight the strong need for intellectual curiosity and a thirst for discovering one's path. Our words can spark the thoughts and ideas of younger Americans because it's true that almost anything we can envision, and commit ourselves to, we can achieve in this society. Through challenging conversation, and a strong vision, we will all grow."

When I was in fifth grade, Uncle Andy urged me to be a student of the world, not limiting my questions to the classroom. As an elementary school student, whenever it was raining outside, he would browse the *Encyclopedia Britannica* for random knowledge. Later, while he was at Howard University, one of his favorite pastimes was to visit the Library of Congress and browse four or five books on various topics. "My grandchildren can do that on their computer. But they must have an inquiring mind. They must want to know something. I want young Americans to understand that a lazy mind is a recipe for failure."

Being curious about the world compels you to find your own path. Andy was curious about faith and God, so instead of becoming a dentist, he turned to theology in 1951 after graduating from Howard University. It was by following his curiosity that he stumbled onto the civil rights movement and struck up a friendship with Dr. King. "Martin and I both thirsted for knowledge," he remembers. Andy began his ministry in the south and ran his first voter registration drive in Thomasville, Georgia, when he was twenty-two. When he was twenty-four, he met Dr. King, who was twenty-seven. Four years later, Andy began to work with him. During the last eight years of King's life, Andy was his aide, companion and friend. "I am probably one of the few people he felt free to show anger and cuss out on occasion. I was one of the few people with the gall and temerity to annoy him with challenging opinions and provocative critiques of his tactics and decisions. Surprisingly, to most people, I knew Martin as a quiet, thoughtful and introverted scholar whose actions might best be described by Gandhi's statement: 'There go my people. I must catch them for I am their leader.' At the same time, he could be the most fiery, articulate and passionate spokesman for the needs, the pain and the hopes of our nation through the difficult times. He never allowed himself to be bitter or despairing even in the face of enormous pressures and persecution by the very government that he sought to save. We both had in common an intense desire to probe our curiosity and find our own path."

Both Dr. King and Andy believed that it is through curiosity and self-discovery that one can find righteousness. Andy is fundamentally a religious person. The most important thing to him is to be righteous. That doesn't necessarily mean being good or judgmental. Righteousness is a combination of a desire for purpose in one's own life as well as a realization that you can never achieve righteousness completely, so you become compassionate toward those who are struggling, regardless of what state of existence they happen to be in.

Dr. King and Andy felt they could take on the world by virtue of their moral power. It was a moral power of forgiveness and understanding. It was the constant conversation and dialogue that helped them understand their self-described enemies. "We didn't say to the J. Edgar Hoovers of the world that we are better than you. We said we understand and forgive you. We want you to understand us. It almost didn't matter whether they did. We continued to extend the hope that we could live together as brothers rather than perish together as fools. The amazing thing is how many responded to us."

Through didactic conversation and debate, Dr. King and Andy crystallized their philosophy of nonviolence. They incorporated aspects of Gandhi's nonviolent movement that would work in the segregated society, like marches and protests, and they rejected parts that wouldn't fit, like excessive piety and material renunciation. "Through conversation we can overcome our greatest fears. We overcame the terror of the Ku Klux Klan with nonviolence. It wasn't the marching. It was the refusing to hate them. It was the ability to see them as our brothers even as they saw us as their enemies," said Andy. He remembers when a fellow crashed through the barriers as Dr. King was checking into a Main Street hotel in Selma, Alabama. "He knocked the hell out of Martin. Martin got up and said, 'Excuse me. I'm sorry if I offended you. Can I help you?' The fellow didn't have anything to say and was cuffed. It wasn't just that he didn't try to fight back. Martin calmed everyone around him because they wanted to beat the shit out of the assailant. That wins people over. Listening wins people over. The success of our young leadership may rest on their ability to listen to others, coupled with active and curious minds."

I interjected, "You and Dr. King are exceptions. Some folks are mature past their years. Dr. King was thirty-five when he won the Nobel Prize. I'm not up for the Nobel Prize, or even a Rotary Club Award, and the last time I checked, neither were any of my friends." He responded, "You and your generation are powerful. It's important for young Americans to realize their power in shaping not only their lives but also world events. And this shaping process is wrought by constant conversation and an appreciation to learn from those who have come before you. Martin once said, 'I want young men and young women who are not alive today but who will come into this world with new privileges and new opportunities, I want you to know and see that these new privileges and opportunities did not come without somebody suffering and sacrificing for them.' It's important to have a firm moral, intellectual, socioeconomic foundation. If you don't know how that foundation was built, you can become arrogant. It's fairly easy to be arrogant in America. It's easy to think your success comes because you are young, smart and good looking. Everyone needs to find someone with whom they can verbally spar and learn from. That's how you crystallize your ideas. That's how you contribute."

Having a reverend-turned-civil-rights-icon urge you to find your moral foundation could put a lot of pressure on you. But instead of reaching for a brown paper bag, I felt at ease talking with him, as if reading a familiar book: "While the youth have an enormous amount of power in shaping the nation, there's no need to be in a hurry. I was a product of a time in American life when folks worshiped the child prodigy. My mother held up to me as examples twelve-year-old concert pianists. Not much has changed. We still revere prodigies. I was not one," he said.

This book is the natural outgrowth of a conversation that started over twenty years ago between a student and his mentor. We bridged my inexperience, curiosity and immaturity with his wisdom, answers and sensibilities. The wisdom in this book comes from Andrew Young. It was his decision for the book to be in my voice, which initially caused me great trepidation: How could I be the translator or ambassador for the Ambassador, someone I admire and love? He calmed my initial worries and urged me to write how I perceived him and our conversations. I began writing the book knowing full well that he was the star, and I was merely the scribe. He got upset with me after reading an initial draft of the text. "There needs to be more of you in this," he said. "Nobody cares about what I have to say," I countered. "That's untrue. I need you to challenge and criticize me, that's how you will form your own opinions and grow." In fact, Uncle Andy wanted me to accurately portray our conversations and how we often disagree and push each other. My role in this work gradually changed from being merely a silent stand-in for those of us beginning to find our way, to someone who prompts, questions and, at times, challenges.

While Uncle Andy wanted me to add more of my personal observations to this text, my self-assigned mission was to ultimately get out of the way. I have tried to minimize personal references in these exchanges. The only time I bring to light my personal views is when I think they can challenge him and elicit more explanation.

A brief bit about me, so that you better understand the narrator. I'm an Indian American born in Atlanta, Georgia, the home of Coca-Cola. One of my friends, who edited my first book, called me a "Coca-Cola Curry Cowboy," a label that I like. I spend my days (and some nights) working at a Wall Street investment bank. I'm a jazz bassist and still play professionally; hence these pages are filled with occasional musical references. I work with a music charity that I helped to start, Music for Tomorrow. I have a deep but waning interest in politics. I got involved in the John Kerry presidential campaign while I was in college and served as a special assistant and speechwriter to Senator Max Cleland. While studying for my postgraduate degree in London, I worked at the Labour Party headquarters. Andy likes to call me an overeducated overachiever. But the sad thing is I still don't know where I'm going, like a tourist without a map.

I hope you sense my nervousness about being perceived as trying to upgrade myself by collaborating on a book with Ambassador Young. Let me be clear: I seek neither fame (I learned from the letter he gave me on my college graduation day) nor fortune (I don't depend on writing books for income). It was Uncle Andy who asked me to help him formalize his beliefs for the next generation. I was certainly excited at first but had reservations about whether I was the right person to collaborate with him. I gradually grew to see this work as a tribute to my intellectual giant and godfather.

This intergenerational exchange is divided into three sections: (1) Civil Rights, (2) Race, Faith and Love and (3) Leadership. In the first section, we speak of Andy's involvement in the civil rights movement and the still unrealized aspects of Dr. King's aspirations. Andy's anecdotes about his involvement reveal the fissures among the top ranks of the civil rights leadership and how Andy learned to make peace with his peers. He offers a compelling vision of how to strive to improve economic equality for minorities not only in America but around the world. He sees Dr. King as a macroeconomic thinker and makes a strong case for creative and compassionate capitalism. He urges us to understand the civil rights movement as a campaign not only for racial equality but for creating jobs and economic opportunity for the poor.

In the second section, Andy teaches us about how to deal with race and racism. He believes racism stems from personal insecurity and sees it as a disease that must be treated with the medicine of love. Later in the section, he instructs us to believe and have faith in something, to live with conviction and passion. To live a meaningful life, he asserts, requires faith and love.

In the last section, Andy teaches us about leadership by invoking past leaders, like Dr. King and Mahatma Gandhi, and those of the future, like President Barack Obama. He distills the most important lessons we can learn from those who are at the forefront of our society and explains why even top leaders need mentors and contrarian counsel. He advises us to "look up, if you want to go up."

I want to highlight that this book is not exclusively about race or African Americans. Many civil rights leaders like Andy Young weren't just thinking about the conditions of African Americans. Their concern was the human condition and civil rights everywhere. They were, to borrow Albert Murray's term, Omni-Americans. And this book is not a biography. See Uncle Andy's books *A Way Out of No Way* and *An Easy Burden* for further reading about his life. I hope that you will detect not only the timelessness of Andrew Young's wisdom but also its universality: We can all learn from his words. From him we can learn how to get involved in public service and how to invoke faith as we grow older. We can reject the cynic's view of the world. We can learn that when a challenge arises, we can rise to it.

I also want to highlight the tone of this book is meant to be conversational and playful. While some may think I'm not sufficiently deferential to Uncle Andy, we both wanted the tone to match that of our thousands of conversations throughout the years. We wanted to capture our friendly intergenerational dialogue and better articulate the complex ideas with which we struggled.

Andy Young's mind sparkles with facts, anecdotes and good humor. Like an expressive jazz musician's improvisations, his comments can veer off-topic and even dart wildly, but he always comes back to the theme. The topics and conversations in this book are far-ranging. I find some of his best moments are when he solos off-key, alluding to an esoteric story or peripheral point. I ask for your patience as our conversations unfold in each chapter. The takeaways don't explicitly hit you over the head. It's up to you to interpret and work out your own meaning from our conversations. That's part of the fun. Part of the excitement in conversing with Uncle Andy is hearing what he will mention next, whether he will be brisk like a butterfly or brave like a samurai.

Andy Young hasn't just inspired me. He has influenced and inspired millions. It is our hope that our conversations will spark more conversations and refresh our collective memory of the civil rights movement. We hope these conversations will be particularly helpful to those in my generation who only know about the civil rights movement from the last few chapters in American history books. We hope that our conversations can help others find their own sources of knowledge—their mentors and sparring partners.

I wasn't able to witness firsthand one of America's finest moments, the righting of many wrongs that had plagued America for hundreds of years, but we can learn much from the moral courage of those who led the movement. As we prepare to assume leadership positions in the world, no matter how big or small, we should revisit those who exhibit the timeless qualities of moral courage and strength of character. Before history marches on, we need to hear Andy Young's poetic and lyrical words. They can serve as our compass. His anecdotal vignettes not only entertain but teach.

Andy always likes to tell me, "It's necessary to be prepared for when your time comes. All of Dr. King's acolytes wanted to be Dr. King. But I say, don't get your fifteen minutes of fame until you know what you want to say and who you are. We used to joke about the free speech movement at Berkeley: After the students won, they didn't have shit to say." We can learn from this battle-tested voice. With a solid understanding of our past, when our time comes, let's have *something* to say.

1 SLEEP IN, DON'T BRUSH OTHER PEOPLE'S TEETH AND FIND YOUR OWN WAY

Don't let the noise of others' opinions drown out your own inner voice. And most important, have the courage to follow your heart and intuition. They somehow already know what you truly want to become.

—Steve Jobs, cofounder and CEO of Apple[1]

I was en route to Uncle Andy's house. There was a traffic jam on I-285, the highway that encircles Atlanta. Luckily my mom was driving. She knows the shortcuts you'll never hear from a GPS, the ones that send you zooming through a BP gas station parking lot and puffing for air. Even though I'm perfectly capable of driving, she always insists on taking the wheel. Whenever I visit my folks in Atlanta, I try to swing by Uncle Andy's. "Make sure to ask him about his parents and how he learned to respect them," my mom grinned as she drove. I rolled my eyes. "As if the commandment to honor our father and mother wasn't enough," I thought.

We pulled into Uncle Andy's narrow driveway. The cracked, dark gray pavement was kissed by the weeds in his front lawn which was browning in the middle. Eight Japanese maples surrounded his house. Andy planted them after spending time in Japan to court the International Olympic Committee in the late 1980s. He used to have several bonsai trees which he bought in Korea during the 1988 Olympics. He took the trees to a monastery during the 1996 Olympics in Atlanta because he couldn't devote the almost daily care needed to maintain them. The ninety-year-old monk who was looking after them died, and then torrential rain destroyed the trees. The camellia bush he brought from the home of his late wife, Jean, in Marion, Alabama, has grown more than ten feet since it was moved.

He's lived in the same house since December 1966, when he bought it for $32,500 on a plot fifty feet wide and four hundred feet deep. He's installed ramps and rails in his backyard and jokes he is building his own retirement village. It's a small house with a main floor and basement. He had to expand it because his mother moved in after his father passed away, and because of his blossoming collection of African art and odd gifts from his extensive travels. Even his artwork is humble. Well, besides the statues of naked African women. One might easily think that Andy didn't have much money or he had simple tastes. Both are true. "Better to have wealthy friends," he's always advised me.

I waved good-bye to mom and was greeted by booming barks from Andy's two tall and tan Rhodesian Ridgebacks. He named one Nzingha after the seventeenth-century Angolan warrior queen who fought the Portuguese. The other he named Simba after the protagonist in *The Lion King* and because Rhodesian Ridgebacks were used to chase lions. "If we had smaller dogs, then my wife would want them to sleep in our bed," he once explained to me.

"Whatcha know?" Andy called out. That is Uncle Andy-speak for "How's it going?" The front door swung open. I heard the hiss of the television in the background. "Since when do you watch Fox News?" I asked. "Got to listen to everybody," he smiled.

While speaking about the upcoming Atlanta Falcons season, he ushered me into his living room, poured pink fruit juice over crackling ice for me, muted the forty-two-inch Panasonic television and sat down. The glass table was covered with unorganized newspapers and memos. I counted two glass figures he had recently been awarded. One of them read, "Award Presented to Andrew Young for His Distinguished Career in Public Service." He saw me eyeing it.

"Do you want it?" he asked. He was serious. Andy always gives. The lyrics from one of his favorite hymns are, "You can't beat God giving, no matter how you try. . . . The more you give, the more he gives to you." At first I joked with him, "Maybe we could sell it on eBay." But I thought better of it. "No thanks, just checking out your latest trophies," I replied.

"What's on your mind?" he asked, while craning his neck to see why Simba was still barking. I sat back in the couch.

"I've been thinking a lot about my next career move. I'm in the same place as many of my friends—recently graduated from college, working a decent job, wanting to make a difference in the world but not sure how to do it. It seems like everyone else has an idea on what I should be doing though."

"How's that?" he asked.

He always asks questions first. Though he's very much a conceptual and thematic thinker and speaker, he likes to get down into the weeds. He likes facts. They help him tell better stories.

A colleague thinks I should apply to business school or take the chartered financial analyst exam. Another thinks I must try my hand at management consulting. You know—Goldman, McKinsey and Harvard Business School, the trinity of overachieving conformity. When you make a little success, people expect you to succeed. I've even started to put pressure on myself, as if my next career move must place me closer to the mountaintop. The problem is that I'm not sure what I want to do or which mountain to climb.

I asked, "How do you escape these great expectations? How did you deal with other people's expectations of you?"

"Your question reminds me of some advice I gave to a bright young man in the tenth grade at the North Atlanta High School," he responded. Uncle Andy advises by anecdotes, like Jesus, who instructed with parables. There always seems to be a fitting story in his museum of a mind. "Everyone was putting pressure on him. He's tall, articulate and good looking. And he's a leader in the school. But there was so much pressure on him that he was breaking out in hives. The doctors couldn't find anything wrong with him," he said.

His classmates were teasing him about not picking a sexy topic like robotics or information technology for his science project. He had chosen biodegradation and composting. Andy urged the kid to stick with the project, especially since much of our future fuel may come from composting.

"I took him aside and said, 'Look, you are letting people put too much pressure on you.' I chose my words very deliberately. I said, 'When people begin to bug you, you can't say it out loud, but you can say deep in the back of your mind—go fuck yourself.' I said it that way because that is a very masculine rejection. 'And you don't need to be wishy-washy about it. If something doesn't seem right to you, don't let it pressure you. Go on about your business.'"

"You told a tenth grader what?" I asked. I can't say I was shocked. I've come to expect jarring honesty from Uncle Andy, but I wanted to make sure I'd heard him right.

"Remember, if you say it aloud, you'll turn people off. You have to say it to yourself. It will actually empower you when you say it in your head," he said.

"I'll practice that at work," I interrupted. Actually, the tough part isn't saying "fuck you" while working on a trading floor, it's saying it in your head.

He ignored me and continued, "I guarantee you those hives went away. It was the emotional pressure and the expectation of his parents and his teachers. Everyone might give you hell. But if this is what you want to do, then believe in yourself. Don't let anyone else tell you what you need to do with your life. I always saw great expectations as conformist pressure." His voice crescendoed as he reached his point, "Find your path."

"How did you find *your* path? So many of us are directionless and rudderless. How did you determine the path that took you from New Orleans as a boy to New York as US ambassador to the UN?" I asked.

"I stumbled to find my path," he started. "I'm a leaf in a divine wind, just floating from one thing to another." I liked his imagery. If he was a leaf, I was crazy kudzu not knowing which way to grow. A divine wind could explain why Andy never enlisted in the military, for example. He broke his arm when he was a kid and it never set correctly, which made him unable to join. Andy was destined to be a peacemaker from the beginning.

Most importantly, he believes that whatever one does should come from within—there is a spiritual core in every human being. He can recite perfectly a quote that he came across in the 1950s from Thomas Kelly's *A Testament of Devotion,* which is about the Quaker philosophy: "Deep within us all there is an amazing inner sanctuary of the soul, a holy place, a Divine Center, a speaking Voice, to which we may continuously return. Eternity is at our hearts pressing upon our time-worn lives, warming us with intimations of an astounding destiny, calling us home unto Itself."[2] I'm impressed with his recall. I can barely recite the Lord's Prayer.

The message that he infers from this passage is that there is something in all of us. We must wake up and listen to this quiet, sometimes brooding voice. He admires other leaders and philosophers who discovered their inner voice and followed it. In the New Testament, Jesus was tempted with power, money and supernatural claims. And he rejected it all. Jesus said the "kingdom of God is within you."[3] German philosopher

Paul Tillich, whom Andy read closely, believed that the search for ulti-mate reality must occur within as well as without.

"You don't find your calling immediately. It's one step at a time, one day at a time," Andy stated slowly. "It takes time to discover your inner voice." I thought about the movie *What About Bob?* in which Bill Mur-ray's psychiatrist recommends that he take baby steps toward goals. It seemed like Andy was saying the same thing—take baby steps toward your aspirations.

I argued that some might think that his career was premeditated. Be-coming a reverend was excellent preparation for getting involved in the civil rights movement. And being involved in the civil rights movement prepared him well for the United Nations, just like working at an invest-ment bank could prepare one well for working at a private equity shop or hedge fund.

"Except I made all the wrong choices for an up-and-coming bour-geois black preacher. I should have gone to a big church, but I went to a little one. I should have gone to Yale, where my pastor went, but I went to Hartford Seminary. I had a small, intimate experience with my profes-sors at Hartford that I couldn't have gotten at Yale because I would have just been another number. But I wouldn't say that my career happened by accident either. I borrow the term from Adam Smith—I felt an invisible hand has guided my life from within," he replied. "I had no idea I would get involved with the civil rights movement and become a trusted advisor and friend to Martin. But the civil rights movement wasn't concentrated in the church. It was fomented in law schools and universities."

In 1955, the year Andy graduated from the seminary, Rosa Parks sat down in the bus and sparked a national debate about civil rights. That's when the church started to get more involved. It wasn't until the early 1960s that Protestants, Catholics and Jews came together and created the National Council on Religion and Race in Chicago, which was the first large, organized, ecumenical attempt to discuss civil rights.

"My interest in civil rights didn't get activated in school. And even my getting interested in theology took some time."

"How did you work out what you wanted to become?" I asked.

"You've got to remember where I started," Andy declared. "My father wanted me to become everything he wanted to be."

Andy's father, Andrew Sr., wanted Andy to become a baseball player. Andrew Sr. was a good baseball player, but blacks couldn't get into the major leagues when he was growing up. His dream was that Andy would become the next Jackie Robinson. But that's what *he* wanted to do, and Andy understood that at an early age. And then Andrew Sr. wanted Andy to become a dentist like him. Andy knew that his father had rebelled against his father too. Andy's grandfather Frank was a businessman. He owned a pool hall and grocery store. He was the treasurer of several burial societies and Masonic orders. Frank wanted Andrew Sr. to carry on the family businesses, but Andrew Sr. left home and enrolled at dental school.

"Your papa wanted to live vicariously through you, but you rejected his aspirations for you," I said, trying to capture the facts like a photographer trying to snap the perfect sunset.

"Hell yes! I had to break away from my father. I didn't want to brush anyone's teeth," he chuckled. He leaned forward and spread his wrinkled hands.

Andy believes that rejecting your parents' aspirations doesn't mean rejecting them altogether. He understood at a young age that his father was a very thoughtful, pastoral and socially sensitive man. Many of his father's patients came to his office not only to get their teeth cleaned but to speak with someone at a high moral and intellectual level. Andrew Sr. had a powerful commitment to the truth. Once as a boy, Andy bragged about getting more change than he was supposed to from the butcher. Andrew Sr. started to take off his belt and demanded that Andy return the money immediately. Andy hauled ass back to the butcher not wanting to be whipped by his father.

"That's just who he was. I wanted to be those things too, but I didn't have to become a dentist to do so. His motives were sound. My dad wanted me to be secure with a job that paid $10,000 per year," he explained. In the 1930s, when Andy was born, a job that paid $10,000 gave one security and the ability to educate one's children. Andy's younger brother, Walter, however, became a dentist, which was his calling.

"In a way, you were like the kid who was breaking out in hives," I said.

"Yes. It's tough to say 'fuck you' to your parents or anyone else. When you do, you can go the other direction and wander aimlessly."

As a young man, Andy was sent by the United Church of Christ to San Francisco. The Church was one of the sponsors of the famed City Lights bookstore, where beat poets performed. Andy envied Jack Kerouac and the other beat poets and their freedom. The free booze was tempting. The free sex was very, very tempting. But he had to cut his trip short. It was just too wild. It was too free. "You can't say 'fuck you' to everything. I realized that a life dedicated to partying was no life for me," he said.

While in San Francisco he went to a shop in Chinatown to buy a silk dress for Jean. The Chinese clerk disappeared behind a curtain of beads, and Andy started to panic and ran out of the store, not wanting to be shanghaied. He had seen many kung fu movies in which a hand appears from behind a beaded curtain and drags the unwitting patron away against his will. Upon reflection on the incident, Andy realized that he was guilty of stereotyping and could better understand the prejudices some whites had against blacks.

I've lived in San Francisco and thoroughly enjoyed several carefree moments. I explained to him "Bay to Breakers," the city's annual seven-mile footrace in which participants dress up in costumes, tap kegs and just revel. My favorite costumes were the seven fish running in the opposite direction followed by a bear.

I returned to the subject at hand. "Did Dr. King start with the end in mind? What did Dr. King want to become?" I asked.

"When he first started to preach, Martin's ambition was to teach at a top-notch seminary and become the preacher at a place like Riverside Church, the big church on the Upper West Side of Manhattan, which was financed by the Rockefeller brothers," he replied.

Just before Dr. King was killed, the leaders of Riverside offered him a year's sabbatical from the movement to be the interim pastor at Riverside. Andy and other civil rights leaders encouraged him to take the offer, but he declined because he was too involved with the movement.

"Did he want to be the Rick Warren of his day?" I asked.

"Not exactly. Martin thought he wanted to become a pastor of a large church, but he later found ideals to which he could aspire. That is something very important to learn from Martin—to follow an ideal like service, nonviolence, love. And then life becomes an innovative effort to try to achieve these ideals," he said.

"If my ideal is generosity, then I can try to be generous in my vocation, family life or in some other way," I replied. My mom encouraged me to read Rabindranath Tagore's *Gitanjali* and *The Religion of Man,* in which he describes kindness and love as the ultimate religion. I've tried to internalize kindness and love as personal ideals. I'm no paragon, however. Far from it. "So you think I need to worry less about my actual job but try to use whatever I'm doing now to achieve my ideals of love and kindness?" I asked.

Andy grinned. "I couldn't have said it better. You're listening to that voice within." I was actually listening to his voice. After listening to a mentor for years, his voice can merge with yours.

Cool. This was actually helping me. If I tried to pursue my ideals with actions both big and small, I might feel as if I were making a contribution to the greater good. I didn't need to rescue puppies from burning buildings to exhibit my kindness. I could open the door for girls everywhere. I said, "I have to ask you too—what did you want to become?"

"I didn't know. But I needed to get away from those great expectations. I had a strong interest in theology, but my father warned me that he wouldn't pay for seminary. He thought seminary was a waste of money. So I went on my own," he replied.

"Is that where you found your calling?"

"By that time I had started to feel like there must be some God-given purpose in my life. I wasn't just on earth to be my father's son. I was on earth to do something really profound. I was put on this earth for something different. Something unique for which only I was specially created. It's my conviction that this is true for everyone. Everybody has a purpose," he responded.

"I think the only profound thing I've done in quite a while is to chat with you," I said. He paused for a moment and didn't smile. Andy's always been better at giving compliments than receiving them.

When Andy graduated from college, he didn't know what he wanted to do. He felt that he had committed fraud with his dad's money. After college, he thought he was supposed to know what he wanted to do. On the drive back to New Orleans after graduating from Howard University, Andy's family stayed at a church camp. In the segregated South, blacks had to stay at churches or with friends. While at the camp, Andy went on a morning run. Inspired by Jesse Owens, Andy harbored Olympic ambitions and wanted to make the 1952 American Olympic track squad. He pushed himself to run to the top of nearby Kings Mountain. He reached the summit exhausted and thirsty. He sat shirtless and surveyed the picturesque landscape. Everything seemed to have a place and purpose. Andy had a sudden awareness that if everything in the world had a purpose, there was certainly a purpose for him. It was his epiphany and his moment of enlightenment.

After he returned to the camp in the afternoon, he joined a baseball game. He was playing in the outfield with his white camp roommate John Heinrich, who had a degree in divinity from Yale and one in agriculture from Cornell and was about to leave for Rhodesia to be a missionary. Andy was in shock because it was the first time he had heard of a white person going to Africa to help people. He grew frustrated that no-body had suggested that he should go to Africa to help others. "That white roommate's life became a judgment on mine," he said.

"Did you go to Africa?" I asked.

"No, but learning about him was another gradual step to under-standing what I wanted to do with my life. It helped me hear the voice within me," Andy responded.

When he returned home from his graduation, Andy's minister, Nick Hood, asked him to accompany him on a trip to Texas to participate in an interdenominational and interracial conference for young people at Lake Brownwood. Andy saw the trip as a good opportunity to drop off Nick at the conference and then spend some time with his college room-mate Bob Hilliard, who was from San Antonio. Andy and Nick drove to Texas and didn't see a single black person along the way after leaving Houston. When they arrived at the conference, which was out in the sticks, Nick said to Andy, "You really need to stay at least one day." Safety in numbers, like a herd of gazelles trying to avoid a hungry lion.

Andy promised to stay one day and ended up staying the entire week. He was fascinated with how many of the white folks at the conference had a strong sense of mission. Some were going to India, others to Latin Amer-ica to help the poor. He remembers one young student from the Univer-sity of Texas who said if her father knew she was at a conference with two black people, he would disown her. She came to the conference because her understanding of the Bible was that Jesus said we are all brothers and sisters and that we are all God's children. The University of Texas student and John Heinrich sparked Andy's curiosity, so he took a job working with young people in Rhode Island and Connecticut to get them more in-volved in local churches. Andy was dipping his toe into the sea of service.

"It seems to me," I said, "that seminary is a place where you intro-spect and discern a path. If I spent years considering my faith and the world, I'd have a better idea on what I should be doing. How do you wake up someone to find their calling? How do you stop substituting other people's opinions for your own?" I asked. I'm not a monk, but I still seek a sense of purpose and enlightenment.

"You've just got to look around. There are always clues. I've always thought you would excel in public service. But instead of listening to me, you must see where you are. You've been in the eye of the dragon working at a bank during a great recession. In spite of all the people who've been fired, you haven't lost your job. There must be some reason or calling for you to be there," he said while he wagged his left index finger at me.

"I'm cheap," I smiled. "But aren't you just trying to ascribe greater meaning to something that doesn't warrant it?" I asked.

"There is a larger purpose for why we are here. I believe things don't happen by accident," he responded. "Coincidence is God's way of remaining anonymous."

"Didn't Einstein say that?" I asked.

"I said it too. I believe it."

I thought about the coincidence that led to my job. I started working at J.P. Morgan in the London office in a technology role, writing computer scripts for traders. I was as bored as Paris Hilton in a library. Completely out of the blue I ran into a young J.P. Morgan equity salesman named Luke, who took me under his wing and helped me find a better position in San Francisco. Now that I think about it, maybe that was God's way of remaining anonymous. I never wanted to become a banker. I needed some income to fund my farfetched dream to create an Internet startup with my friend. But becoming a banker has helped me to understand the world in a new and important way. Sometimes it's the coincidences that have the most significant influences on you.

Andy glanced at the television. Bill O'Reilly was on.

I said, "Central bank chairman Ben Bernanke became an eminent scholar of the Great Depression, which inevitably prepared him for the 2008 credit crisis. The person with perhaps the most comprehensive knowledge of the Great Depression helped America avert another. You would infer greater meaning to his story, right?"

"Yes, he followed his clues."

"What were your clues?" I asked.

"They were all over," he summarized.

Andy's introduction to homelessness was at Union Square in New York in 1957. He was supposed to meet someone there, and a bum came up to him. He was a true New York beggar because he asked Andy for not a nickel or a dime but a dollar, which was a lot of money back then. He desperately needed a drink. He said that he knew who John F. Kennedy was, but this was well before Kennedy was running for president. He had attended Choate boarding school and Harvard with Kennedy. But he'd flunked out and his family had disowned him. He lived in the streets as an alcoholic. He had no place to go.

"It sounds like he was putting you on," I interjected.

"He may have been a charlatan, but he had a good story," he responded.

The bum made Andy realize something: "Even though I was black and middle class, I realized I was blessed because I had unconditional love from my parents. Here was someone who came from an upper level of society. He went to better schools than me, and I was a successful young church executive, and he was the bum."

Andy realized that poverty was everywhere. Even those who came from higher parts of society are in need of healing. Soon thereafter Andy committed himself to the idea of service—the idea of working not toward profit but healing others spiritually and emotionally.

"For me, the clue walked up and asked me for a dollar," he said.

"Did you take your own advice? Did you put too much pressure on your son? Did he follow the Young family tradition of rebelling against father figures?" I asked.

"Because my father pushed me to follow in his footsteps, I took the opposite approach. I always told my children that they didn't have to do what I wanted. They needed to figure out what God wanted them to do." He mentioned that his kids wanted him to be more positive toward them, but he resisted. "It's obnoxious and self-serving to constantly praise your own children. I'm very proud of my children but I want them to stand on their own." He resisted finding his children easy jobs. He almost wanted his kids to rebel against him.

"I always felt that you do what you love. And if you do it well enough, you will make enough money to get by. You will make all the money you need. I never made a decision just to make money. I turned out okay," he said.

"Sometimes taking a job for money is a necessity after student loans. Call it the money trap," I stated.

"Well, the key to Bo growing up was when he realized that I couldn't make him a millionaire. He said I gave him fame without fortune, but I could give him a good name that could open almost any door. Like me, Bo wanted to be the opposite of the father figure. Money is no doubt important. But I learned to live without much of it. To feel that money is the only objective is cause for concern. I know a young lady with a PhD who says that she wants to be Oprah Winfrey. And I said, 'The hell you do. You want to be who Oprah is now, the most beloved and famous woman on the planet who is also a multimillionaire. But you don't want to be beaten, raped or struggle, suffer and lead the brutal life that Oprah had to lead to develop her strength.' The young lady is still restless. She is like every other young person. She wants to get rich and be famous quick," he said. Even having a PhD doesn't entitle you to instant wealth and happiness.

"Many ambitious people are in a hurry. Is that sometimes to their detriment?" I asked.

"It always amazed me how few talented students survived the South in the 1960s. I know so many who had nervous breakdowns and developed ulcers. They were always in a hurry," he said.

They wanted to change the world in one semester, one summer, or one year. The problem is that the world doesn't change that quickly. Andy argues that the world doesn't change: It grows. And growing takes time, like a lad who drinks lots of milk. You can't dramatically change the world during sophomore summer. The folks who made a real contribution to civil rights committed themselves not to a time frame but to ideals like nonviolence, equality and justice. If you commit your life to an ideal, Andy believes you will grow, and your possibilities will grow with you. Your opportunities will inevitably grow. They did for Andy. His grandmother quoted Matthew to him: "Therefore do not worry about tomorrow, for tomorrow will worry about its own things. Sufficient for the day *is* its own trouble."[4]

"Each day brings its own problems. So worry only about today," I said quizzically. I wanted him to confirm my quick paraphrase, which he did.

"If you do a good job today, you'll be led to where you're supposed to be going. I never understood politicians who spent so much time worrying about the next election," he observed.

When he was a congressman, Andy didn't worry about joining the president's cabinet even though he was an ardent supporter of Jimmy Carter. He just did his job well. Dr. King stuck to this philosophy of patience too, which he learned from Dr. Benjamin Mays, who was his mentor and the president of Morehouse College in Atlanta. Dr. Mays had a saying: "I have only a moment. Only sixty seconds in it. Forced upon me, can't refuse it. Didn't seek it, didn't choose it. But it's up to me to use it. I must suffer if I lose it. Give account if I abuse it. Just a tiny little minute. But eternity is in it."[5] Dr. King heard that when he was fifteen and internalized this message for almost twenty-five years.

"How are you and your friends using your minutes?" he asked.

"I don't think I'm using all of them efficiently," I said. I spend way too much time at sports bars watching Atlanta's teams lose.

"I'm not trying to deny anyone a good time or urging anyone to get more serious about life. I'm saying, use the minutes for what you want to do and not somebody else. You really can't blame anybody else for wasting your time. Dr. Mays used to tell us, 'By no fault of yours or mine, we

African Americans find ourselves three hundred years behind. No use in blaming anyone.' He wanted us to use our minutes and not complain about the past many years. But the second someone else tells you how to use your minutes, you've got to say to yourself what I told that tenth grader," he said. "My challenge to you and all young people is to develop the vision, discipline, and courage to try to catch up in the next twenty-six years."

Andy told me how he walked away from other people's expectations his entire life. While others pressured him to run for office, he came to the decision himself. He didn't overload or burden himself while making the decision. Civil rights leaders thought it was very important for there to be an African American congressman from the South, and the best opportunity to win was the fifth congressional district of Georgia. His friend, and later Georgia congressman, John Lewis was searching for someone who could represent that district: someone who could raise money outside of Atlanta and was comfortable speaking with white people as the district was only 32 percent black. Julian Bond, who later became the head of the NAACP, passed on the opportunity because his family didn't want him to run. He had received several death threats and had several young children. Andy entered the race against conservative Republican Fletcher Thompson because "there really wasn't anyone else, at least nobody who could win," he said. He lost the election in 1970, but he ran again in 1972 and won.

He won not just because Thompson ran for the Senate and therefore the seat was open, but because he laid the groundwork between elections. Mayor Sam Massell appointed Andy cochair of the Community Relations Commission for the City of Atlanta. The archbishop of the Catholic Church was the other cochair. There were several labor strikes at the time. Andy had learned from Tony Zivalich, a burly friend in the Teamsters, that strikes were never about money but a lack of communication. The workers demanded a four-step wage increase, but the mayor offered only a three-step increase. The workers rejected the increase. Andy visited with the workers and drew a line down the blackboard. On one side he put everything the workers wanted, on the other he wrote what the mayor was offering. When one considered that the mayor would pay the workers for the time they had missed during the strike, it was effectively a four-step increase. So the workers re-voted and the strike ceased. Andy earned a reputation as a peacemaker. He had settled several strikes in only a few weeks.

Andy had won a friend in the mayor of Atlanta and several more in the business community. Andy kept the black vote, earned the labor vote, garnered the support of Catholics with the help of the archbishop and received support from several prominent Jews. The Jewish community had always been in the forefront of the civil rights movement. They too offered strong support to Andy's efforts to get elected. Rabbi Jacob Rothschild, a leader in Atlanta's Jewish community, supported Andy. His son and grandmother canvassed rich and poor neighborhoods for Andy. Uncle Andy's win helped to usher in the "New South" in which African Americans and more tolerant whites were in power, like Jimmy Carter in Georgia, Reuben Askew in Florida and Dale Bumpers in Arkansas. There were great expectations and hopes among fifth-district constituents now that a civil rights luminary was their new congressman. But Andy didn't let it get to him. He was effectively representing the entire south for African Americans and the poor because there was no other black congressman from the region. Andy still didn't let the expectations get to him. One baby step at a time. He didn't pressure himself.

It's one thing for Andy not to follow his dad's wishes to become a dentist. It's quite another that he kept a level head during the tumultuous civil rights movement. He never wanted to brush anyone else's teeth.

"What about the pressure to carry on the legacy of Martin Luther King?" I asked.

"I certainly didn't feel any pressure. I wasn't a Baptist like several of the other civil rights leaders. Very few people knew me. I wasn't in many of the photographs. It wasn't great expectations but great ambitions that destroyed our movement. Everyone else wanted to take Martin Luther King's place. They felt the pressure. Ralph [David Abernathy] and Jesse [Jackson] wanted to be Martin Luther King. I didn't want to be Martin King. I wanted to be Andy Young. They hungered for the recognition and fame. I've always believed that affirmation can only come from within you. It's not from what everyone else says about you," he said.

"Since you didn't come across as a ruthless go-getter, did others try to recruit you or try to pressure you into helping them become the next Dr. King?" I asked.

"Ralph once said to me, 'If you wrote speeches for me like you wrote for Martin, you could help me to become Martin Luther King.' I said to him, 'Bullshit! I never wrote speeches for Martin. You are a great preacher, Ralph. But you aren't and will never become Martin. You need to become Ralph David the Great. The most I would do for Martin was the sort of thing you do for me: look something up and give me a couple points of background. Speeches didn't make Martin.' There were thousands of preachers that were as good as or better than Martin. Few if any were willing to listen to their inner core and follow a spiritual path to help the less fortunate of God's children."

"I get it. We must look inside. We must march to our own conga drums. Is there any way to quicken the self-discovery process?" I asked.

"You need to think of twelve to thirty as the Jesus years. We don't hear anything about Jesus during those years. At twelve he was talking back to his mother. He would run away from his mother and go to the temple. He was beginning to assert his own independence. And even later he said, 'Who is my mother? Who is my brother? He who does the will of my father.' The years between twelve and thirty were his years of spiritual pilgrimage. Some people say he may have gone to India. Others say that maybe he went down to Egypt. It's clear that he was on a spiritual journey. And I think everyone's got to take their own spiritual journey."

Andy turned to the teachings of Plato and Paul as a young adult. He read devotional and mystical literature because it helped him to question his life and find clues to help determine where he wanted to go. Reading a broad range of literature enabled Andy to survey a vast variety of interests. He drew inspiration from Paul Tillich's *The Courage to Be,* which explains how to summon the courage to conquer anxiety and doubt. He also read Gandhi's *Autobiography* and collected works. He drew the most inspiration from Matthew, chapters five through seven of the Sermon on the Mount. Andy later named his second book *An Easy Burden* after a passage from the Sermon: "For my yoke is easy and my burden is light." He references the Book of Matthew as the "book of nonviolence."

He encouraged me to use my minutes pursuing what I love. And not to take orders. Ever since I was a kid, my teachers, friends and parents have urged me to focus on one thing and do it well. I tend to be a multi-tasker, sometimes to my detriment, like someone who texts while driving a car. Whenever I try to buckle down and focus on only one project or cause, I'm miserable. After reflecting upon Uncle Andy's plea to listen to my inner voice, I realized I am most happy when I have a lot of pots on the stove: I'm the master chef in my kitchen.

Andy was one of the main reasons I pursued my deep interests of technology and jazz music. He pushed me to follow my interests. Some of those interests, like jazz music and entrepreneurialism, became passions. He added gasoline to my little sparks of interest. He always knew there was a place for school, but there was a larger place for the classrooms of life: "Your time on the streets of Atlanta, New Orleans, New York, London and everywhere else you've lived are more valuable than your Dartmouth, London School of Economics and J.P. Morgan education. You are developing the full breadth of your abilities." He favors the wisdom of life over the facts of knowledge.

"I always thought those Ivy League schools were overrated," he jibed. "Smart and overeducated young people like you need to be careful not to chase something because other people think it's prestigious. It's not a bad thing to feel guilty for your success either," he said.

"What do you mean?" I asked.

"One of the keys to our success as civil rights leaders was that we felt guilty about our success. We were as prone to materialism as anybody else. The only reason we didn't succumb was because most of us were born middle class in the midst of poverty. The civil rights movement was a calling to share our success. I don't know whether many Harvard Business School [HBS] graduates feel guilty enough about their success to share it, nor do they realize their acceptance into HBS is often a blessing of birth," he said.

At first, I thought that was an unfair remark. But I realized how few of my peers who attend top-rated business schools (or work at investment banks and consultancies) want to do something more than make money. I'm not much better.

"What do you think the civil rights movement would have looked like if the leaders had attended HBS?" I asked

"We wouldn't have had one," he replied. I chuckled.

"You spent your little minutes sharing your success," I said.

"Yes, we listened to the voice deep within us and tried to make our own path. And we didn't follow orders too well."

"I hear you," I confirmed. "Isn't the inner voice just your intuition?" I asked.

"Call it whatever you want," he said, not answering my question. I think he was getting a little tired.

So I did, I call it my intuition.

Maybe Uncle Andy's advice can be considered cliché and traditional. Is his "find your inner voice" any different from the *Star Wars* exhortation to "trust the force?" When taking a test, my teachers taught me to trust my gut and follow my hunch. His advice is not as distinct as a blue rose, but I think a difference is that Andy sees intuition as Tagore did when he called it "God's alphabet," a distinctly divine and spiritual creation. He also wraps his advice in the packaging of punchy bravado, which is sure to wake up any tenth grader or young banker. Above all, Uncle Andy's counsel to discover my intuition has been a settling influence on me. It has helped me to slow down and think deliberately about what *I* want to do, and not chase the foolish mirages of excessive prestige and profit. I don't want to go to business school, so I won't. Elementary. The nonelementary part is that it's not enough to just listen to your heart—sometimes you have to take a leap of faith and risk failure. If you feel called to do something, you may need to risk failure.

"The path will light up for you as it will for your generation. You're bright. You are interested in music, public service, finance and people. I don't know anybody else—I really don't—with a combination of those gifts. So I always thought there was something special for you. But I would be the last one to try to tell you where it is or what it is. You work out your own salvation with fear and trembling," he said. I appreciated his comment. Sometimes I think Uncle Andy has a higher opinion of me than my own parents.

All Andy knew was that he didn't want to become a dentist. When he was nineteen, he decided to give himself time to evolve and not rush it. He let his future find him, and it did. In his twenties, Andy came across the teachings of St. Augustine. He paraphrases one of St. Augustine's prayers: "Save me lord, but not right now." St. Augustine wanted a wild, youthful life. He was thirty-five before he settled down and accepted his role in the church. Albert Schweitzer was a Nobel Peace Prize winner who was a concert organist and physician. He had three or four careers. At fifty-five, he went to the Belgian Congo and started a hospital, and decided that was his calling. Andy always looked at great men and realized they each had their own schedule. He chose Albert Schweitzer and thought he could wait until his fifties to figure out what he wanted to do.

"Here I am at seventy-six, and now my role model is Moses, who didn't start leading the Children of Israel out of Egypt until he was eighty. He lived a screwed-up life along the way. But from eighty to one hundred and twenty, the years in the wilderness, that is when his life began to define itself and he defined the people. I've always used this belief to curtail the influence of pushy parents, friends and blind ambition."

Andy was tired. He tries to fill his downtime with power naps. Sleep was his bane in college, but now he has trouble. "I'm no Michael Jackson," he made clear to me, referring to the late pop star's insomnia. I walked toward him and patted his shoulder. He closed his eyes, and his big belly moved up and down. I let him sleep. I needed time to think. I needed time to listen.

2 SLIDE OVER, ROSA— WE YOUNGSTERS CAN HELP

And in the end, it is not the years in your life that count. It's the life in your years.

—Abraham Lincoln[1]

We sat at Uncle Andy's narrow kitchen counter. I had brought mouthwatering sashimi with ponzu sauce and spicy tuna rolls from Pacific Rim Bistro, his favorite sushi spot in Atlanta. We wolfed down each bite without using chopsticks and soon ran out of wasabi, so I searched for Tabasco in the pantry.

Both of us had reason to be gluttons for zesty pain. He grew up eating spicy New Orleans gumbo—his mom liked to include peppery Mexican chorizo, and, when he was little, she added spices to keep the food fresh since his family didn't own a refrigerator. I grew up eating my mother's fiery saag paneer and baingan bartha. Andy also loves Indian food. He likes to tell the story of dining at the Indian ambassador's house in Washington, DC, in the late 1970s. He was served mild curry and said to the ambassador, "I'm from New Orleans, so I can handle more zing." Andy was given some peppers, which he crushed and sprinkled into the curry. He got some of the peppers on his napkin and made the mistake of wiping his face with the napkin. When telling me the story, he adds, "Whooh! My face was hot!" He also mentions that he rushed to a bathroom, removed his shirt and wiped himself down with a cold towel while the ambassador graciously waited. "I'm just glad it wasn't my crotch," he laughs.

While we ate sushi in Andy's kitchen, the television boomed in the other room. A local news reporter detailed the violent death of an Atlanta teenager. The next story was about another teenager who had been murdered only a few days earlier. The television station's reporting was no surprise: It was the standard "if it bleeds, it leads" approach to local news.

"There's no good news on television. That's why I'm trying to make documentaries," said Andy. He helps to create documentaries on topics that interest him, like the economic opportunity in Africa and the bad-boy rapper T.I. turning good. In these documentaries he highlights underreported but illuminating stories. I describe it as PBS with a kick. He's looking for a sizable grant to produce a documentary on Nile Valley civilizations. He's even trying to help the King family come together to make a movie on Dr. King, a project that has piqued Steven Spielberg's interest. (Intellectual property rights can get extremely complex, and, Andy says, "people can get obnoxious by asking for the moon. This story must be told. I trust Spielberg to do the best job.")

I responded to his television comment, "Depends on how you look at it. If you see advertisements as good news, then there is good news all the time. The bad news of teenage murders lures the audience so that station operators can sell airtime for good news."

"I never thought about it like that," he said. I felt good about myself, like a schoolboy who gets an A+ on a test.

He continued, "What I don't like is all these young people getting killed. Young people are important, usually more than they realize. These murders make me sick to my stomach."

I didn't want to get into a long conversation about teenage violence, so I changed tack, though eventually we went back to the subject of why young people are important.

"What are you up to next weekend?" I asked blandly.

"I'm going to see some old friends," he replied. Most of his good friends are schoolteachers. "I'm comfortable with teachers because they are fairly well educated, attuned to politics, but they aren't extravagant, so it doesn't cost me a lot of money to entertain them," he said in his low voice. He speaks slowly with many pauses between words. The silence adds to the profundity of his remarks.

Both his late wife, Jean, and his current wife, Carolyn, were elementary schoolteachers, down to earth and not extravagant. Jean was a fourth-grade teacher and reading specialist. Carolyn taught for thirty years in the Atlanta public school system. She integrated Goldsmith Elementary as one of its first black teachers, and later taught for eighteen years at E. Rivers Elementary, where she was also one of its first black teachers.

His love for teachers goes way back. He had a crush on his fourth-grade teacher, Ethelyne Jones Acox, who taught him how to write. In an old crowded New Orleans public school, she was the only one who encouraged him. She put her arm around him and said, "You certainly form your letters well." Andy's penmanship is worthy of praise. He likes to use black ink in calligraphic pens to sign his name but keeps losing the ones I give him. While Andy was opening a bank account in New York as a young man, the branch manager said he wouldn't accept his signature because it was right out of the penmanship book. The manager gave him a yellow legal pad and made him develop a new unique signature that is a combination of cursive and print. To this day he uses the same signature. He slants his letters to the right and loops the downstroke of the A in his first name to cross it.

"Has spending so much time with teachers helped to shape your thoughts toward young people?" I asked.

"Oh, yes. The more I hear of young people having trouble, I can't help but think about those Jesus years of twelve to thirty. So often the answer is just more patience. Young folks need not hurry. My teacher friends agree with me," he said.

In my household as I grew up, patience was like a four-letter word: lazy. My father taught me to pursue anything I wanted—a job, game or girl—with active persistence. Jazz ballads like "Body and Soul" and "Here's That Rainy Day" are even tough for me to play. I usually want to rush the beat. To hear Uncle Andy urge me to take my time, to take breaths and slow my motor goes against my natural inclination. I've struggled to follow his prescription for patience in my personal and professional life.

"I understand that life is a protracted journey, but why do I have to wait to make a contribution?" I asked.

"You don't," he responded. "But you need to take time to determine the appropriate action in your situation. Take the tragic example of the Black Panthers, who were essentially young students and dropouts. They got themselves all worked up and got themselves shot."

Founded in Oakland in 1966, the Black Panthers sought to promote black power and self-protection. Some of the Panthers resorted to violent means to propel their agenda. Many Panthers read Robert Williams's *Negroes with Guns,* and they protested white-dominated police forces by ambushing officers with weapons. Some even turned on their own members, torturing a nineteen-year-old New York chapter activist who was suspected of being a police informant. While some may think the Panthers hunted their goal of black power with unhinged abandon, the organization started several programs to help local communities. Andy posits that a combination of frustration, despair and desperation led to the creation of the organization.

I observed, "Weren't the Black Panthers just angry at their situation? In other countries, young rebels use weapons to fight for their cause. They want a better life and take matters into their own hands."

"They were in a hurry to get killed," he countered.

During the years of the civil rights movement, Andy would ask the tough kids who didn't believe in nonviolence, "How many people did you kill last week or year? If you are so violent, why aren't you busy being more violent?" He criticized them: "You aren't violent. You're cowards because you aren't doing anything." Those who claimed they couldn't accept nonviolence were nonetheless experiencing the systematic injustices of racism. The nonviolent movement gave them an opportunity to resist those injustices. Andy often said that it didn't make any sense to throw rocks at someone who had a machine gun. "That isn't militancy. That's stupidity. We had to confront the tough kids who were in a hurry," he explained. Movement leaders once convinced black gang members in Chicago to join a march in Mississippi. The gang members were scared stiff and gained an appreciation for the Southern Christian Leadership Conference (SCLC) staff who were unfazed while marching in unfriendly quarters.

"But sometimes young people's impatience can help them make a positive and meaningful impact on society," I replied.

I got a crash course in the benefits of impatience from several young Silicon Valley entrepreneurs while living in San Francisco in 2007. They hatch an idea, and a month later they launch their product. And a year later, several million people are using it. Many of these entrepreneurs are in such a hurry that they launch products that have bugs and security problems. They rely on user feedback and rapid iteration to catch and debug their source code. It's a fast process but one that is valued in the valley. I draw inspiration from LinkedIn founder Reid Hoffman who says, "If you're not somewhat embarrassed by your 1.0 product launch, then you've released too late."[2] Amen.

In summer of 2006, my college buddy David and I traveled to India in order to build a social networking Web site for young Indians that would help them with their educational aspirations. The educational services market in India is huge. Indian Internet penetration, however, is not. David moved to India to lead the local development and marketing of our product. A former professional basketball player in Germany and MVP of the Dartmouth basketball team, he soon acquired the nickname "Vanilla Gorilla" because of his imposing height of almost seven feet. After draining our financial reserves, I took a job at an investment bank in London to finance our operations. When a job opportunity arose in San Francisco, I jumped at it.

I fell in love with the entrepreneurial ecosystem of the Bay Area. I was young and in a hurry. I pitched top venture capitalists on Sand Hill Road and shady angel investors. I mostly got "no's," but we saw some success with a modestly growing user base. AOL even offered us an international licensing deal. I wish I had done some more homework! Like many entrepreneurs, I failed because I ran out of money. But you also find accomplished self-starters in Silicon Valley like the founders of YouTube and Google. The successes of these entrepreneurs convince me that young people who are in a hurry can change the world for the better.

"Ideas are currency in the Bay Area," Andy commented. "The more you have, the richer you are. I wish every young person could experience the start-up culture out there. In the 1960s, Martin and I really tried to encourage this type of innovation by building a supportive ecosystem. We didn't want to step on the fresh ideas of the many students who were involved."

"Did young people have a significant impact on the movement?" I asked.

"Young people were the civil rights movement," he declared.

He stopped for a moment, wanting his words to sink in, like pebbles thrown in a pond. He looked up from his empty plate, "We civil rights leaders didn't take any credit away from them. In Selma, young people started the movement because they were pissed that their parents couldn't vote. In Greensboro, North Carolina, young folks started the sit-ins, and then there was Claudette Colvin."

"Who's that?" I asked.

"The girl who wouldn't give up her bus seat."

"I thought that was Rosa Parks, or at least that's what Trivial Pursuit says," I said.

Andy explained. Fifteen-year-old Colvin refused to give up her seat on March 2, 1955, claiming it was her constitutional right. The Montgomery police yanked her from the bus, kicked her and arrested her. Colvin was wound up because black history month had just ended, and she had just finished learning about the Fourteenth Amendment and significant African Americans like Harriet Tubman. Colvin was a member of the NAACP youth group, and Rosa Parks was a mentor to her and a friend of her family. Colvin's arrest was practically ignored by most black leaders even though they were looking for a test case. Yet some black leaders were galvanized; even Dr. King, who was a new resident of Montgomery and was bogged down trying to finish his doctoral dissertation, rallied in support of Colvin.

"That little teenage girl must have had a steel testicle," laughed Andy. Southern black women were true militants because they were frequently on the front lines, cleaning white folks' kitchens and mopping white folks' offices. They experienced abuse firsthand.

But Colvin was too young, too early and too unknown. Some African American leaders thought she wouldn't be a good public face for the movement because she was still a student and recently impregnated by a married man. Some blacks even blamed Colvin for provoking the police officers. They wanted a sure-fire winner for their public face. Enter the unassailable, forty-two-year-old Rosa Parks. Nine months later, when Parks refused to give up her seat, black leaders were ready like a football team about to take the field.

"I think more people should know about Colvin. Maybe Snapple can make her a Snapple Fact, or Google can change its logo for a day in her honor. Did you ever meet Colvin?" I asked.

"No, not as a youth" he said. "I met her later, at an event where she was honored by Evelyn Lowery and the SCLC women."

"How has history treated her?" I asked. I was curious to learn whether he agreed that many had forgotten about a young person's critical contribution to the civil rights movement. I was pleased to discover that historians have not forgotten. In 2009, Phillip Hoose's excellent *Claudette Colvin: Twice Toward Justice* won the National Book Award for

Young People's Literature, which led to a picture of Colvin appearing on the front page of the *New York Times*.

"Claudette is like America's Winnie Mandela. Winnie was as much or maybe more of a hero to South Africans than Nelson Mandela or Archbishop Desmond Tutu, yet the outside world didn't give her any credit or consider her for a Nobel Prize. The ANC [African National Congress] beat up on her too," he said.

Winnie Mandela is the ex-wife of Nelson Mandela. When Nelson was sentenced to life imprisonment, she carried on his cause to end apartheid. But she called for militant methods to attain freedom. In 1988, Winnie's bodyguard implicated her in the beating death of a fourteen-year-old who was thought to be a police informant. She was also accused of corruption. Despite her sullied reputation, she was elected president of the ANC Women's League.

"The ANC was really afraid of Winnie," Andy continued. "She was living in South Africa alone, without any support or money, and was totally exposed to the brutality of the apartheid regime. She was cracked and shattered. But she never gave up. She kept her husband's cause alive. Like Colvin, she went underappreciated." But among the rank and file of Soweto, a shanty town neighborhood of Johannesburg, she remains "our beloved Winnie."

Andy's daughter Andrea visited South Africa while working as a legislative aide to Senator Ted Kennedy. Winnie was under house arrest, surrounded by barbed wire, with spotlights focused on the house twenty-four hours of the day and police peering in, completely isolated from her ANC supporters in Soweto. Winnie thanked Andrea for crying because she said all of her tears had dried up. Soon after her meeting, Andrea made a commitment to work on African issues as the Secretary for Africa with the United Church of Christ Board for World Ministries, where she supervised the church's missions in Africa. She even got involved in the Free South Africa efforts in America that eventually led to the passage of sanctions legislation.

"Unlike Colvin, the student leaders of the sit-in movement are widely celebrated for their role in civil rights," I observed, rescuing myself from an Uncle Andy tangent.

"That's the best example of how young people helped to define the movement," he said.

The student sit-in movement began in earnest in February 1960 when four North Carolina Agricultural and Technical College students sat at a Woolworth's lunch counter. The store employees refused to serve the students at the counter until the store closed. The next day more than twenty students showed up. And the day after, more than eighty students came. The sit-in movement snowballed, adding dozens of students throughout the South as the weeks and months passed.

"Is that where John Lewis got involved?" I asked.

A son of the South, Lewis played a principal role in organizing the sit-in movement in Tennessee. Lewis got involved in the movement while a student at Fisk University in Nashville, Tennessee.[3] He famously led the march in Selma where he was beaten over the head. Now a congressman from Georgia's fifth congressional district (Andy's old seat), Lewis has earned the reputation of the "Conscience of the Congress." He also shops for ties at Neiman Marcus (I ran into him there once)—that should be a Snapple Fact.

While living in New York in 1961, Andy watched a story on NBC that profiled the student leaders of the Tennessee sit-in movement, one of whom was Lewis. Andy was very inspired by Lewis, Diane Nash, Bernard Lafayette and their peers. They motivated other students, both black and white, to create their own sit-ins to protest segregation. They had started a true grassroots movement. Andy also admired the style in which the Fisk kids conducted themselves. The sit-ins had all the right elements: the philosophy of nonviolence, the tactics of boycotts and voter registration drives and the sizzle of good press.

"Were the students local folk heroes?"

"Not really. Girls weren't chasing them. They weren't the football players or fraternity brothers. They were the nerds," he said.

"John Lewis was a nerd?" I asked.

"He was ... and he still is." We laughed. "He's also a saint. After more than thirty imprisonments and beatings, he never became bitter or angry," he concluded.

The students dressed in their Sunday best to contrast with the whites. Many brought textbooks to read during the sit-ins. What made the sit-in movement special was that it motivated young people who were not part of the NAACP to get involved. After Andy saw the NBC story, he knew it was time to return home to the South.

"Something was brewing, and I had to be part of it. Young people lit a fire within me," he said emphatically.

My mom taught a university course on organizational behavior. My sister followed in her high heels, pursuing a doctorate in a similar field. She now works at a consultancy and reviews the structures of organizations. I grew up around business charts and flowcharts. I had to ask, "How did students fit into the structure of the movement?"

"You must first understand the demographics and organizational structure of the entire movement," he replied. I was excited. Forget John Lewis. I'm a nerd.

There were two key groups of activists: the old established group, which included future Supreme Court Justice Thurgood Marshall and NAACP executive director Roy Wilkins, who advocated for incremental, gradual change and had worked for progress through the federal courts since the early 1940s; and the young crowd that demanded immediate social change. Dr. King and other civil rights leaders became the moderate implementers. They navigated between the two groups and brought them together, bridging generations.

"It was the coming together that made the movement work," he declared.

"How did you and Dr. King help the students?" I asked.

"We were their big brothers. We didn't dictate orders. Martin sent funds to the Student Nonviolent Coordinating Committee (SNCC), which John Lewis chaired, for their first meeting, but we wanted them to remain independent, so they could continue their creativity. When you're independent, you're more creative," he said.

"Was there any downside to having students so actively involved?" I asked.

"Well, much of the student initiative was driven out of emotion. Some incident would occur that would galvanize the young community. Of course young people wanted to go faster and do more. Martin and I had to help them to act rationally and not emotionally. Martin had an acute sense of timing. He let the young folks have their space, but would help guide them toward an appropriate path with his words," Andy said.

"Did any students come to you for advice because of your theological grounding?" I asked.

"Not really." He said young folks didn't want to hear about religious or spiritual matters, though John Lewis also had a strong religious and moral grounding.

"Most students didn't pay attention to people over thirty, and I was thirty. But that was what made them so effective. They weren't looking for gradual negotiations with the white establishment. I didn't get frustrated with that. The Bible was written by old people and only has a few stories that show young people having an impact. David slaying Goliath is a good example. I remind young folks that Jesus said don't forbid the children from coming unto him because such is the kingdom of heaven," he said.

"Did students consider you an Uncle Tom?" I asked. (Guess from whom I learned my bluntness.)

"Some did, but they thought anyone who wore a shirt and tie like me was a sellout. But most young people felt that way because they were uncomfortable speaking with white people. Martin always sent me to speak with whites because I was comfortable having spent time in the northeast and in church."

"I would have thought young people would have been more demanding or violent like the Black Panthers," I said.

They might have, Andy recalled, but many of the young leaders were like Jim Lawson, who came to Nashville after serving as a Methodist missionary in India for two years. He also spent time in an Ohio jail for being a conscientious objector to the Korean War. He led workshops on nonviolence in Nashville that started at six o'clock in the morning, so only serious students would come.

History will never know the names of thousands of blacks who went to jail or were killed because they eschewed a nonviolent path. The Black Panthers briefly merged with the SNCC, but they soon realized they held completely different goals and approaches. In 1966, there was a fissure between the SNCC and SCLC. Black power promoter Stokely Carmichael ousted John Lewis from his leadership position at the SNCC. He liked the attention of the press and put forward a militant image of not only himself but the SNCC. On one occasion, Carmichael charged a police officer who had bumped him. Andy was pissed with Stokely because he represented the SNCC and other students looked up to him for leadership. He could have endangered the safety of the entire group of marchers. Carmichael was impatient and annoyed by the persistent calls from Dr. King and other leaders for nonviolence. Andy saw the young people's cry for militancy and black power as impatience and a dramatic overreaction. Andy and his peers in the SCLC learned to hate the sin and not the sinner. They would have to convince the same white people who worked against them to work with them. To be sure, not all young people were alike. The ones who were smart and serious about bringing about change were firmly grounded in Gandhi's philosophy of nonviolence.

Mahatma Gandhi invited several black university presidents, such as Dr. Benjamin Mays of Morehouse, Mordecai Johnson of Howard University and William Stuart Nelson of Dillard University, to India to observe that country's independence in 1947 firsthand. They returned with a strong understanding of how nonviolence can bring about change. These university presidents surely introduced Gandhi's teachings into course curricula, sparking discussion and debate on campus. Higher education was the logical place to teach nonviolence and to instruct the future leaders of the civil rights movement.

"It must have taken some time for such a counterintuitive approach like nonviolence to win support among younger people," I said.

By the time young people started hearing about the Gandhian philosophy in the 1960s, it had already been part of the African American dialogue for a good number of years. Andy summarized the origin of the nonviolent movement, which made me feel like I was watching another of his documentaries with ancient black-and-white footage. I removed my grimy Nike tennis shoes and placed my elbows on the counter. Andy crossed his legs, revealing his blue argyle knee socks.

The Gandhian movement started in 1912 in South Africa where Gandhi spent time, and it didn't reach fruition until 1947 when India became independent. In the 1940s in the United States, early civil rights leaders tried to promote Gandhi's nonviolent methods in the courts, but it wasn't until Rosa Parks, Claudette Colvin and the sit-in movement that civil rights leaders understood how to turn Gandhi's philosophy into dramatic action.

"Were you ever concerned that young people would reject the nonviolent philosophy en masse?" I asked.

"No, because we built a supportive ecosystem," he put it plainly.

Young people were surrounded by nonviolent images and ideas. The schools were teaching the philosophy of Gandhi, the churches were proselytizing about the compassion of Jesus and civil rights leaders like Dr. King were making speeches about nonviolence.

Like YouTube, Andy observed, "we provided the infrastructure and people populated content. Martin articulated the vision and developed the infrastructure of the movement, from securing financing to working with several grassroots organizations. And the students innovated with boycotts and sit-ins, things that attracted the attention of the nation."

I was impressed. Very impressed. "Do you use YouTube?" I asked.

"Oh, my grandchildren have it on sometimes. I like watching funny animal bloopers with them."

"I have to admit, the otters holding hands are adorable," I said quickly, while thinking to myself that at least he wasn't watching the treadmill dancers.

We had skipped around a few anecdotes about why young people are important, but I felt Uncle Andy was contradicting himself. On one hand he said young people are important, which to me means that we should hustle and go after our dreams. On the other hand he said young people should be patient. I decided to get more direct with Andy and ask him to explain his remarks with more tangible examples and anecdotes. I channeled my inner Mike Wallace. I discovered that his answers weren't contradictory, just counterintuitive.

"What should young people today know about young people during the civil rights movement?" I asked.

"The leaders of the sit-in movement understood their shit before they opened their mouths. They had read Gandhi. They had read the Bible. They knew that they were in the midst of the struggle for the soul of America," he replied. Still not concrete enough for me.

"What is the struggle for my generation? How do young people make a difference today?" I asked, looking for him to say something heavy, but he went for funny instead.

"I liken the civil rights movement to the environmental movement. Not everyone needs to join Greenpeace or the Sierra Club. Young folks could do something to impact the environment where they live, like turn off the lights or recycle their old copies of *Playboy*," he joked.

I pushed back. "By telling someone to localize the greater issue, aren't you teaching them to be more parochial? Recycling a magazine obscures the greater cause," I said.

"It doesn't make it more parochial. It makes it more relevant," he stated.

He then said something that is quintessentially Uncle Andy: "You must start where you are." If he has a mantra, that would be it. It's simple—like a Hemingway sentence—but powerful.

He thinks that the biggest problem in any movement is that folks want to know the answers before they know all the questions. He got very upset with the Hunger Coalition because they didn't feed anybody. They raised a lot of money to talk about hunger and nothing happened. He wanted them to address global hunger and do something practical and meaningful. They started with a theoretical problem and nobody got fed. Start with simple problems and build from there. You'll be on much more solid ground.

"That gets back to your message of listening to the voice within you," I remarked, trying desperately to connect the dots.

Those in the movement, Andy said, used to sing the song "Freedom Is a Constant Struggle," which contains the lyrics, "We've struggled so long we must be free." In the Portuguese colonies in Africa, the Africans said, "A luta continua," which means "the struggle continues." The saying, which was coined by Amilcar Cabral, a leader in the nationalist movement in Guinea-Bissau, became a mantra for freedom-seeking people everywhere. There is a constant struggle for justice that will continue regardless.

"I try to get young people to see that life is a struggle. You struggle in many ways. And you don't have to go out of your way to create your own struggles. Be faithful to yourself. Start where you are and you'll hear your inner voice. You'll find your time and your place," he commented.

I wasn't satisfied. I wanted a more concrete answer or anecdote. "What is the student movement of today? I don't see one. Maybe there is a less apparent, invisible one," I said.

"There's not one with the same magnitude as ours, but don't get caught up in the myth that all students were engaged," he responded.

In the early 1960s at Fisk University and other Tennessee colleges, there were more kids sitting on the benches of the football and basketball teams and drinking at their fraternities than involved in the sit-ins. While there were thirty people at the sit-ins, there were three hundred doing other foolish things. Another ho-hum day on campus. There were a few special people like John Lewis who had a special calling.

"I encourage young people to chill out and relax. It's okay to goof off at the fraternity. I look around for the kids who were with us in Mississippi and Birmingham, and a lot of them are dead. They died because of ulcers and heart trouble. John Lewis is one of the few that survived the movement. Marion Barry, who was involved, is still alive, but he has been shattered and shaken for the last twenty years. It takes special people to help lead and inspire dramatic change," he said.

"Every movement needs its special agent of change. The colonialists had Alexander Hamilton and Thomas Jefferson, for instance. Enlightened activists inspire their sluggish followers," I said.

"There is a spiritual logic to our history that we seldom understand while it's going on. True leaders tap in to this spiritual awareness of what ought to be happening right where they are, like Thomas Jefferson and Martin. But also, the followers aren't lazy. Maybe they aren't inspired by the cause or don't know their calling. Martin and I were not activists in college. We took our time. We finished our schooling, got married, settled down and then our time came. We couldn't have forced it. Young people can make a difference now. But don't worry if you aren't ready right now," he affirmed.

Andy once told me that he and Dr. King identified with Jefferson and Hamilton—young men trying to create a new America. In their rebellion against England they never wanted to destroy England. They wanted to be free and to partner with England because it was still a powerful economic force. That was a much more fitting model for civil rights leaders than a revolution. Dr. King and Andy were not trying to overthrow the government. They were trying to get the government, as Dr. King said, to "live out the true meaning of its creeds." Dr. King constantly quoted from the Declaration of Independence and Constitution.

"Jefferson and Hamilton started where they were, and so did we," Andy said.

Start where you are. It's a settling mantra. Instead of huffing and puffing, Uncle Andy has been the calming coolant to my sometimes overheated hopes. He urged me to relax and just enjoy high school and college. Your time will come, he said, but don't wander aimlessly. You start with that man in the mirror and take practical, relevant steps to make a difference.

Practical steps. Andy mentioned how before the movement the communists had identified several race problems in the South. They came to the region with theoretical ideas and suggestions. Nobody paid any attention to them, and they finally gave up. The last thing that any social scientist or civil rights leader would have suggested to start a movement was for Claudette and Rosa to sit down in a bus. It made much more sense to start with the educational and economic issues. And the movement began in earnest when someone just started where they were, in the back of a bus. Civil rights leaders responded to the practical actions of Claudette and Rosa as if they had internalized Gandhi's comment, "There go my people. I must hurry and catch up to them for I am their leader."[4] Instead of starting with a middle-class theoretical framework, civil rights leaders responded to people's needs and immediate concerns.

"Look around and see where you can start," he suggested to me as he parted his hands.

Still, I wanted him to offer concrete suggestions on how I could make a difference at a young age. "Several of my friends entered the Peace Corps and Teach for America because they saw it as a way to address immediate problems. Is that an appropriate path?"

He thinks the student movement of today needs to be centered on education. He used to say to his first wife, Jean, that teaching is the most important movement we have. If we don't find a way to educate the next generation, then the many civil rights protests will have been in vain. What good is it to have racial equality when minorities still have a terrible time getting a job or finding affordable housing? He advises students to see the next step in the civil rights movement as the education of tomorrow's leaders.

"It doesn't matter how young you are. Keep passing down your wisdom to the next generation," he said.

"Is there a young person that you've come across recently who is making a difference, someone who is passing down wisdom at a young age?" I asked.

He spoke of an eleven-year-old that he honored at a ceremony in Washington, DC. The kid went to Africa and saw the difficulty so many had in traveling from one town to the next. He came back and sent over 2,000 bicycles to Africa with his program, Wheels to Africa. Now he is fourteen and is calling on people to send 10,000 bikes to Africa. He's just a nice little clean-cut kid who wanted to do something. He is passing along wisdom to his peers by his sheer actions.

"I got it. You're never too young to contribute," I remarked.

"You've encouraged me too," Andy said. I can live three days on a good compliment. I waited for him to continue, "You responded to Katrina by helping many musicians return to the city. Katrina sparked more sustained activism than any other event I can remember in this century, more than September 11th. What was it about that hurricane that compelled you?" he asked.

"I think New Orleans is one of the most beautiful and soulful places in the world. I became friends with many folks down there before Katrina. That we would let a city that has contributed so much to American culture die seemed wrong to me," I said. I started where I was. I am a jazz musician and I've worked hard to save the home of jazz music.

"People get involved when things are obviously wrong, like a catastrophe or moral crisis like segregation," he observed.

"Why does it take a catastrophe to get young people to care? Or is that just human nature?" I queried.

"Yes, it is human nature. We tend to get upset when things go wrong. We're usually okay with the status quo. Such was the case in the civil rights movement until people started to realize slowly the wrongs of segregation," he said.

"Maybe we need to find a new crisis every few years to reawaken us."

"You may not find a new crisis, but young people can find a new location to be reawakened and challenged. In the 1960s, it was the South. In the 1980s, it was South Africa," he noted.

"In the 1990s you had the fall of the Berlin Wall and spread of democracy. And now?" I asked. I answered my own question, "We are in a new global environmental movement in which young people can participate. Al Gore sounded the alarm about the issue. Maybe it's the crisis of our time." Maybe not.

Whatever crisis our generation confronts, Andy urges us to remember that we can always make an impact. I've always thought politics was a good way for young people to get involved because you can learn about almost any issue—racial equality, economics or the environment. Andy's father taught him to read editorials when he was a boy, which got him interested in public service years later. Every four years the same question is raised: "Will young people vote?" Andy thinks there are other significant ways for us to participate in our democracy than just voting.

Not only did young people vote for Andy, they volunteered to work during his campaigns for elected office. Most of the energy and vitality in his campaigns came from young people. Almost every successful campaign is powered in part by the enthusiasm of young people. It was young people who helped their parents to see Andy as a potential candidate and congressman. The way young people responded to him made older people take him seriously. That is true for Barack Obama too. Hillary Clinton was polling better among older people, but the younger people arguably convinced their friends and parents.

"And getting involved in public service at a young age has enormous benefits for the rest of your life," he added.

There was a twelve-year-old kid named Wallace who helped Andy during his first congressional campaign in 1970. Andy gave him the job of organizing kids to put stickers on cars and explained to him that he couldn't just put them on the cars. Wallace had to ask people for permission, explain why they should vote for Andy, wipe off the bumper and then stick one on. Wallace recruited fifteen kids to frequent parking lots on the weekends and talk to people. When Wallace finished high school, Andy was in his second term in Congress. Wallace wanted to attend college and called Andy to ask for help, and Andy obliged.

Finally Andy had given me a concrete anecdote, some tangible advice. If I had a nickel for every time I heard about a young person getting hooked up because of their involvement in a political campaign, well, I would have a lot of nickels. Wallace eventually had a lot of nickels too.

When he finished university, Wallace asked Andy for help in getting admitted to law school. Andy was serving as UN ambassador and had enormous clout, which helped Wallace gain admission despite his mediocre college grades. Later, when Andy served as mayor of Atlanta, he went up to Wall Street to sign bond certificates which totalled $300 million for an airport runway. It was Andy's first time in a Wall Street conference room, and who was sitting next to him? Little Wallace all grown up. Wallace had become a junior partner in a law firm on Wall Street and was making more money than Andy's paltry $50,000 salary.

"What's the moral of that story?" I asked.

"I use Wallace's story to show that if people understand politics at an early age, they can benefit their whole life. Politics is really about access to power and money. You get involved to do good. Little Wallace really believed in the causes for which he campaigned. But if you keep doing good, you will probably also do well. You're a good example of that. You were knocking on doors in the New Hampshire presidential primary, and the next thing you know, you are a special assistant on the John Kerry campaign," he said.

I started where I was. I went to university in New Hampshire, one of the most important states in presidential primaries. Almost every day there was another presidential candidate on campus or in a nearby town. My involvement in the Kerry campaign has helped me in other parts of my life, or so I think. But I get queasy thinking about supporting a candidate for an ulterior motive. Being so transparently ambitious about using politics to attain other things leaves me unsettled.

Andy understood. "You get involved for the right reasons. And just by being active and getting involved, opportunities will emerge. Sure, you can smell the young ambitious people and that can be off-putting. The more you lean forward, the more the person you are talking to leans back," he said.

Words to remember. The more you hustle someone and get in their grill, the more they are apt to recoil. Taken another way, the more you lean back and say and do things for the right reason, the more someone leans forward and wants to help you. So getting involved in public service at a young age for the right reasons can help you in unknown ways. You become a leaf in the divine wind. Getting involved in public service provides a terrific window not only to the issues of the world but to how it works—money, connections and influence.

"But remember," Andy admonished, "while I urge you to take your time and find the speaking voice in your heart, it doesn't mean you shouldn't look for ways to contribute to society today. And then there is the other problem . . ." he trailed off. Sometimes you don't know if he's lost in thought or done with it.

I pushed him. "What problem?"

"When you get older and wiser, one of the hardest things you can do is to listen to young people," he said.

I liked where he was going. "Young people have the ideas, older people have experience and power," I said.

"That's what Martin and I realized. We were the ones that tried to fuse youthful zeal with old-fashioned methods. If we listened too much to young people, we might have rushed things. If we listened too much to the old farts, we wouldn't have supported the sit-ins that were so dramatic and successful. That's why I like talking with you. You challenge me," he said.

I nodded. He was on a roll. I felt like I was in a snow globe with bits of knowledge sailing around me. Andy slowly stood up. He's not too tall, about five feet eight inches. He waddled to the bathroom, shifting his weight from one knee to the other. He's determined to avoid knee replacement surgery. He's waiting on research to determine how stem cells can grow new cartilage.

I exhaled and reflected on our discussion. I felt relaxed. Rome wasn't built in a day and neither was the Lego replica of Rome I once saw in a museum. A teenager galvanized a community by refusing to give up her seat. College students captured the attention of the nation with the sit-ins. A young preacher inspired and challenged our nation.

I wanted to learn more about the young preacher. But that would have to wait for another day.

3 A MACROECONOMIST TEACHES A NATION TO FISH

[Economic] statistics are like a bikini. What they reveal is suggestive, but what they conceal is vital.

—Professor Aaron Levenstein[1]

"Cast! Cast!" the guide yelled at me. "Cast! Cast!"

The blue boat tipped as I leaned forward and threw the fishing line upstream. The Missouri River seemed angry. Its heavy current splashed against the boat and took the line back downstream. It was running very high because of the extremely warm weather—the snow was coming off the mountains faster than usual. I cast the line once more and caught a green sprig on the bank. "You're a natural," Andy joked. Fly-fishing is hard work. I prefer the simplicity of ordinary fishing—beers and boys, slurp and burp.

Andy wasn't faring much better. He hooked two branches and the guide. I actually caught a silver trout, which we named Secretariat after the 1973 Triple Crown winner. We released it after Andy took photographs. He is a keen photographer with a camera always at hand. We cruised down the river under the azure Montana sky. It was a warm day in May 2004, and we were out for a little exploration and adventure. We looked the part. We wore beige waders, and Andy wore a tan cowboy hat with sunglasses. Our families had traveled to Montana together to take part in a community service award ceremony organized in part by my mother. Andy was a featured speaker at the event, along with former United States senator George McGovern.

It was there and then that Andy and I had the first of our series of winding conversations on civil rights and economic empowerment. I was in college, and I failed my first economics exam and dropped the course, so I tried to learn the material on my own. I began to read the works of important economists like Adam Smith, David Ricardo, John Maynard Keynes, Friedrich August von Hayek, Milton Friedman and Amartya Sen. Uncle Andy thought I should read the works of another "macro-economist," Dr. Martin Luther King Jr. He believes that many overlook the economic goals and dimensions of the civil rights movement. A firm understanding of Dr. King's speeches and writings would show that economic opportunity was at the heart of the movement.

"What books did you read in high school English class?" Uncle Andy asked.

I didn't know where he was going, but I answered. *"To Kill a Mockingbird, Catcher in the Rye, The Scarlet Letter, Wuthering Heights, Beowulf, Brave New World,* several Shakespeare plays like *Hamlet* and *Julius Caesar,"* I said. I've still never read *Romeo and Juliet.*

"Every prep school kid in the country reads basically the same stuff," he responded. His wry, withering and mocking critique disappointed me. I liked many of those books (and their CliffsNotes).

"Isn't that a good thing? There is a common body of work or national vocabulary that I can discuss with my peers. It's good to have some standardization," I retorted.

"If you read what everybody else is reading, you don't really learn anything unique. That's why I have encouraged you to read mystical poetry. It's the same thing with all the economists you're reading. Every student who takes an economics course reads one of those authors. But if you want to learn something new about economics, something stirring and less theoretical, you should read Martin's speeches," he returned.

"I'm pretty sure he wasn't an economist. I've never heard any economics professors mention him or seen his name in economics white papers or textbooks."

The boat idled while the guide checked his small map. A robust gale of wind brushed the boat against the bank.

"He was one of the finest macroeconomics thinkers that this nation has seen," Andy said.

I didn't argue with him. I chalked his comment up to his wild bending of the term "economist." Reverends like to widen the meaning of words. It gives them room to interpret, entertain and embellish. As for me, I stuck to the strict definition: An economist is someone who makes weather forecasters look good.

Several years later I was in graduate school in London, auditing a corporate finance course and not understanding most of it. A classmate asked me whether Barack Obama shared Martin Luther King's views on economics. Obama was still a US senator from Illinois, and I wasn't familiar with his views on economics. For that matter, I didn't know much about Dr. King's views on economics either. So I did what most diligent students do. I Googled for answers.

Dr. King delivered his "I Have a Dream" speech at the March on Washington for Jobs and Freedom in 1963. Jobs. The word stuck out. I reread the speech. Dr. King used a financial metaphor to describe the misfortune of African Americans: "America has given the Negro people a bad check, a check which has come back marked 'insufficient funds.' We refuse to believe that there are insufficient funds in the great vaults of opportunity of this nation. And so we've come to cash this check, a check that will give us upon demand the riches of freedom and the security of justice."[2]

I could see that Dr. King had a strong desire to create jobs for minorities. This one paragraph in a monumental speech made me remember

Uncle Andy's remark about Dr. King the macroeconomist. Andy had decided at first not to attend that speech. He saw no reason to attend and didn't think the march would become iconic. Luckily, Dr. King convinced Andy and Jean to come, so they witnessed the events firsthand. The march was organized by six large civil rights groups: the Southern Christian Leadership Conference (SCLC), the Student Nonviolent Coordinating Committee (SNCC), the Congress of Racial Equality, the Urban League, the National Council of Negro Women, and the NAACP. It attracted middle-class blacks and white liberals. That such a broad coalition of groups and individuals rallied to the cause of jobs and economic opportunity is telling.

There's an old proverb that my mom taught me: When the student is ready, the teacher will appear. I wasn't ready to understand Uncle Andy's remark in Montana, but a few years later I was ready, and I asked him for a full explanation. Of all the topics I've discussed with him, I find his commentaries on Dr. King as an economics thinker and his own thoughts about economic empowerment the most germane to who I am. I work at a global investment bank and see the Bloomberg terminals blinking relentlessly with financial news and numbers every day. Our conversation helped me understand the significance not only of creating jobs but of my job. Our discussion helped me see Dr. King as a powerful economic thinker and provided an insightful, practical tag to my understanding of the civil rights movement.

"You've finally come around to it," said Andy with a hint of satisfaction.

He had wanted me to ask about Dr. King and economic empowerment for years, but he gave me the space and time to stumble upon my own questions. Andy was eager to speak. Even though he calls himself a "slumdog economist," not having taken economics courses in school or studied it formally, it is one of his favorite topics. It's hard to get through any conversation on civil rights without his mentioning jobs, capitalism and economic opportunity.

"How was Dr. King a macroeconomics thinker?"

"It's best if I tell you a story," he said.

I exhaled and furrowed my brows. I wanted to squeeze a direct answer out of him, but I've learned that the real gems are found in Uncle Andy's stories. I rested my head on my hands. That's my "go ahead, talk" prompt—he's very familiar with it.

He told me the story about the time he was scheduled to preach about the Christian family at his small church in Thomasville, Georgia, in 1957. On the day of the sermon, one of his deacons came to the church with a black eye. Andy investigated and discovered that the deacon's wife had hit him on the head with an axe handle. Both the deacon and his wife were fifty years old and upstanding members of the church. The deacon had worked on a plantation for almost thirty years. He had run the entire plantation on a salary of $45 per week. He had just discovered that a young white boy who had much less experience than he had was earning $75 a week at the plantation. The deacon was more experienced, but the white boy was paid more simply because of his skin color. The deacon proceeded to get drunk, and his wife got mad at him.

"I realized then that no matter how much I preach, if I don't change that system that made him a second-class citizen, I'm not going to help change the quality of life for the people in that community," he said.

Andy moved to the poor rural town of Thomasville in 1955 thinking that the citizens would be less materialistic than his peers in the black middle class. He thought it would be a perfect place to build his congregation and focus on the teachings of Christ. He quickly learned, however, that his parishioners aspired to become like his peers in the black middle class. Young people were leaving town to find jobs elsewhere. They wanted more money to afford a better lifestyle with the same materialistic things as the middle class. They wanted the freedom to thrive economically.

His comment reminded me of how President Kennedy ended his inaugural address. "Here on earth God's work must truly be our own." I said to Andy, "Instead of talking about God, you wanted to do his work here on earth."

"I was tired of doing church work and wanted to do the work of the church."

"And Dr. King?" I asked.

"Oh, Martin felt the same way," he replied.

Dr. King told Uncle Andy that while he admired the Good Samaritan he didn't want to become one. Andy says it shocked others to hear a prominent southern minister like Dr. King say that he didn't want to be a Good Samaritan. Blacks were raised to be Good Samaritans and to offer help to the person bleeding on the street because it was usually a black person who had been beaten up. Dr. King said that he respected the Good Samaritan, but he didn't want to spend his life picking people up from the streets after they had been beaten and robbed. In Dr. King's "I've Been to the Mountaintop" speech that he delivered the day before he died in April 1968, he described the dangers of the actual Jericho Road. Dr. King had visited the Jericho Road in Israel and knew it to be a snaking and twisting route that enemies could easily attack. It was once known as the Bloody Pass.

There is also the metaphorical interpretation of Jericho Road: The journey ahead is dangerous and susceptible to all sorts of pitfalls and pratfalls.

"Martin wanted to change the Jericho Road so that people didn't get beaten up in the first place. He wanted to put traffic lights and police officers on the Jericho Road. We felt that the way to bring about comprehensive civil rights was macroeconomic social reform," he said.

He later came to see Dr. King's metaphor as a macroeconomic take on civil rights problems, including the joblessness that plagues not only African Americans but all Americans. Indeed, Andy recognizes that there are plenty of problems in the world, from hunger to disease, water resources and trade subsidies, but that day he focused my attention on economic problems.

"Dr. King wanted to get to the root of the problem. I've heard folks say that about terrorism today. The way to beat terrorism isn't to kill terrorists but to kill their ideology. It's difficult to do, not only to ameliorate that which causes the problem but to determine what the causes are," I observed.

I reminded Andy that Dr. King made use of a financial parable or metaphor in the "I Have a Dream" speech, when he mentioned the "bank of justice." We often use financial metaphors to describe things in our life. After a friend has done a favor, we say, "I owe you." We use words like "debt" and "repay." We talk about "spending" time. Linguist George Lakoff calls it our "moral accounting."[3] Not only do we use these metaphors, they inevitably frame our thoughts and shape how we think.

"That's why he used that metaphor. The only problem is that nobody remembers that part. People only remember the 'I Have a Dream' cadences," he replied.

"Why's that?" I asked without thinking.

"It was the most eloquent part." Realizing the obviousness of his statement, he continued, "It tied the movement for black people directly to the Constitution and Declaration of Independence and the beliefs of Jefferson and Lincoln. Though he wanted to talk more about his economic vision, we really had to keep it to politics." Civil rights leaders dovetailed themes of racial justice with religious rhetoric much like the Abolitionists had done a century earlier.

"Why didn't he describe his economic vision more fully?" I asked.

"We were just exiting McCarthyism, especially in the South. We didn't talk much about economics because that meant talking about redistribution of wealth . . ." he said.

I interrupted, "You didn't want to be called communist?"

"Almost everybody, including J. Edgar Hoover, tried to label us as communists. But Martin decided to emphasize his desire for political freedom and equality. We said we just want the same thing everybody else had. Martin's decision not to talk economics put the country very much at ease," he said. J. Edgar Hoover, the first director of the FBI, was a thorn in the side of the civil rights movement leaders. He authorized surveillance of

Dr. King and others and was generally, as Andy puts it, "a paranoid old transvestite crank." There have been a series of rumors since Hoover's death that he liked to wear women's clothes. Hoover didn't seem to be able to tell the difference between an angry kid throwing a Molotov cocktail in a riot and the disciplined civil rights marchers who believed in civil disobedience.

I concluded, "Voting rights were enacted and civil rights legislation was passed. The political dreams of Dr. King were realized. But I presume the little financial nugget in the speech shows us the unrealized part of his dream."

"As good church folks would say, Amen," he said.

While the civil rights leaders didn't talk much about economics, it was a cornerstone of the movement. The slogan of the SCLC was to "redeem the soul of America" and to cure the triple evils of racism, war and poverty. Desegregation was the answer to racism. Ending the Vietnam War was a partial answer to war.

Andy continued, "I've spent my entire life trying to work toward what Martin was talking about the whole time—curing poverty with economic empowerment."

"If you and Dr. King were so deeply concerned about poverty, why didn't you start with working toward comprehensive solutions to help the poor like organizing job fairs, working with politicians to extend health care benefits?" I asked.

"We couldn't," he said with a long, loud sigh.

I could tell I'd hit a chord. He looked pensively at the ceiling. They couldn't because people were angered and humiliated with signs that said "whites" and "colored." The blatant racism was the most immediate grievance. It bothered students that they could spend their money in department stores everywhere except the lunch counters, hence the sit-ins. It made more sense to start with educational reform, but it wasn't their decision. Claudette Colvin and Rosa Parks sat down on the bus and started the movement. They responded to immediate grievances, such as the "legal" humiliation of forcing blacks to sit in the back of the bus. Experiences dictated strategy. It was pragmatism defined.

"And those experiences convinced you that one first needs police officers on the Jericho Road before one can provide jobs," I summed it up.

"Well said," he confirmed.

The response to Rosa Parks's actions was the Montgomery bus boycott. Civil rights leaders used several boycotts to protest blatant racism. I said, "You gained the right to vote through engaging the business community. Your political goals were achieved by flexing your economic muscle." I had it. Or so I thought.

"In part."

"In part? What am I missing?" I asked.

"We recruited folks to boycott because the mobs and police in Birmingham were flagrantly abusive toward almost all black citizens. Bull Connor was a terror," he said.

Bull Connor was head of the Birmingham police department and involved with the Ku Klux Klan (KKK). He used police dogs and fire hoses to scare and attack African Americans. He was a public face for the ugly race relations in the Deep South. Black homeowners were making good money at Birmingham's steel mills, and they built small white frame houses with gardens and jungle gyms. Such socioeconomic progress was threatening to the KKK, so they bombed more than sixty homes in one year on what became known as Dynamite Hill. There were dozens of unsolved bombings. Birmingham was burning. In another instance of ugly brutality, white hoodlums knocked a black teenager from his bicycle, castrated him and left him there to die. This open belligerence toward blacks provoked many to sign up for the boycotts. It wasn't about economics. It was about ending the humiliation and mortification.

"I know you wanted all that violence to stop, but what else did you want to accomplish with the boycotts?" I asked.

"There was no justice for the bombings. But we didn't focus on that fact. We tried to address the underlying problems and create a compelling solution. It took a tremendous amount of strength to focus on the central issues and not get distracted by violence."

Andy and the other leaders articulated four goals: (1) desegregate stores including lunch counters and signs, (2) hire blacks as clerks, (3) drop charges against folks arrested for nonviolent demonstrations and (4) work toward desegregation of schools. They sent a letter to the mayor but, of course, he didn't respond. Before they demonstrated, they conducted workshops and trained demonstrators in nonviolent tactics. Blacks wouldn't buy anything but food and medicine. Whites were deterred from going to the stores because they wanted to avoid the demonstrations.

"Segregation was bad for business—businesses offended a large segment of their customers. The boycotts were even worse for business," he observed.

The demonstrations started with twenty-five to fifty people marching each day from the Sixteenth Street Baptist Church to city hall. No white politician would negotiate, so Andy turned to the business community. But he first turned to an unlikely broker, the church. He knew the director of Christian education for the Episcopal Diocese of Alabama, who was a young woman he had met at a conference at Northwestern University. He asked her to arrange a meeting with the Episcopal bishop. When Andy met with the bishop, he explained the purpose of the boycott and requested a meeting with Dr. King, Ralph David Abernathy, Reverend Fred Shuttlesworth and five or six local business leaders. The bishop obliged. It was the ensuing conversations with businessmen that led to results. But it was also the dramatic imagery that depicted economic conditions for blacks in the South. Andy, for instance, led a small group of blacks to a bank. He asked to speak with the bank's management about hiring black people, but nobody would meet with them, so they took a knee, like a vassal before a lord, and prayed.

Andy and other civil rights leaders recognized that it wasn't enough to bring about racial equality. They needed to demonstrate for fair economic opportunities. In 1966, Dr. King and others looked to replicate in the North the success of the movement in the South. They picked Chicago for several reasons—many leaders who were involved in the movement in the South hailed from Chicago, and the Coordinating Council of Community Organizations (CCCO), an amalgamation of several civil rights groups, invited the SCLC to the Windy City. Andy was against taking the movement to the North because there was unfinished business in the South. But to Chicago they went. They worked closely with Operation Breadbasket, an organization that Jesse Jackson adopted from Dr. Leon Sullivan, who founded it in Philadelphia. The organization aimed to find jobs for blacks in the city.

The tenor of the movement in Chicago was much different from that in the South. In the South, civil rights leaders invoked religious imagery and spoke to the self-respect and self-worth of blacks. In Chicago, however, Andy found that poor people, while no less religious, responded less to religious and spiritual ideas and more to talk of economic empowerment. Their experience in Chicago convinced civil rights leaders that the next chapter in the civil rights movement should be focused on economic empowerment.

In 1968, the SCLC launched the Poor People's Campaign. It was the second part of the civil rights movement and, arguably, the part that has not been fully achieved. SCLC leaders pushed Congress to consider an economic bill of rights and a multibillion-dollar antipoverty package. Unfortunately, Dr. King was killed while the campaign was still in its infancy. Civil rights leaders pushed ahead with the campaign despite Dr. King's death. Before they took the campaign to Washington, DC, the leaders issued a declaration of their desires that included a fair job and living wage, an income for those who couldn't find jobs, the right to use and access land and the right and access to capital.

"How did you know that a boycott was the right solution? How did you know the business community was important?" I asked.

"The businessmen are the ones who pave and clean the Jericho Road. They are the ones who control who can cross the road. They control the flow of capital. They collect the tolls. We always knew that money is color-blind," Andy said.

Green sure is color-blind. Working at a bank, I'm often amused at how money brings together people from peculiar and different backgrounds. I routinely attend investor meetings for, say, a Brazilian company in which all ten investors are from different countries. Why is a Malaysian asset manager interested in a Brazilian company? Why is a Chicago-based hedge fund manager interested? For one reason and one reason only—to determine whether they can make money investing in it.

Businesses in the South were the propellants of an integrated society. Coca-Cola urged Atlanta city officials to integrate the city. Coke managers were embarrassed when they brought important black clients and customers from Latin America and other countries to the segregated South. They joined Mayor Ivan Allen and pressured the chamber of commerce to integrate. The business community brought about social change in Atlanta. Perhaps that's why Atlanta became known as the "city too busy to hate."

"Atlanta had plenty of problems, but you're precisely off and approximately correct. The business community is the agent of social change. I learned that from my granddaddy," Andy partly agreed.

His grandpa Frank Young ran several successful businesses in Louisiana. His white competitors were allowed to keep their businesses open on Sunday, but he wasn't, so he decided to move from Franklin, Louisiana, to New Orleans. He was the treasurer of several black Masonic organizations and controlled their funds. When he notified his bank that he wanted to withdraw his funds and move to New Orleans, they were alarmed, especially because he was the bank's largest customer. The bank officials had a word with the Franklin sheriff and Frank was able to keep his business open on Sundays. The bankers were the real sheriffs of the town.

Andy also learned the importance of the business community down in Thomasville, Georgia, where he pastored a small church. In Thomasville, Andy was organizing a voter registration drive in 1956, and the Klan came to protest it. He went to the mayor, who ran the hardware store, and told him about the Klan's plans. He convinced the owners of Flowers Bakery, Sunnyland Packing Company and other business owners to reject the Klan. The mostly white-owned businesses urged their employees not to participate in the rally. They told the sheriff that the Klan could have a meeting on the courthouse steps but couldn't parade in the black community.

"That was a tremendous victory in 1956. And it came because the people who employed the most people in town spoke up," he concluded.

"That's how you realized business matters?" I asked.

"Yes. I learned from that ordeal that the business community could act quicker, more effectively and spur more dramatic change than government. Years later, in Birmingham, we kept the boycott going for ninety days between Christmas and Easter, and it was 90 percent effective," he replied.

After ninety days, the white authorities were ready to talk. Andy and the other leaders were very pragmatic about the solution. They asked the stores to take down the "whites" and "colored" signs without making a public announcement. They asked store owners to recognize that while they had a problem with high turnover among young white store clerks, the black maids in every department had been there for several years longer and knew the stores better. It made business sense to hire black maids as clerks. The stores complied, and there was no resistance to these moves. After thirty days without any incidents, everybody just relaxed.

"I understand that the business community was important to your efforts in attaining civil rights. But you've lost me on how Dr. King wanted us to achieve his macroeconomic vision. How do we help and heal the Jericho Road?" I asked.

"Not so fast," he advised.

Often during our chats Uncle Andy tells me to slow down. He really wants me to listen to the entire arc of his explanation. There's no jumping to the end.

He didn't miss a beat: "Martin and I had a tough time understanding capitalism." They both started as New Testament socialists. They believed that in order for the poor to have more, the rich must have less. Like Gandhi and the Jesuits, they believed in an equitable distribution of wealth. They knew the type of capitalism that African Americans were experiencing was unfair: Blacks were locked out of economic opportunities. There was no equal opportunity.

"You know what they say about socialism: You must choose between a hungry mind and a hungry tummy," he said.

We laughed.

I added my two cents: "My piece of the pie doesn't come at the expense of your piece. You can create new markets, discover a new pie." I winced at my half-baked pie metaphor. I simply wanted to make a point that capitalism isn't a zero-sum game.

"I'd love some peach pie," he said. He was serious. If I didn't get him on topic soon, I would be driving to Kroger or another supermarket hunting for peach cobbler. "Keep going," I said. "I want to make sure I understand."

Uncle Andy's attention snapped back.

"We really wanted a piece of the pie. But I started to realize exactly what you explained. It doesn't take anything away from the rich for the poor to have more. You get what Martin and I liked to call capitalism with a conscience or humanitarian capitalism. Ever since I was in Congress, I've advocated that we grow capitalism inclusively. Instead of taking from the rich and giving to the poor, urge people to come into the economic fold," he said.

"Let me get this straight. Instead of advocating a Robin Hood approach, you support expanding capitalism to attract and include the poor?" I asked.

It surprised me to hear him talk about enlarging capitalism, especially because he is a Democrat. Liberals look to tax and redistribute wealth as a means to evening the economic landscape. While I grew up believing in this philosophy, I've gradually moved to embrace a purer capitalist philosophy. And so has Uncle Andy. My automatic assumption was that Uncle Andy saw the worst in capitalism, but our discussions taught me to see how capitalism can grow millions out of poverty. He actually has a profound understanding of what it takes for capitalism to succeed (and it isn't excessive taxation).

I should note, however, that Uncle Andy thinks my characterization of liberal policies as tax-and-spend is "completely and absolutely bullshit." He impressed upon me his belief that most Americans forget that their success was built on Roosevelt's New Deal, Eisenhower's interstate highways, state universities and rural Hill-Burton hospitals, while using public infrastructure such as waterways, sewer systems and electricity grids. He thinks rich people don't want to admit that it was big government that made their parents rich after the Second World War. He questions those involved in the 2009 and 2010 tea parties. The original Boston Tea Party was a protest against the British who were taxing the colonies. American taxes go toward bettering America. "Americans are more tough minded and tender hearted. Tea party organizers are tough hearted and soft minded," he explained. Andy wants people to board the free-market train but not to forget who laid the tracks. He's procapitalism and pro–public funding. He calls it public purpose capitalism. He wants to have his pie and eat it too.

"In order for capitalism to succeed, it has to grow and needs to tap new markets. There is a constant need for new markets. Instead of trying to fight each other for a bigger share of the existing market, let's look at the inner city as a new market," he said.

I told Andy about the pending Hawaii ordinance that would ban those who don't wear deodorant from riding the bus. I even worked in a pun. "Instead of organizing a stinky boycott, an entrepreneur can envision an opportunity to sell deodorant in Hawaii. Instead of seeing Africa as a place where people walk around barefoot, why not sell good but cheap shoes there?" I asked.

"That's how macroeconomic visionaries think. I can see you are starting to understand Martin's macroeconomic prescription," he said.

Andy sees entrepreneurialism as a significant part of Dr. King's macroeconomic dream. Loans are the lifeblood of the entrepreneur, but African Americans have historically encountered difficulties in securing them. He brought up his problems with Atlanta banks during his tenure as mayor during the 1980s. The banks redlined the area in which he lived in southwest Atlanta and wouldn't loan money. The banks felt there was too much risk despite high education—six colleges in that part of Atlanta—and high per capita income levels.

"How the hell can an entrepreneur feel empowered when he's living in a safe place and can't get a loan?" he once asked me.

"The entrepreneur can apply for a nonprofit grant," I replied.

"No, no, no," he declared. "Charity is not the answer. It rarely is the answer."

He got my attention. Andy feels the response most people have to the world's problems is micro-oriented. When you help the downtrodden by being the Good Samaritan, it doesn't solve the problem at a macro level.

"What? You've got to connect the dots for me. How is charity a problem?" I asked. I didn't want him to sneak a point by me like sunshine past the rooster.

"My problem with charities is that the people who manage and control the charities usually don't know what it takes to make money. They are usually dilettantes who come up with idiotic ways to spend money someone else earned," he opined. He added more color to his remarks, "Giving ARV drugs to people with no food or clean water is self-righteous and not helpful." He argues that President George W. Bush's $15 billion that was allocated to fight AIDS in Africa would have been better spent if $5 billion had gone to providing clean water, $5 billion to agricultural development and $5 billion for HIV work.

"Okay, but what of top philanthropists like Bill Gates who is very involved in what his charitable organization funds?" I asked.

"I get very upset with Bill Gates and Jimmy Carter. With their brains and access to money, they should have been able to do more than provide charity in the developing world," he responded. He posits that Jimmy Carter in a second term could have made a major economic impact on Africa and the world. He did impact the development of democracy and governance in southern Africa.

Many large philanthropists were capitalists first. Their genius is making money. Andy wants these philanthropists to share their genius to help poor people make more money, a sustainable solution to eradicating poverty. He has long wished that America's top philanthropists like Warren Buffett, Bill Gates, Jimmy Carter and Bill Clinton would focus like a sniper on job creation in developing countries. But I'm not convinced.

Bill Gates and Microsoft have created thousands of millionaires across the world. Microsoft has developed software that has helped nongovernmental organizations and governments in emerging markets. Pension funds, teacher retirement funds, college endowments and mutual funds have all invested in Microsoft and seen dramatic appreciation in their holdings. It's a very stable company that could even issue a dividend.

"Why are you knocking Bill Gates and his brainchild?" I asked.

"He received little input from the people whom he was trying to help." To be fair, Bill Gates has opened several offices in developing countries. He has also been one of the strongest advocates of "creative capitalism," an effort to make capitalism work for those at the bottom of the economic pyramid. Indeed he thinks Bill Gates is well prepared to help with creative capitalism but thinks Gates should focus on food, water, electricity and roads. Even if the infrastructure projects are small, it is a starting point. The water pumps must be linked to irrigation and communities. It may not be a massive Marshall Plan but tourism and village development is a good start. Giving people ARV drugs without proper food and nutrition isn't a well thought–out approach. In 2008, Gates detailed his ideas regarding creative capitalism in a speech at the World Economic Forum in Davos, Switzerland.[4] In his speech, Gates clearly states the difference between economic demand and economic need.

There is economic demand to develop Viagra or hair-growing formulas for balding men because there is an affluent group of people who can pay for the development of these things. However, there are millions who have economic needs, such as better medicine or clean water, but they aren't able to articulate their needs in a market-friendly way. That's where savvy entrepreneurs and creative capitalists come in. They figure out a way to make capitalism work for those who have economic needs but can't find sustainable solutions to address those needs. It may seem counterintuitive to couple the self-interested system of capitalism with the altruistic motivations of philanthropy. But Gates (and Uncle Andy) believe there are ways to direct the self-interest of capitalism toward benevolent and altruistic goals.

Detractors of creative capitalism argue that corporations should focus on their main mission: maximizing profits for shareholders. It is up to the shareholders to invest their money as they desire in charitable causes or other self-serving projects. Corporations that don't maximize profit are in violation of their fiduciary responsibility. Others say that corporations that engage in creative capitalism are only seeking positive public relations.

Andy believes the best way to help people is to provide jobs so they can lift themselves out of poverty. He criticizes Bill Gates further because Gates spent most of his early donations on AIDS research. It's not enough to give people a cure for AIDS. To be sure, one must try to stop the spread of deadly diseases. Andy calls the motivation for antidisease initiatives not born from charity but out of the need for "self-preservation." Instead, give poor people clean water and good nutrition. And if you provide good jobs, they will eventually build up a health care apparatus to at least mitigate the effects of deadly diseases.

"Does money taint the motivation of those wanting to help?" I asked.

"Money taints only if you don't share it. You have to help people make money. Everybody needs sustainable income and you can't do that through charity. Ending poverty has to be about generating wealth, not about only sharing profits. Those profits need to be passed on to other people to help them generate wealth in their own way," he said, adding, "If you see someone drowning, you can throw them a life vest or teach them to swim before they wade into water."

"In a world of hungry people, we can provide them fish or we can teach them to fish," I said. We were trading metaphors. "And Dr. King wanted to make fishers out of men?"

"He wanted to make them prolific fishers. Fishers who caught, fried and sold fish. There is a biblical undertone to our fishing reference. Jesus says to his disciples 'I will make you fishers of men,'" he commented. He is gung-ho on economic sustainability. In order to improve the Jericho Road, we have to look for creative and sustainable solutions. Help people help themselves.

"Isn't it Ted Turner who sees money as weed? You have to pass it around, share it so that everyone can take a hit," I said.

"We used to get high on our hopes," he said. I rolled my eyes. I'm usually the cheesy one.

It's difficult to see where Andy picked up his probusiness, strongly pro-capitalist sentiments. He and the other civil rights leaders didn't have much money to run their organizations. Dr. King ran his organization on less than $500,000 a year. They depended on financial contributions and fundraisers organized by singers Harry Belafonte, Aretha Franklin, even Frank Sinatra and others. Dr. King decided to give away the money he received from the Nobel Peace Prize to other civil rights organizations. He was engaging in charity. Would Andy criticize Dr. King? After years of reflecting on Dr. King's "dream," Andy has come to embrace the macroeconomic interpretation.

"I take it the challenge of my generation is to reinterpret the civil rights movement of today to help the poor make more money?" I waited for him to resume speaking but he didn't. I could almost hear him thinking. He and I now believe somehow democracy and free enterprise must learn to work for the poor in the twenty-first century. We need to make free enterprise work for the billions in China, India, South Africa, Egypt, Mexico and Brazil, and the thirty million poor in the United States. Jobs and education are more effective than police and prisons in stabilizing the poor and offering hope.

"I want to be very clear about this," Andy began. "The challenge of your generation is to realize the full extent of Dr. King's dream. How can you help poor people make money? How can you empower people economically? How can you build the Jericho Road?"

"Can you think of good examples of that dream being realized?" I asked.

"Some say Carlos Slim is a good model. He's done more to end poverty by being a greedy son of a bitch."

"Huh? The Mexican multibillionaire Carlos Slim?"

"His telephone network in Mexico has created five hundred thousand jobs that are sustainable. The question I have of all charities including my own is how do you keep them sustainable? The only way is by letting someone invest their life and make a profit."

"There has to be a better example than Carlos Slim," I remarked. Slim is one of the wealthiest people in the world and receives much criticism because his companies comprise a virtual monopoly of the Mexican telecom sector. It's probably unfair to criticize Slim. He and other extremely successful capitalists are the most prominent and largest philanthropists. The same corporate executives and bankers who make significant money also contribute substantially to charitable organizations.

"The person who best exhibits the idea of empowering poor people to make money and lift themselves out of poverty is Muhammad Yunus," Andy said.

The recipient of the 2006 Nobel Peace Prize, Yunus is the founder of Grameen Bank, which provides small loans to poor entrepreneurs in Bangladesh. The entrepreneurs usually don't qualify for loans at traditional banks. Andy saw the success of small loans in Vietnam firsthand. He met a poor farmer who borrowed $50 to buy two pigs. The farmer raised the pigs, which had eight piglets. The farmer sold a few piglets to pay off the original loan, ate a couple, and bred the rest. Microloans are a sustainable approach in global macroeconomic development. Grameen Bank has loaned poor people billions of dollars. There are drawbacks, however. Grameen and other microfinance organizations charge large interest rates, sometimes over 20 percent. Andy gave me a copy of Yunus's *Banker to the Poor* in 2000. I was young and didn't read it.

"Have you heard of Kiva?" I asked. He had a vague idea.

Kiva.org uses the Internet to microfinance poor entrepreneurs in developing nations. It was created by former PayPal employees, who understand online transactions. Kiva has had terrific success, was featured on Oprah and has raised almost $100 million in loans. Andy especially liked learning that the average Kiva loan is around $400 and 95 percent of the loans are repaid.

"Your generation is already onto Dr. King's macroeconomic vision. We need more Kivas, Grameens and McDonald's," he said.

"What do Big Macs have to do with alleviating the world's poor?" I asked. Andy's roving mind sometimes takes wild leaps. This time I had to ask him to slow down.

"I'm guilty of an occasional Big Mac or Chick-fil-a sandwich. McDonald's deserves credit for their operational systems. It has trained more black businessmen than any other organization in the world. Warren Buffett said that if you run a business like McDonald's for six months, that's as good as an MBA," he said.

Whenever a youngster says to Andy that he wants to become a businessman, he advises him to work at McDonald's. At McDonald's one learns customer service, inventory management and maintenance, personnel training and quality control—almost all it takes to run a business. Most of the millionaires that Andy knows started as McDonald's operators. Among them is Hank Thomas, formerly a Freedom Rider, a civil rights activist who rode interstate buses to test unjust segregation laws. He couldn't afford graduate school so he got a job at McDonald's and eventually bought several restaurants. While he was mayor, Andy occasionally went to Hank's restaurants, made biscuits and flipped burgers. Hank eventually did so well that he sold his string of McDonald's and bought a group of Marriott hotels.

"McDonald's has opened several locations in the inner city. It has seen tremendous growth in other countries too. In a weird way, you are saying McDonald's is part of Dr. King's macroeconomic dream," I commented.

I added to Andy's McDonald's example, connecting it to the issue of peace, which was central to Dr. King's message. Tom Friedman suggests that no two countries with a McDonald's have ever gone to war with each other. He calls it the "Golden Arches Theory of Conflict Prevention."[5] Others call it globalization or the integrated supply chain. Business brings peace and prosperity. The theory has its flaws. Russia and Georgia, two countries with McDonald's, went to war in 2008 and it wasn't over the Hamburglar's loot.

"Capitalism promotes peace. I know some people think big business is bad or overly greedy, but look at how much capitalism has helped black people and minorities in the last century. And I am heartened by how much more it can help," Andy said.

Andy and the chap who ran Dollar General stores used to serve on the same board. The man was doing well financially and wanted Andy to suggest where he should donate his excess money. Surprisingly, or maybe not so surprisingly, Andy said he didn't want the chap to donate any of his money to a charity. Not even to the United Way or the Humane Society. Andy urged him to put his money in a "high-risk account": go into some neighborhoods where there were no Dollar General stores and risk money in hiring black and Hispanic clerks, accountants and managers.

Andy wanted Dollar General senior management to teach minorities how to run a store. He reminded the man to be prepared to lose money but also to be prepared for the stores and employees to make money.

"I imagine you must be out of step with your full embrace of business and procommerce views. Do other civil rights leaders criticize you?" I asked.

"I catch a lot of heat for my probusiness views. Other civil rights leaders think I've sold out. But all they want is charity and government grants. Instead of free money, I say earn it. It is better to build your own business. Government must assure us that banks and capital are available. Being in capitalism with no access to capital is just as bad as being in a democracy without the right to vote. Both are slavery." Both are, as Dr. King would put it, bad checks.

Andy probably caught the most heat when Nike hired him to investigate their overseas factories in 1997. Nike had received negative press for the working conditions in its factories in Southeast Asia. Ultimately, Andy defended the company's operations, after seeing globalization at work for himself.

"Didn't you deserve the heat for defending the sweatshops?" I asked. I wanted to ask whether sweatshops were part of Dr. King's macroeconomic dream, but he derailed me.

"I didn't see sweatshops. In China, they were laid out like college campuses," he responded. He took pictures and published his report on the Internet. He went on to explain that he found the dormitories had running water and toilets. Many of the workers were women and were served two meals a day, which was more than they could arguably receive anywhere else in the country at the time. By working at Nike, employees learned the discipline and knowledge to move up and make more complex and lucrative goods like electronics. Just like working at McDonald's, the so-called sweatshops of Nike were the bottom rung of the job ladder. Andy found that most of the female employees were working to amass a dowry in order to get married, and many faced a choice between working at Nike or being sold into prostitution. "While there were certainly some problems in the factories, working at Nike looked pretty good," he said.

Consider the cost breakdown. Of a $100 tennis shoe, $18 was spent in Asia, $25 in Oregon at Nike's headquarters and the rest at Sports Authority or another shoe retailer. There were more jobs created in the United States than in Asia and most of the profits came back to communities in America. The labor and commerce commissioners for China and Vietnam told Andy that the only problem they had with the new jobs was that there weren't enough of them. Working in a shoe factory could actually be more profitable than becoming a doctor in either country.

In 2006, Andy received heat because of his involvement with Wal-Mart. The president of Nigeria asked Andy to lobby Wal-Mart and the Home Depot to enter Nigeria. Andy met with Wal-Mart senior management and learned that they were interested in Africa but too bogged down in Europe and America. They asked if he could help, so he became the chair of Working Families for Wal-Mart.

In his neighborhood the small stores and drugstores were sold to bigger companies who made bigger profits. But the community is much better served by three chain drug stores, two first-rate supermarkets, many more jobs and lower prices. He explained his views to a local newspaper writer over three hours, in which he feels he was misunderstood. He apologized for his remarks and resigned the post.

He explained his remarks to me, "I was talking about my neighborhood. Instead of three or four mom-and-pop stores, we have CVS, Walgreens, Rite Aid and Kroger. Our neighborhood hasn't stayed stagnant. Those four chains ensure competitive pricing and quality products in my neighborhood," he said.

One of Andy's acquaintances wants him to buy a group of twenty-five gas stations. Gas station employees sometimes have to face violent crime, so Andy is thinking of taking on the project in order to provide jobs for ex-convicts. "Nobody would mess with them. And it would create much-needed jobs for the communities."

"You're saying economic isolation isn't possible?" I asked.

"Exactly. People somehow like to force economic isolation on poor people. Remember, I ran a ninety-day strike and boycott organizing hospital workers in Charleston and even went to jail with garbage workers in Atlanta, so I'm not ignorant. I wanted Wal-Mart to help provide jobs and quality merchandise at affordable prices to poor people, which they do. It's rank hypocrisy to be against increasing local footprints of Wal-Mart. They provide goods at affordable prices to poor people."

Indeed, there are concerns with the way Wal-Mart does business, but opening Wal-Mart stores and making Nike shoes have spawned thousands of jobs around the world, many in poor countries. Like Kiva loans, they give poor people a chance to clasp onto the bottom rung of the global economic ladder. In this new economic system, much as Andy found with the boycotts in the South, the only color that matters is green.

"Dr. King's macroeconomic dream requires a great deal of work. You can't just create jobs out of thin air. Sometimes a society lacks proper infrastructure like roads, computers or even centers of higher education. His dream can't be attained by one or two federal laws," I observed.

"You're right. There are thousands of little things that young people can and must do. Just like the folks at Kiva or other West Coast start-ups—start to envision new markets. Look at Africa, that's a great example," he said.

Andy's preferred way to alleviate poverty is tourism and his favorite example is Africa. Many African countries lack the modern infrastructure of clean water and power grids. But he believes that tourism is a way not only to habituate foreigners to Africa but to attract foreign capital. He is such a strong proponent of the tourism-as-development idea that he lobbied Delta Air Lines to open routes from the United States to Nigeria in the mid-1990s. Today the route from Atlanta to Lagos is the most profitable for Delta. But the violence in the Nigerian Delta inhibits the country from deriving even more profits from tourism. Many Nigerian tourists are the second generation born in the United States but are beginning to return home with talent and money.

A significant amount of oil is concentrated in the Nigerian Delta, and local rebels resort to violence to voice their discontent at multinational oil companies. Sectarian violence between Muslims and Christians threatens to rip the country apart. Without the promise of safety, tourism in Nigeria will be limited. It was at Murtala Muhammed International Airport in Lagos that a security guard offered to let me through the security check point without X-raying my bag if I gave him $40.

I was horrified.

Other countries have seen success with tourism. Andy also points to Rwanda, which is on track to quadruple its GDP thanks in part to the dramatic increase in tourists. The country is building a convention center and hundreds of new hotel rooms. As a result, the government is spending more on its education initiatives, trying to ensure universal education for primary school students.

He is such a strong proponent of tourism because he saw it work in Atlanta while he was mayor. Near the beginning of his tenure in 1982 there were 2 Marriotts. At the end, in 1990, there were 74. The total number of hotel rooms grew from 3,000 in the 1970s to 120,000 in the twenty-first century, with a near 70 percent occupancy rate. Each hotel room creates about two jobs. The folks who work in the hotels require little training and almost no formal education. All you need is to be nice, polite and efficient at your work to get a job.

Andy understood the true value of bringing more tourists to Atlanta when he gave the bellman of the Hyatt in downtown a dollar for parking his car. The bellman said, "Mr. Mayor, I know what you make. I make more than you in tips each year. Please keep your money." Making $50,000 as mayor of Atlanta, Andy didn't doubt the bellman.

The Atlanta airport generates billions a year in revenue for the city and employs tens of thousands. I haven't even mentioned the effect it has had in attracting businesses and capital to Atlanta and the region. During Andy's tenure as mayor, the airport shoeshiners were making almost $100,000 a year (before all the security reforms that resulted from the

September 11 attacks). Andy actually had to cut the hours that shoeshiners work to four hours per day because they were making too much money. The shiners were making $5 every ninety seconds. They were sending their kids to college without any problem. The most memorable complaint Andy received from city workers was that they wanted him to give them city golf course passes because they had plenty of time to play.

"What do you tell young people who want to start or join a non-profit?" I asked.

"I tell them not to. I tell them to make some money. If you make more than you need, start another business and create some jobs in places that don't have many, like Africa. Use tourism to attract jobs to the inner city. If you really want to help the poor, work at an investment bank. Learn how the financial system works. Learn about capital markets and asset allocation," he said.

When Andy's daughter Andrea finished law school and wanted to help the less fortunate, Andy suggested that she work at Merrill Lynch to learn about finance. Instead, she went to work in Washington, DC and helped the poor through her advocacy of public policy. It's unusual for me to hear someone defend investment banking, especially on the grounds that the profession can help one learn about alleviating poverty. But Muhammad Yunus showed us that even a banker can win the Nobel Prize.

Finance and commerce arguably play the most important role on the Jericho Road. And young people are at an advantage to help shape the Jericho Road and work toward Dr. King's macroeconomic dream because, as Andy says, "Young people don't know any better, so they fiddle and create. They create the Kivas and the solutions of tomorrow." The Jericho Road will be paved with business, commerce and youthful innovation.

4 YOU'RE AN INSECURE TEACHER (AND SO IS THE NEXT GUY)

Few of us realize that racism is man's gravest threat to man, the maximum of hatred for a minimum of reason, the maximum of cruelty for a minimum of thinking.

—Rabbi Abraham Heschel, theologian[1]

"I can't date white girls," my roommate Clayton said in his unexcitable voice. He nibbled at his messy beef burrito. We were at La Cocina on Third Avenue in New York, and the topic *du jour* was women. It usually is with him.

"Why not?" I asked.

"They haven't experienced enough pain. As an African American, I can tell you that the black experience is one of struggle and grief. If I tell a white girl that I was pulled over by a cop for no reason, she may not understand. Plus, when I dated a white woman, I got many disapproving looks from white guys," he said.

"We aren't in the 1960s," I replied, deciding not to point out that some women think they suffer more discrimination and pain than any man regardless of race.

Clayton and I have a long history together. We attended the same K–12 private school in Atlanta. We attended the same college, and we work for the same company. We're almost the same person, except he is taller, faster, stronger (and more intelligent) than I. I'm his Mini-Me. Over the years I've heard many of his stories of racism, and they always bug me. In our high school, one of our classmates frequently referred to Clayton as "boy" and once called him a nigger while in math class. When Clayton got a higher score on his math exam than the classmate, Clayton told him, "You're dumber than a nigger."

"Racism may not be as apparent as it was in the 1960s, but it's hard to shake completely from our society," he said to me, while continuing to munch.

His comment reminded me of Andy's aphorism that he had learned from his papa as a kid and passed down to me: Racism is a sickness. It's hard to shake and rid someone of it quickly. "Racism doesn't have anything to do with you or me. It's a problem with the racist," Uncle Andy once told me.

He suggests that one should treat racism with compassion just as one would treat AIDS with ARV drugs and proper nutrition. You have to try to understand racists since they espouse backward and diseased ideas. I was pleasantly surprised to see a YouTube clip of a KKK demonstration before a 2009 LSU–Ole Miss football game in which several young white folks criticized the Klansmen: "I bet none of y'all have ever attended a class at Ole Miss. . . . You'd flunk out."

I bet Uncle Andy would shy away from such criticism though. He certainly had plenty of opportunities to learn how best to "treat" racism when he was a kid. White boys trolled his neighborhood yelling, "Alligator bait!" at the black boys. He grew up with an Irish grocery store on one corner of the road and an Italian bar on the other. He could hear the shout "Heil Hitler" emanating from the nearby Nazi meetings at the German American Bund headquarters. Most of his father's friends and business associates were Jewish, so he grew up with heavy exposure to Judaism. He interfaced with people from all walks of life. As a boy, he was reprimanded by a police officer for hanging out with a white kid from the neighborhood. I like to call his neighborhood a "jam session" in which he encountered all the hues and saturations of New Orleans residents.

While his grandmother urged him to fight anyone who was a racist, he internalized what his father taught him—"Don't get mad, get smart." His dad once gave him an IBM poster that said, "Think!" It was his first lesson in nonviolence. Instead of violently reacting at every racist episode, he learned how to employ cool reasoning at a young age. It was also a necessity because he was younger and smaller than most of his peers and didn't want to get beat up. He learned that the best defense against racism was to have a strong and prepared mind. A strong and steady mind enabled him to act rationally and not emotionally during the civil rights movement and during his tenures in public office. From his father, Andy learned that it's a waste of time to just complain about a problem like racism. People who have superior intellects should spend time on bettering their education and finding compelling solutions.

To turn the other cheek on racism and not retaliate may seem like an accommodative measure, a continuation of the southern liberalism exemplified by Atticus Finch in *To Kill a Mockingbird* and by many southern politicians of the mid-twentieth century. But neither Finch nor Andy advocates tacit acceptance of racism. Their silence gives them time to determine how to influence the behavior of others.

Andy tells the story about visiting Dr. King in an Albany, Georgia jail in 1962. He had put on his church clothes to command the most respect from the white police officer who received him and said, "There is a little nigger out here who wants to see a big nigger back there." The big-bellied officer had the look of the archetypical southern racist. Instead of getting upset, Andy took note of the officer's nametag. Every time Andy visited he would greet the officer, "How are you doing today, Sergeant Hamilton?" The officer soon warmed up, sharing stories about his family. A spoonful of compassion was the right medicine for the racist officer. Andy considers learning how to treat racists as one of the most powerful lessons of his life. When everyone else was losing their heads, Andy kept his.

Years later while Uncle Andy was lecturing in Maine, a tall, slim and handsome gentleman came up to Andy after the talk. Dressed in white pants and a dapper green sports jacket that made him look like he had just won the Masters, the man asked, "Do you remember me? I'm Sergeant Hamilton from Albany. I had to get out of Georgia. I now run a security firm here in Maine!" Andy's anecdote reminds me of a William Butler Yeats poem that I paraphrase, "Life is a journey up a spiral staircase; we keep coming back to the same points but from a different perspective."[2] Sergeant Hamilton, a racist Andy treated with love, and who reformed himself, is one of those points.

Andy's example has served me well. My college jazz band once had a Latino guest artist rehearsing with us for a week. When I walked into the first rehearsal, he said to everyone, "I didn't know we had a terrorist in this band." His comment was particularly topical because it was a year or so after the September 11, 2001 attacks. I just laughed it off. Don't get mad, get smart. After rehearsal, I took him to the Jewel of India for dinner, and we talked about music history for several hours and eventually became friends.

In July 2009, Andy and I met in the lobby of the Hilton Hotel in New York after the centennial celebration of the NAACP. We sat in the lobby café and sipped warm English Breakfast tea. It was the perfect time to talk about race, racism and race relations: "I think we've come a long way in race relations. A good friend of mine says she doesn't believe in the concept of race. It's an unnatural grouping. There is only one human race," I said.

"She may be right. But we all seem to artificially group human beings. The church talks about original sin—all people are born self-centered and must learn to be civilized," Andy responded.

"Are you saying that we are born with a proclivity for racism?" I asked.

"I'm saying that kids always try to make distinctions. One of my daughters once crawled into my lap and said, 'You and I are brown. We're not yellow like Lisa and mommy,'" he stated.

That was certainly color awareness. There is a history of discrimination among African Americans (and Indians) over the lightness of skin. One of my friends in Brooklyn who is fair-skinned once told me, "I'm a minority's minority," because her darker African American friends didn't accept her as a "true sister." Growing up in New Orleans, Andy was insecure about his color because he was considered dark-skinned by most of his mother's Creole friends. The color consciousness of Andy's daughter would have become insidious if Andy had encouraged his daughter to see herself as better because of her color. Instead, he told her that they are all one family, "You are different because God made you different." Race consciousness is like noticing the differences among vanilla wafers, graham crackers and chocolate chip cookies. They look different but are all sweet and delicious.

God made us all different. But many of us don't want to accept this. Andy brought up the time when he and Carolyn went to South Africa to take part in the opening of Oprah Winfrey's school in early 2007. Mariah Carey was also there. Andy holds her in high regard as one of the most beautiful and talented women in the world. Nevertheless, Mariah must have asked Carolyn over a hundred times how she looked. She was annoyingly conscious and insecure about her appearance. Though this isn't an example of race or racism, it shows how even those at the top can be insecure about their appearance. Personal insecurity, believes Uncle Andy, is the seed from which warped ideas on race stem.

Divas are conscious of their looks since much of their success depends on their beauty. But plenty of noncelebrities are insecure about their appearances and want to change their looks. In 2009, Andy addressed the National Council of Korean Presbyterian Churches in Atlanta and made the same point. He told them black people pay a lot of money to get hair that resembles that of Korean people, and Korean people sell their hair to pay for operations to get big round eyes that resemble those of black people. Plastic and cosmetic surgery is a multibillion-dollar industry in the United States. From Andy's travels to Asia, Brazil and South Africa, he has grown disheartened that so many are unable to appreciate God's creation. "That's a terrible way to live—to want to be someone else," he said to the National Council of Korean Presbyterian Churches. He also believes that too many women feel insecure about their breasts, and men are guilty of encouraging sexist stereotypes. A couple of his friends almost died as a result of leakage from breast implants. "Breasts are for babies to nurse, not to attract *real* men," he explained.

"Did you ever feel insecure about your race and image? Did you conk your hair?" I asked.

"No, but I used a stocking cap to smooth it down. I greased my hair down a little because my daddy did it. When I moved north, I let my hair grow out, but it wasn't any kind of personal rebellion," he said.

In 1953, Andy's wife, Jean, earned a scholarship that allowed her to travel to Europe to work at an Austrian refugee camp full of those trying to flee the communist regimes in Eastern European countries. Andy had saved up some money to afford the $240 round-trip ticket and decided to accompany Jean but work at another camp. At the time, he had a big Afro. He was in an Austrian mountain town and finally decided to get his hair cut. The townspeople had never seen a black person before. He went into a joint barber shop and beauty parlor. All the women gathered around Andy to watch him get his hair cut. He tried to give instructions in German even though he couldn't speak a lick of it. Instead of sweeping his hair from the ground, the sweeper picked up the hair and gave little samples to the ladies so they could feel what it was like.

"I began to be more or less proud of my hair and culture by then. I was unique. I had developed a strong enough self-image," he remembered.

"I'm insecure about my wild and bushy eyebrows. There might be an animal burrowing in them. My left ear is flatter than my right one. How do I get over my insecurities?" I asked. I was only half-kidding.

"I say you look into the mirror and say, 'God, you were showing off when you made me,'" he remarked. His advice doubles nicely as a pickup line.

"You've got to flatter yourself because there are plenty of jackasses who are going to criticize you," he concluded.

Race and image awareness is one thing. Racism is quite another. The roots of racism are found in individual insecurity. Andy defines racism as "the social and economic institutionalization of individual prejudice." Because race and racism are thorny topics, he chooses his words with particular care. He sometimes uses the anthropological term "ethnocentrism," the propensity to focus on one's own ethnicity or culture.

White southerners felt inferior to the whites in the North during Reconstruction and Jim Crow. Whites in the south were discriminated against by northerners both economically and socially,[3] as the industrial economy of the North was far more productive than that of the agrarian South. One of the reasons why white southerners created Jim Crow laws was so they didn't have to compete with northerners. The white southerners felt better because they believed they were at least better than former slaves. Jim Crow gave some southern whites a higher status even if they were poor and uneducated.[4]

The warped race relations during the Jim Crow era became an integral part of the social fabric in the South. It affected the self-image of many blacks. Several blacks were reluctant to visit Andy's father if they were in need of a dentist because even they thought white dentists were better. Jim Crow segregation led to other absurdities as well. During a parade in Thomasville, Georgia in the 1950s Andy saw a float sponsored by the Sunnyland Packing Company that had two larger-than-life-size cartons of eggs. One of the cartons was labelled "Grade A White" and had twelve white children in it, and the other said "Grade A Brown" and had twelve African American kids.

Race becomes demonic when it becomes politically and economically institutionalized, as it was in Nazi Germany, South Africa or America's segregated South. That's why I think Andy was particularly courageous: He wanted to change the South. He wanted to take on institutionalized racism and shake the sickness from society. He drew inspiration from the apostle Paul, who spoke about breaking down the wall of hostility between Jews and Greeks. Andy wanted to tear down the wall between whites and blacks. The civil rights movement was about tearing down the political, economic and social walls that divided and segregated society.

The struggle for civil rights was an epic fight because of the deep-seated pathology that comes with race in America. The colonists who brought slaves to America were very religious and moral people. It's ironic that in order to justify the morality of slavery, they had to proclaim that slaves were inferior human beings. Even the US Constitution decreed slaves as three-fifths of one person.

Andy doesn't blame all racism on colonialism. But colonizers often divide and conquer people based on groupings like race and religion, and sometimes on random things. In Rwanda, Europeans invented the groups "Hutu" and "Tutsi." Originally Tutsi meant anyone who had more than ten cows. The distinction led to genocide. Colonialists turned people on each other instead of toward each other. That makes sense if you are trying to conquer a group of people, but not if you want to build a cohesive culture.

Andy believes racism against blacks has been ongoing for several thousand years. Slavery and segregation in America are more recent examples of a historical prejudice against Africans on the part of Europeans. He points to Pope Nicholas V, who in 1452 gave power to the King of Portugal to force nonbelievers, such as pagans living in Africa, into slavery. Early Portuguese discoverers and settlers were quick to colonize foreign lands and introduce slavery.

Andy said that most people in the United States grow up learning a European version of history. But those who win the wars are the ones that write history, right? Uncle Andy doesn't think this approach is intellectually honest. He has always urged me to study world history, not just European history: for instance, What was happening in Asia and Africa during Napoleon's reign or during the American Revolution? He believes civilization started in the Great Rift Valley in Tanzania, Kenya and Ethiopia, where Lucy and the remains of other hominid ancestors were found. He firmly believes that we all came from Africa.

"People forget that Nubian pharaohs ruled Egypt for several years. Anwar Sadat and I could be cousins," he said. He also believes that the Sphinx's nose was shot off by European soldiers because it had Negroid features.

"I think that's a wacky idea," I said.

"I am a conspiracy theorist," Andy admitted. "Dick Gregory used to say something like, 'If you are black and not slightly paranoid, you are really sick.' Did you ever see the statue of the person who built the first pyramid? You have to go to the basement of the Cairo museum because he probably had thick lips, a wide nose, kinky hair and black blood."

He then cited the parable of the Good Samaritan to illustrate how ethnocentrism occurs even in the Bible. The Jews and Samaritans were enemies. They accused each other of misinterpreting God's word and worshiping false gods. Jesus told the story of the Good Samaritan to the Jews to show how even the people they disliked were doing the Lord's work. Even your enemy can perform saintly deeds.

Andy doesn't even blame all racism in the segregated South on whites. He thinks African Americans were culpable in part because they participated in the system of slavery for hundreds of years. He quotes Frederick Douglass, who said ending slavery was an effort to save "black men's bodies and white men's souls."[5] Dr. King's arrest in Birmingham in 1963 angered several thousands of blacks. In order to restrain the nonviolent demonstrators, the police turned on the fire hoses at full power. Andy and other leaders led protesters back to the Sixteenth Street Baptist Church, and it fell upon Andy to calm the crowd. In his first speech at a rally, Andy asked the protesters if they had been bitten by a dog or hit with a baseball bat before. He then went on to say, "The issue here is not the dog, the billy clubs and the fire hoses. We are upset all right, but we are upset about those scars that racism and segregation have put on our psyches and our souls." He then made the protesters understand the task ahead: "We are marching against an entire system that must be changed. It would do no good to kill the policeman who beats you; he's trapped by the same system. He believes that his white skin makes him superior, and that he's supposed to keep you down. Somehow we've got to help even the racist policeman to see that a man can't keep another man down in the gutter unless he keeps one foot down there with him. . . . It's time for us to get the entire South out of the ditch."[6]

But that was then. This is now. To be sure, America has a pockmarked past, but I reminded Andy that we live in the proverbial melting pot. Even though racism goes back thousands of years, I really believe that twenty-first-century America is one of the most integrated societies in world history. We are closer to building a more perfect union than ever before. I hope my optimism is infectious.

The Hilton Hotel café was almost empty and the tea now cooled. But Andy was just warming up to the subject.

"We didn't melt. America is more like a gumbo than like a soup. The individual ingredients are easily identified in the gumbo. The diversity of spices and tastes make the gumbo rich. I use that analogy with race relations. While I live and work with white people, I also live in a black world. There is a difference," Andy remarked.

Andy learned to live in three different worlds. His parents brought him up in an integrated middle-class world. He also learned to live in a world that was full of vulgarities and trash-talking street bullies. From this world he learned what it takes to survive tough situations. "I grew balls thanks to public schools," he says. Finally, he learned to live in the white corporate world. When he visited his father in downtown New Orleans, he put on a shirt and tie and spoke in a completely different manner. His mom said to him, "If you aren't well dressed, whites will accuse you of stealing. With a tie, at least you'll get some respect." My father always said Andy put people at ease during their executive meetings.

"Minorities have a hard time growing up. But they are stronger when they do because they've learned how to navigate several cultures and worlds. Their minds are more flexible. They are more dynamic. It's what helped me see common ground at the United Nations," he said.

While he was US ambassador to the UN in the late 1970s, Andy didn't experience many racist episodes. On one occasion, however, he was waiting for his car at the Waldorf Astoria. A Texan came up to Andy in the lobby and gave him his keys to his car, assuming Andy was the valet, saying, "Take this, boy." Instead of getting angry, Andy said he would take care of it. He walked to the bellhop and gave him the keys. The next day, the Texan and Andy were waiting for their cars. Andy's limousine pulled up, and he overheard the Texan asking the bellhop who he was. Andy walked over to the Texan and asked, "Did they take good care of your car?" The Texan apologized profusely, realizing he had embarrassed himself in front of the US ambassador to the United Nations.

The same sort of thing happened while Andy was in Congress from 1973 to 1977. He was scheduled to address a YMCA conference in North Carolina. When he arrived at the airport, he couldn't find a driver, so he called the conference organizers. They said the driver was waiting at the airport. Andy had seen a driver circle around several times. The driver didn't expect "Congressman Young" to be a young black man wearing a sports jacket.

"He was looking for someone who looked like Colonel Sanders," Andy laughed.

The problem, though, is that not every minority is given access to all three worlds. Many poor black kids are exposed only to poverty and can't see what the world looks like on the other side of the street. They have no concept of another way to live.

"I think that every individual is born insecure and isolated," Andy said. "If they have two loving parents who give them a strong self-image in the first few years, they develop a personal security that makes them a potential leader. Young people who are not given a sense of worth and security with their mother's milk really have a hard time finding it."

"Wait a second. Bill Clinton and Margaret Thatcher had tough one-parent households. And they turned out all right," I countered.

"Bill Clinton had a phenomenal mother. Barack Obama did too. Margaret Thatcher had a strong father. Sometimes that's all it takes," he allowed.

"And Dr. King?" I asked.

"Oh, he was born a king," he responded.

Dr. King was the star of his family. He was the standout of three children and was named after his father. His grandfather was a prominent preacher of Ebenezer Baptist Church, which was one of the more leading churches in the United States at the time. He was also the treasurer of a national Baptist organization that had six million members when King was born. Dr. King's mother was one of the first people in Atlanta to get a master's degree in music. But King was like many of us: He focused on his shortcomings. When he was a small child, he thought he was ugly. He grew up black in a white world. But he had the blessings so many young folks are without today: loving and financially secure parents and a supportive extended family.

One of the challenges in life is to turn insecurities into assets just as Dr. King did. Andy speculates, "Dr. King may have had a Napoleon complex" since he was only five feet seven inches. King worked hard to overcome his insecurities at a young age and resented those to whom success came easy. It was his intense work ethic that helped him produce some of the most memorable speeches of all time (even though he received a C in speech at university). In fact, few if any of the top civil rights leaders were six feet or taller. Indeed, they cast larger shadows.

"You and I were born into loving families with two strong parents. Strong parents can shield any young person from the racist sickness of any society," Andy said.

My friend Samantha was raised in apartheid South Africa by her black mother and white father. She didn't realize that South Africa was a segregated society, and when Nelson Mandela won the presidency in 1994, she thought it was "just another election." Some may think she was raised to be ignorant, but I believe her parents raised her so that the sickness of her society didn't affect or influence her self-image.

"The problem is that many young people don't receive a decent education from their school or their parents. Instead, our views on race are shaped by entertaining image-makers like angry and violent rappers," I said to Andy. I was about to get on my soapbox on the ills of rap and popular culture. Andy, however, threw me a curve ball.

"Well, there are some reasons I'm glad we have angry rappers in our society," he said.

Andy knows something about rappers. It's not that he enjoys rap music. He doesn't listen to it. He prefers the music of Ray Charles and Aretha Franklin, and he loves jazz. I turned him on to my favorite jazz pianist, Bill Evans. He keeps *Everybody Digs Bill Evans* and Miles Davis's *Kind of Blue* on his iPhone. He even presided over Miles Davis's marriage with actress Cicely Tyson at Bill Cosby's house. But Andy is seen as an elder statesman in the African American community, and a bevy of young black stars such as Chris Tucker, Ludacris, T.I., Usher and Tyrese have come to him for counsel. Once, when Andy was exiting a bookstore in New York after a book signing, Tupac Shakur's limousine was just passing. Tupac stopped the car and got out to talk to Andy. Tupac wanted to talk longer and promised to be in touch with Andy the next time he was in Atlanta. Unfortunately, Tupac was killed a few days later.

Recording artist Chris Brown even called Andy after his ugly fight with R&B singer Rihanna. Andy pressed Chris to turn away from violence and toward love. If you treat a woman right, you don't have to fight.

He also told him to listen to the music of Otis Redding every night. His songs "Respect" and "Try a Little Tenderness" evoke a calmness that puts the soul to peace. "Otis will just make you feel better," he told Brown.

It's one thing to have the ears of successful black hip-hop stars. It's another to push them to be more than an angry black stereotype and to use their influence for good, as Uncle Andy does. For instance, when Clifford Joseph Harris Jr., also known as T.I., was arrested and pleaded guilty to federal weapons charges in 2008, Andy invited T.I. to church to listen to his Sunday sermon. Andy then took him to Goldwater Memorial Hospital in New York to meet with some victims of gun violence who had been gang-bangers in the 1960s and 1970s. Several victims told T.I. about the negative impact of guns. It totally changed his perspective. Andy produced an Emmy Award–winning documentary, *Walking with Guns,* that details T.I.'s trip to the hospital. The film grabs your heart as each patient tells his story, and one gives marching orders to the young rapper to change his ways. T.I. has committed to talking to students about the dangers of guns and to use his influence for good.

Andy paradoxically wants to use rappers to help reverse the angry black stereotype that some rappers helped to create. Uncle Andy doesn't see it as a paradox. He doesn't see T.I. and other hip-hop stars as only rappers. They are victims. In the case of T.I., he was a victim of gun violence who can speak meaningfully about the dangers. Because these stars have the ears of millions of youngsters across America, they can promote a more positive image. It's a lofty goal to try to reverse the black stereotype, and I'm unconvinced recruiting rappers to the cause is the best way to accomplish it. I must admit, however, I don't have any other ideas besides the platitudes of better education or creating economic opportunities for minorities.

In autumn 2009, I was seated next to rapper Akon's brother on a plane. We started talking about baseball and quickly moved onto music. I asked him two simple questions. "Why do rappers with so much sound so angry? Aren't they happy with their success?"

"My man," he began. "Rap and hip-hop ain't music. It's a way of life. It's about how you wear your hat. It's about your jeans. It's about the Benjamins. Being angry is just how we do it. It's how we get people to listen." To each his own.

One day Andy and Carolyn were walking down Fifth Avenue in New York and passed by a Gucci store. Two rappers whom Andy didn't know and their wives came out with seven shopping bags each. They urged Carolyn to go in and buy a new $1,200 pair of jewel-encrusted shoes. Carolyn said she couldn't afford them because she was a schoolteacher. The wives were shocked. One of them said, "You need to get a man who can buy you them then."

Many people who grow up in poverty have a problem dealing with money once they have it. "T.I. has first-generation money. He is unfamiliar with the wealth and stature that comes along with his stardom. I've spent a lot of time with him. He's actually a smart fellow. We're lucky that he turned to rap music though. In countries where there aren't free societies, he might have turned to terrorism. The angry, bitter rappers and youngsters in other countries sometimes become the terrorists," he observed.

"Rappers are American terrorists?" I asked bemusedly, wondering whether he realized the bizarreness of his remark.

"Not exactly. They just don't know how to cope with their success. They exhibit the same nihilism that many blacks felt after Dr. King's death," he said. He motioned for the waiter. He wanted a cold glass of water.

At first blush, it sounded like an inflammatory point. He thinks that rap music helps young African Americans cope with their experiences. It offers them a shot at making it big. Rap is one of several creative (and potentially profitable) outlets for young, disaffected African Americans, whereas in developing countries, young malcontents turn to violence. I think it's a tenuous point at best, but he stands by it.

Then Andy contrasted successful rappers with young civil rights leaders in the 1960s. Even though many of the leaders were well known, they stayed in their communities. As they earned more money, they endeavored to make their communities and schools better. Andy had plenty of opportunities to move to a house in a more affluent neighborhood but remained in southwest Atlanta. The key difference between the civil rights leaders and several rap stars was that the civil rights leaders were essentially middle class. There was a history going back three or four generations that taught them how to act and harmonize with society.

"Why are you helping someone who makes his money in propagating a dangerous black stereotype? As a lion in the nonviolent movement, why defend someone who raps openly about violence and criminal activity?" I asked.

Andy recognizes that music has always been a nonviolent way to voice frustration, but there is a difference between music that articulates frustration and music that advocates violence. Blues musicians like B.B. King and Muddy Waters sing out their frustration without encouraging brutality or violence. While Andy doesn't support T.I.'s venomous lyrics, he recognizes the potential positive influence the convicted rapper could have on young people. When T.I. shows up at an elementary school to talk about gun control, the middle and high school students want to attend as well. T.I.'s lyrics might not be peaceful, but he can certainly use his platform to advocate good causes to our country's youth. That is the only way Andy believes T.I. will grow up and move on.

Andy learned how to act properly from his parents, church and then school. The principal of his high school, Mrs. Margaret Davis Bowen, held several assemblies in order to stress how students should behave. She told them how to dress, how to speak and how to get along in polite society. It was a real world education in the comfort of a New Orleans high school. T.I. never got that education.

Andy is trying to help the hip-hop community get that sort of education. In 2009, he hosted the Andrew Young Men's Leadership Forum, an intergenerational forum among members of the Civil Rights, Boomer and Hip Hop generations. It is designed to promote dialogue and understanding among the generations as well as increase community engagement and political involvement. He lauded the wives and girlfriends of the rappers and entertainers for pushing them to recognize and embrace family values. The symposium was an attempt to help the hip-hop community see how they can collectively help young people overcome personal insecurities, deal with being black in America and, even though it wasn't an explicit goal of the gathering, reverse the angry black stereotype.

The symposium organizers also helped the rappers understand how to invest their earnings. The rappers learned that they didn't work for money, rather money could work for them. With a little guidance, I suspect, these rappers could be top clients of the private banking arms of Wall Street investment banks.

"I've seen tremendous growth in T.I. just by his talking with me about his life. I've never heard him talk about anyone except his grandmother. He is a good person in a sick society," he said.

"What does that mean?" I asked.

"It means you should hate the sin but not the sinner," he said. He referenced the civil rights movement in Birmingham, where he learned to see racist whites who supported segregation not as bad people, just people in a terrible situation. By being respectful of those who sin like Sergeant Hamilton, you may be able to win them over with compassion and love. It was seeing people for who they are that has helped Andy to keep calm and not overheat. We're all God's children.

He believes T.I. and some youngsters may lead wild, undisciplined and at times sinful lives, but one need only look to their upbringing for answers to why. T.I. is no different from thousands if not millions of young black people who grow up without a solid sense of family and community. Andy thinks that, generally, African Americans never reconstructed the sense of community after slavery.

"The slave plantation gave slaves an artificial sense of security. But that's how you can get phenomenal leaders growing up in slavery. They understood basic security and shared it with others," he explained.

There were many things that broke up the basic family unit for African Americans: government policies, migration patterns and urbanization, among others. As a result, we ended up with a society in which thousands of teenage mothers raise their children in poverty. It's no surprise that many who rap vulgar rhymes haven't learned how to live in society. If I've learned anything about Uncle Andy, it should also be no surprise that he is recruiting the image-makers of the angry black stereotype to undo the image. That's like asking cigarette companies to debunk the cigarettes-are-cool image of the mid-twentieth century. Andy is making an unusual request to these rappers, but maybe they can have a positive influence on young African Americans.

"What would you say is the sickness in today's society?" I asked.

"Even though segregation doesn't exist, we still have sickness. There is silent racism. It happens every day and in every way. It's hard to fight because humans tend to group things into subgroups," he observed. "I've always said that in the North like Chicago and New York, whites didn't care how large you got, they care how close you get. In the South, however, they didn't care how close you got, they care how large you get."

The silent racism he encountered during the 1950s and 1960s still lingers. He encountered silent racism while living in New York in 1957. Mortgage officers stalled Andy's application citing several reasons, but the implicit reason was clear—race. Andy's manager at the National Council of Churches, who was white and bought a house three blocks away from Andy's desired house, intervened. He was disgusted with the mortgage officers. Andy was even initially reluctant to take the post with the National Council of Churches because he didn't want to be the token black person, which he felt was just as bad as silent racism.

In 1966, civil rights leaders went to Chicago to take part in a march to end slums. It was in Chicago that Andy realized that after you peel away the scab of racism, you are left with the sore of poverty. He discovered that in Chicago it was profitable to keep blacks in poverty and in the slums. Many slumlords who were white inherited the slums from their parents and grandparents. The slumlords simply collected checks from renters. They didn't care about maintaining or improving the property. The private sector resisted the efforts of civil rights leaders to improve living wages of poor blacks. They didn't see the slums as their problem. Even many labor unions turned a cold shoulder. Civil rights leaders organized a rent strike and received a HUD grant to renovate the slums and turn them into condominiums for first-time home buyers. The condo fees were usually less than the rental fees. This story didn't get publicized because young black militants in Chicago didn't want to give credit to HUD or any other government organization since they were supposed to be antigovernment (anti–Mayor Daley and HUD) and antiestablishment.

There was also clannishness among the civil rights leaders—the civil rights movement leadership was Baptist. Joseph Lowery, who spoke at President Obama's inauguration, was Methodist, Hosea Williams was a Presbyterian and Andy was a United Church of Christ Congregationalist, so they sometimes felt at odds with each other and recognized that a Baptist would always be the leader of the movement. It seemed like everyone was part of a smaller group or cult based on a variety of things, like religion or alma maters. Dr. King teased Andy for not going to Morehouse. The civil rights leaders had their own little groupings that made them feel more secure. They were also mostly part of a larger group: men. Women in the SCLC often felt underappreciated by King and others.

"I'm still guilty of stereotyping. It's almost impossible to eradicate," Andy admitted. He told me about the time he preached at an army base in Korea. The gospel choir, which was behind him, was really jumping.

The pianist was stomping and swinging, leading the singers. Andy remarked that the pianist must have been from Mississippi or Alabama. The pianist-and-choir director was actually a petite Filipino woman.

"Not all stereotyping is bad," I interjected. This time I gave him the curve ball.

I was performing in New Orleans with my friend's funk band, which was called "Dr. Funk" because all the members were students at Tulane Medical School (except for me). After a show at Tipitina's Uptown, several people asked me what type of medicine was my specialty. After I told someone repeatedly that I wasn't a doctor, they responded, "You're an Indian American, you must be a doctor!" It's a benevolent stereotype that many people think all Indian Americans are doctors, engineers or entrepreneurs, even if that means hotel or gas station operators. Apu, the Kwik-E-Mart operator in *The Simpsons*, probably makes the most money after Mr. Burns, Smithers and Moe the bartender (depending on Barney's drinking tab). Ironically, Dr. Hibbert, the family doctor in *The Simpsons*, is an African American.

"Asian Americans undoubtedly benefit from positive stereotypes. Unfortunately, blacks are stereotyped in a negative way. Part of this silent racism is propagated by the rappers you mentioned. They are rewarded handsomely for continuing a tragic stereotype. Without a solid education, I would have ended up angry and bitter at life just like many of these rappers," Andy said.

He seemed to be putting his finger on the need for better education. But that seemed like a common answer. I wanted something more specific.

"Is there something we need to do on the federal level to help? What is the race relations bill of the twenty-first century supposed to be?" I asked.

"I'm not so sure there is a federal solution. It's easier to combat racism on a personal level—just be happy with yourself," he said. But dissatisfied with the brevity of his answer, he continued, "Smart affirmative action like we enacted in Atlanta could be a model for the future."

Affirmative action is meant to give minorities an essential leg up. In Atlanta, city planners innovated and turned affirmative action into a way to make minorities work together. The city mandated joint ventures for building projects. In 1977, Mayor Maynard Jackson refused to build the city airport unless every contracted process had been at least 25 percent completed by someone of a different race. If a black contractor won a job, they had to find somebody of another race to do 25 percent of the job and vice versa.

"We institutionalized positive race relations," said Andy. That's a formula that has worked in several places around the world. Nigeria has been compelled to share oil revenues with all thirty-six states. Sudan, South Africa and even China and Russia must learn to share the wealth with minorities of every class and creed, he posits.

Maynard and Andy consciously structured the local economy so everybody was able to participate in the growth and development. The practice was old hat by the time the preparations for the 1996 Olympics began. Over time city leaders created a social acceptance and economic appreciation of different races.

In fact, Atlanta used its diverse and successful business community to intimately woo members of the International Olympic Committee (IOC). European IOC members were entertained at prominent European businesspeople's homes. African IOC members were entertained at important African American businesspeople's homes. My parents entertained Indian members of the IOC at our home. An Indian member of the IOC, the Maharajah of Patiala, taught my mom to add ketchup to her dal tadka while they were cooking together in the kitchen. Diversity in business is just the way commerce works in Atlanta. Some of the same Atlanta business leaders who entertained IOC members were initially against the games because of fiscal concerns. But Atlanta citizens banded together and made a grassroots effort to win the games.

I moved on. "We had a diversity dean in college, which stinks of political correctness. Regarding your Atlanta example, why did the government get involved with social engineering? In a meritocracy, the person who is most talented wins the project—and doesn't need to enter into a joint venture with someone else," I commented.

"That's true, when you start with a level playing field. But when you start with four hundred years of legal exploitation, discrimination and deprivation, and you want to correct that, you have to compensate for it," he said. Other countries, like India, have instituted programs similar to affirmative action to help the Muslim and poor minorities.

I wonder whether there will ever be a day when affirmative action will not be needed. Andy doesn't think so because there will always be a need to assist those at the bottom of the ladder. There will always be someone else in the underclass. The economy has to work from the bottom up or the people left out will plot to destroy it either individually or collectively through a revolution, terrorism or crime.

"The challenge of your generation is to be aware of people's differences but not discriminate because of them. The challenge is to include all stripes into the broader economy. That's how you get poor kids off the street and give them meaning. That's how you help people who suffer from institutionalized racism and poverty," he remarked. He paused. He wanted to make sure I understood, so he gave me a brief history lesson.

In the 1960s, there were riots across America. Black and white businessmen in Atlanta got together to prevent riots. Their solution was to create summer jobs. The presidents of Delta Air Lines, Georgia Power and a few banks called their suppliers and clients and urged them to create summer jobs for black students. They put together a temporary program of 6,500 jobs. The 6,500 kids who may have been leading troublemakers instead put on a shirt and tie and went to work. That gave them hope and money to begin to think about attending college.

One of Andy's friends got involved in one of these summer jobs programs. He started as a Coca-Cola truck driver. He then interned with a program called INROADS. When he left, he went to the Maxwell School at Syracuse University. He earned a master's degree and got a job at Coke. He worked his way up to be a Coke executive in south Florida.

"We talked about it before, but this is the beauty of capitalism," Andy commented. Coke realized they must have a diverse workforce to get into diverse markets. People who don't understand a market have trouble doing business in it.

"It seems to me you are embracing capitalism again. You see it as a tonic for race relations," I observed.

"I do. I always liked trade because it brought people together. But you must ask yourself, who sets the rules? If the people who are already in charge are the ones asking the SAT questions, then those at the bottom will rarely get to the top. We need to help the people at the bottom get exposed to more than they know. We must plug them into the business world," he said. We must also help businesses to see that poverty is an unexplored market and the new frontier of economic growth. The fortune really is, as Professor C. K. Prahalad famously contended, at the bottom of the pyramid.

Markets are based on finding common ground. Buyers and sellers have to come together on a price. Many capitalists look past the geography, race and religions of counterparties. The increasing number of Westerners who moved to the United Arab Emirates in the mid-2000s to work illustrates Thomas Jefferson's remark, "Merchants have no country. The mere spot they stand on does not constitute so strong an attachment as that from which they draw their gains."[7]

Andy firmly believes that we live in a white world. We wear a suit and tie to work because it's a British tradition. There are still many British and European cultural traditions and images in our society. Many young minorities are not exposed to these traditions. But in order to be taken seriously by white corporate America, young minorities need to learn how to harmonize: how to dress and how to speak. The Japanese quickly learned how to harmonize. They wore dark suits and ties, sending the signal that they could blend into the business world.

Andy wants young people to learn how to live in two or three different worlds like he did. By living in a few worlds, young poor people gain an intellectual breadth or at least aspire for something better. I would say it works the other way too. Middle-class or wealthy young people certainly gain from volunteering in poor areas. They develop a broader understanding of life that can help them become more compassionate.

"I do think there is a key to curing the sickness of racism," he said.

"Which is . . ." I trailed off.

"Somewhere along the line I learned that I could learn something from anyone. I really mean that," he finished.

When you look at people who are different from you as teachers, you learn to respect them for their knowledge and wisdom. You develop a hunger and curiosity for knowledge of who people are and what you can learn from them. You begin to appreciate the fact that every person and culture has value. There is something to be affirmed in everybody you meet. What is the unique thing in this stranger?

When Andy was in third grade, he and his classmate Lincoln were sent to the principal's office for playing mumblety-peg with an ice pick. Both were expelled from Valena C. Jones Elementary School with the instructions to bring their mothers to school to talk to the principal. Andy's mother went to the school, and Andy was reinstated. Lincoln's mother, who had to support several children, was unable to go because she was a full-time maid and couldn't forgo her day's salary. Years later, Andy was thinking about dropping out of college because he thought it was a waste of time. He was a lifeguard at Hardin Playground the summer before his senior year. A person fell into the pool and was clearly struggling, so

Andy pulled him out of the water. It turned out to be Lincoln. Lincoln told Andy that he had been unable to matriculate again at Jones Elementary. He had been sent to reform school and had been recently released from Angola state penitentiary. He had been a serious heroin addict and had the arm sores to show for it.

Lincoln lectured Andy about his responsibility to go to school and finish because he needed to find a way to make the world a place where guys like him wouldn't be put out on the street. He said, "I'm probably as smart as you are." He might have been even smarter. He had survived the criminal justice system. Andy couldn't find any capacity to pronounce judgment on him. It wasn't because Lincoln's mom or family loved him any less but because of economic circumstances that Lincoln did not go back to Jones Elementary. Andy thought to himself, "There but for the grace of God go I."

"What could I learn from a dropout and heroin addict? Lincoln taught me to count my blessings. To see everyone as a teacher will help you see everyone's value and importance," Andy explained. Lincoln helped Andy see the merit in W.E.B. Du Bois's theory that the top 10 percent of Africans Americans could help all African Americans. The betterment of a few could advance the rest insofar as the few remember the masses.

Andy has urged me to renounce my personal prejudices and come to every situation with an open mind and heart. You don't have to agree with another person. You can't lose your identity in trying to agree with them. The idea is to understand and get to know the positives and perspectives of each person and culture. Learn from everyone, and see everyone as a teacher.

It was a shock for Andy to move to New York in 1957. He was just twenty-five and many people who worked with him were gay. But he didn't feel threatened. He was happily married. Instead of eschewing gays, he learned from them. He learned how gays coped as minorities and protected each other.

"I began to really appreciate them. I appreciated their strengths and saw them for who they were because I was comfortable with who I was. They were confident in being themselves," he said.

It all comes back to personal confidence and individual security. We must be happy with who we are. And when we find someone who isn't secure, we must nurture, include and help create opportunities for them— or we may all pay the price down the road. Andy believes that if you aren't comfortable in your own skin, then you may fall prey to whatever sickness that still silently (and, at times, not so silently) pervades our society. To see everyone as a potential teacher is an instructive way to get past our prejudices.

What's that old phrase? "Minds are like parachutes. They work best when they are open."

5 SEEKING THE UNKNOWN AND EMBRACING FAITH

Go out into the darkness and put thine hand into the Hand of God.
That shall be to thee better than light and safer than a known way.

—M. Louise Haskins, poet and teacher[1]

"I don't fear death. But I don't want to get hit by a truck," said Andy, in a light-hearted soft voice. He was trying to get me to smile. It was spring 2002, and my grandfather Dr. Piara Singh Gill, or Nanaji as I called him, had passed away hours earlier. My father dropped me at Uncle Andy's house while my mother and he dealt with Nanaji's death. I didn't cry. I was in college and had known the day was coming, as Nanaji's health had worsened over the previous few weeks. It was the first time that someone so close to me had passed away.

"I'm sure Dr. Gill would agree that not even science can fully explain death and the thereafter," Andy remarked.

Nanaji had been an eminent particle physicist, professor and science advisor to Jawaharlal Nehru, India's first prime minister. After being introduced to him by my parents, Andy grew very fond of Nanaji. He respected Nanaji's rigorous scientific views and love of teaching. I wish I could have taken one of Nanaji's courses or been a few years older so that I could have learned more about advanced science from him.

Nanaji's passing taught me a great deal about death. Uncle Andy seized the teachable moment and helped me to see death not as a period but as a comma in the story of life. Several years later, I revisited the topic of death with Andy. Our conversation started with this gloomy subject but quickly broadened into a dialogue about faith and spirituality. Our conversation helped me see the need for faith in my life and that a life without faith is a lonely life indeed. I've come to see the validity in Kahlil Gibran's words, "Faith is a knowledge within the heart, beyond the reach of proof."[2]

Andy's grandmother lived with his immediate family throughout his childhood. She began to lose her eyesight when he was about eight. She lost most of her sight, so Andy read her the newspaper and Bible everyday. She had been very active her entire life. She had raised eleven children, and only five of them were hers. She always cooked enough dinner in case anyone dropped by. Andy's house became known as the neighborhood soup kitchen because she never turned anyone away, not even the homeless. When she could no longer cook and serve, she used to pray that she would die: "I've done all that I can do." She had a firm faith in the afterlife. For six years Andy heard his grandmother say almost daily, "God, I'm ready to come on home." Andy grew familiar with death and the concept of the afterlife from that early age.

"Did Dr. King ever talk about death?" I asked.

"For the nine or so years that I knew him, he talked about his death all the time. He knew he was going to get killed," he said. King openly joked about how he would eulogize his lieutenants, including Uncle Andy, at their funerals with jarring and uncomfortable honesty.

"Did you or someone else take precautions to protect him?" I asked.

"He was more committed to his values and beliefs than his physical well-being. He knew some of us would be killed," he commented.

But Uncle Andy tried his best to protect Dr. King. In March 1965, Andy and others planned to march from Selma to Montgomery in support of the Voting Rights Act. United States Justice Department officials John Doar and Ramsay Clark warned Andy that they had received reports of snipers lurking to kill Dr. King. Andy couldn't convince him not to participate in the march, so he did the next best thing. He convinced a group of ministers who were wearing blue suits like King's to walk with him in the front row. The ministers were delighted to be leading the march. Little did they know that they were acting as decoys for snipers.

"I would have taken a bullet for Martin," whispered Andy.

"Would he have done the same for you?" I asked.

He took a moment. "I don't know. But that doesn't matter because he was the chosen one whom God had ordained. He was the one uniquely prepared to move history, not me," he said thoughtfully.

While Andy's grandmother dealt with death through prayer, Dr. King dealt with it through humor. He joked and laughed about death—perhaps because he had come close to it on several occasions. In 1958, when King was in Harlem to promote his book *Stride Toward Freedom,* a deranged African American woman stabbed him. He said he felt as if he had an out-of-body experience in which he was aware of all the preachers in the room praying for him. He joked to Andy that all of the preachers wanted him to die, but now they were praying like they wanted him to live. Dr. King said he knew that he had upset the applecart and they would have just as soon gotten rid of him. King wanted to tell the preachers not to worry and that he would be around for a while. He once told Andy that if you're going to get stabbed, make sure it's in Harlem because they have experts there on how to deal with it. He dealt with it all very playfully.

In 1960, Dr. King was arrested in Georgia for violating probation for driving without a state driver's license. The police fitted him with handcuffs and leg irons and threw him into the back of a paddy wagon with a German shepherd that growled every time he moved. The drive to Reidsville took several hours and was hellish because of the many hills and curves along the way. Dr. King said it was the worst night of his life and that it was worse than death. He felt helpless, alone and full of fear and anxiety. He was convinced that he would die. In those days, there were many instances of black men who had been taken from prison, dumped in rivers and left to die.

"It was the exact kind of intimidation that occurred at the Abu Ghraib prison in Iraq," observed Andy. "He would have been content to die. I actually think he came close to a nervous breakdown."

"How did that experience shape Dr. King's perspective on death?" I asked.

"He realized that our physical existence is temporary. Martin said, 'Everybody has to die. You can't say when you'll die, but you have a say on how you live.'" At the suggestion of his advisor Harris Wofford, presidential candidate John F. Kennedy took the courageous step to call Dr. King's wife, Coretta, and helped secure King's release from Reidsville.

"Did the realization of his own mortality and imminent death catalyze Dr. King to be bolder?" I asked.

"Yes. We chose to challenge American society, and we were prepared to die for it. You can choose to push history and society to the point where it will lash back at you and destroy you. That's ultimately what happened to Martin," he said.

"Dr. King was pushing society to change too fast? Why didn't you slow him down?" I asked.

"Oh, we tried at points. He knew that the only certainty in life is death. You live your life so that you can die for something worthwhile—if you choose to. Martin helped me see the inevitability of death and the necessity to face it head on if you are going to change the world and be true to your own beliefs. Don't let the fear of death limit you," Andy explained.

In 1963, Annelle Ponder and Fannie Lou Hamer were arrested for using a public restroom that was meant for whites in a Greyhound bus station in Mississippi. A member of the SNCC went to bail them out but he too was jailed. The next day, Medgar Evers, Mississippi state field director for the NAACP, was killed, shot in his own driveway. Andy and other leaders feared that fighting would erupt, so they went to bail Ponder and Mrs. Hamer out of jail. They asked Dorothy Cotton, the education director of the SCLC, for her car, but she resisted because she didn't feel included in the action. The men got all the show and fun. She ended up driving Andy and SCLC staff member James Bevel to the jail at a high speed. They went around a bend and saw two trucks passing each other. Cotton, who was usually a good driver, drove the car off the road. Andy belted out, "Let the white folks kill us. Don't you kill us. We need to die for something!"

High on Andy's reading list is economist Robert William Fogel's *The Fourth Great Awakening and the Future of Egalitarianism.* Fogel contends that several "great awakenings"—periods of heightened religious activity—in American history brought about broad social reforms. The first Great Awakening in the 1740s formed part of the background to the American Revolution, and the second led to the abolition movement and Civil War. Andy believes a third awakening that began in the late nineteenth century helped to bring about the New Deal and the welfare state years later. A fourth awakening ostensibly started in the 1950s and gave rise to the civil rights movement as people started to realize their identities and self-worth. Fogel suggests that universal education was critical to making American society more egalitarian.

Andy sees the civil rights movement not only as benefitting from the fourth awakening, but as part of it because it helped to spread a new religious sensitivity across the land. Blacks who were born into segregation started to think of themselves as children of God and brothers and sisters who believed in the gospel of Christ. "We began to take seriously the teachings of Christ," Andy explained. This newfound awareness led many to unearth their basic human rights: "We challenged society to accept us as full-fledged human beings." The poor started to consider themselves as worthy of rights. Women began to shake off their second-class status. It's no surprise that the leaders of civil rights movements such as Nelson Mandela, Archbishop Desmond Tutu, Martin Luther King, Andrew Young and others studied scripture and attended church schools established by American and English missionaries. Dr. King consciously used religious vocabulary to highlight the spiritual implications of the struggle for human rights. Civil rights leaders targeted African American clergy to help them garner broad support for the movement. The clergy influenced the African American social networks. If the Internet had existed back then, they would be the ones with the most Facebook friends, AIM buddies and Twitter followers.

He credits Judaism with playing a strong role in the movement. The whole narrative of the civil rights movement and American life comes out of the Jewish notion of escaping from oppression in Egypt. That was true in the Pilgrims who were trying to escape from the oppression of the Anglican Church. That was true of black slaves who identified with Moses. And that was true of civil rights leaders. He looks at Judaism with a certain fondness. In his church, as in many black churches, black spirituals are simply Old Testament stories put to music: "Let My People Go," an old favorite, for example.

Andy said, "Black churches practice essentially a prophetic Judaism that adds Jesus. And the Jesus that is added is not the same Jesus that most white churches add. We in the movement owe a lot to Jews and the Jewish faith for inspiring us and standing with us."

In February 1965, Jimmy Lee Jackson, a civil rights protester, was killed by an Alabama police officer. In March, a protest demonstration was planned as a response. As many as six hundred protesters walked in the direction of the Edmund Pettus Bridge that connected Selma to Montgomery. Alabama police intercepted the marchers and beat them with clubs. The march, which happened on a Sunday afternoon, became known as Bloody Sunday, and it was televised. As Americans came home from church, they witnessed the juxtaposition of the teachings of Jesus and the cruel brutality of the segregated South. Andy thinks many whites started to see for the first time the situation of blacks in the region as tantamount to an "American holocaust." Civil rights leaders' basic understanding of the movement was that God was with them. They knew they didn't possess the strength, wisdom or courage to bring about change on their own. They were acting on faith.

"Jean always reminded me to look to scripture for guidance and support," remembers Andy. He made sure that Jean and the kids were self-sufficient because he was sure he wouldn't outlive Jean or make it to forty.

"What did you learn from the passing of your wife, Jean?" I asked.

I didn't know whether he would answer. It was a sensitive and deeply personal topic. I thought about recanting my question, but he replied. Jean's illness that led to her death materialized suddenly in 1994. She rarely got sick. She was a strong woman. She had four children by natural childbirth without any anesthesia. One morning she was having severe abdominal cramps. The pain persisted for hours. She and Andy had recently returned from a trip to Zimbabwe with my family, so he thought it was just a bug she picked up. But the paralyzing pain did not relent, so he drove her to Crawford Long Hospital at Emory University in Atlanta. After thirty minutes of tests, the doctors confirmed she had a tumor ten or eleven centimeters in size blocking her intestine, and the tumor could break at anytime. The doctors needed to operate immediately because she was almost certain to die. After the tumor and a part of her intestines were removed, the doctors confirmed that the cancer was malignant and that it had spread throughout her lymph nodes. They gave her six months to live. She was a real fighter and wouldn't accept defeat. The doctor that operated said there really was no cure. Chemotherapy and radiation would not do any good; they would just make her miserable. Subsequently, Dr. Levi Watkins of Johns Hopkins Hospital discovered she had five quarter-size malignant tumors. Johns Hopkins was one of the few places where they could remove the liver tumors. So they did the second operation.

"That was really devastating to her," remembers Andy.

She never gave up. She was determined to push herself and live out her life. Both Andy and Jean were members of the Friendship Force, an organization that promotes cultural exchange in order to bring about peace. The organization was planning to send twenty blacks and whites to South Africa for two weeks to educate its citizens and exemplify how an integrated society can work. Despite her illness, Jean led the group to South Africa and wouldn't let Andy join the trip. She wanted to help South Africans cope with the future of their newly integrated society.

Jean talked to the children before she left. "She told our daughter Lisa, 'I cried when I let you go away to college because I knew when I saw you again you wouldn't be my baby anymore. But I knew I would see you again. So I let you go. Now you have to let me go,'" Andy recalled.

Shortly after Jean returned from that trip and was hospitalized again, my father and Andy were supposed to travel to South Africa for business. My dad insisted that Andy stay with Jean at the hospital in Atlanta, but Jean insisted that Andy should go, inquiring, "What's Andy going to do here?" Jean held my papa's hand and promised to keep them fully informed of any developments. On the flight from Miami to Cape Town, Andy paced through the aisle, asking my dad many times if he had made the right decision. Every day, Andy's children would call both my dad and Andy to relay information about Jean's health. One morning, Andy went to the customary breakfast meeting with my papa and said he didn't feel well and wanted to return to the states five days early.

"I think Andy had an inkling. He had a strong mental connection with Jean," remembers my papa.

My dad agreed to pinch hit for Andy's many speaking engagements in Durban. Two hours after Andy departed for America, my father received a phone call from one of Andy's children informing him that Jean had passed away. My father called Lufthansa and paged Andy at the airport in Frankfurt, Germany, where he was connecting to Atlanta.

"Do you have bad news for me?" Andy asked my father.

"I'm sorry, she's gone," he answered.

It was Jean's passing that cemented Andy's belief that death is not a morbid end. It is a transition from one state of existence to another. We sometimes think we are human beings who have an occasional spiritual existence. In contrast, Andy agrees with Deepak Chopra's view, which is grounded in the Hindu philosophy, that we are in reality spiritual beings who are enjoying a brief physical existence as human beings.

Andy sees Christianity as a worldly religion, but one that has lost its emphasis on the transcendental. Most people, he thinks, attend church to be socially respectable and be part of the religiously aware middle class. He has attended thousands of services. He has reached the conclusion that black churches have had more success in retaining transcendentalist aspects of the Christian faith than white churches. The black church has lived with slavery and suffering and realized that only the spiritual life can free one from troubles of this world. The lyrics from a favorite African American spiritual bring home this message, "Soon I will be done with the troubles of the world. I'm going home to live with God."

"I've been around a lot of people dying, but I've never been around anybody dying that has been afraid in those moments. I think there is an acceptance that they are moving on toward another type of existence," said Andy.

"How can you be so sure that death is a transition to another existence?" I asked.

"That's where faith comes in," he responded.

"Well, why does God allow people to suffer?" I asked.

"I don't know," he began. "But I think God is beyod good and evil."

His remark reminded me of Gandhi's comment, "[God] directs the assassin's dagger no less than the surgeon's knife."[3]

Andy continued, "As you meet the struggles of your life, you are elevated to new levels of spirituality. Without faith, it would be difficult to heal. We grieve for our lost loved ones, but there comes a point in grieving where you realize you haven't lost them at all. There is still a spiritual connection with them. I can't make a speech, or we can't talk, without my quoting Martin. Spiritually he is more powerful in my life now than he was when we were traveling together," he uttered quietly.

"Where does your spirituality come from?" I asked.

He explained that death and spirituality are an integral part of the African tradition, that your ancestors never leave you. Andy was flying from Nigeria to Senegal in 2000, and the windshield of the plane shattered like a plate at a Greek wedding. The plane landed immediately. At the airport, an old traditional healer calmed Andy. The doctor said that nothing would happen to Andy while on the African continent: "When you come to Africa there are 50 million of your ancestors' spirits who gave up their lives in passage to slavery, and they aren't going to let anything happen to you."

"I had never thought of it that way. In some ways, it is very comforting," Andy said.

"Are you saying that the spirits of Dr. King, your wife and my grandfather are still with us?" I asked.

"Yes. We couldn't stop the complex plan to kill Martin. I surmise that his death was a well thought-out plan of action that involved a lot of people. It wasn't James Earl Ray. We civil rights leaders have had people come to us and tell us that they were involved. They asked for forgiveness. We were always willing to forgive. I don't feel any resentment toward anybody because I think his death released his spirit. Martin's spirit has accomplished more in American politics than his life ever could have," he replied.

Moments before his death, Dr. King was joking around with Ralph David Abernathy and Andy, and they engaged in a pillow fight. After the fun, King and Abernathy went upstairs to the room they were sharing.

Andy remained downstairs to wait for Reverend Kyles, who was hosting a dinner for Dr. King and his cohorts later in the evening. Andy killed time by shadowboxing with his colleague James Orange, a gentle giant, in the parking lot. Then a quick shot rang out. Andy looked up to the balcony on which King had been standing. He could see that King had fallen back. Andy ran up to King's room and saw blood around his head. As soon as Andy looked into his eyes, he knew the famed civil rights leader wouldn't survive.

"It's still tough for me to talk about Martin's death. I tear up almost every time," whispered Andy. This time was no exception as he dabbed a lone tear on his cheek with his pearl-colored handkerchief.

Civil rights leader Ralph David Abernathy eulogized Dr. King at his funeral by comparing the slain leader to Joseph in the Book of Genesis. Joseph's brothers considered killing Joseph and called him "the dreamer"— Joseph's brothers said, in Andy's paraphrase, "behold the dreamer, let us slay him, and see then what shall come of his dreams." Andy explained the significance of King's death: "Many of us, including Dr. King, felt that dreams have to be liberated from the mind and the body. For Dr. King to give his life for his beliefs gave a spiritual authority to his life. We see him for his strengths and not the many flaws that he had."

Andy believes that death makes us more mindful that people are spiritual beings, which is ultimately what's important. A person's weaknesses, shortcomings and failures are less important than their spiritual reality. There was a gambler on Auburn Avenue in Atlanta who ran an illegal lottery. At his funeral, Andy eulogized him as the forerunner of the HOPE Scholarship, a merit scholarship in Georgia that is funded by the state lottery. He sold lottery tickets illegally, but he used the money to educate his children, and he was a very generous man who would help almost anybody in need. He gave money, all gained illegally, to the YMCA and the churches.

"I dressed him up and made him look like a holy figure in spite of the fact that he was something of a rogue. When a person is physically gone and can't do us any harm, then we can finally appreciate the good. Then we see the person as a human being," he explained.

"Is death the only time you are aware of spirituality?" I asked, changing the subject.

"No, I get spiritual when I think about my purpose in life," he responded.

Andy has been aware of his spirituality since he was a kid. He felt that he was more than just one hundred pounds of flesh. He wanted to be something more than he was. He had dreams.

"Once I started to focus on my purpose, I became aware of my spiritual existence. I realized my soul was merely resting in my body for the here and now," he explained.

"Looking back at your life, what has been your purpose?" I asked, hoping he wouldn't give me a series of platitudes.

"My purpose has been to serve humanity," he began. I waited for him to explain. He didn't.

"That's broad," I prompted.

"It's simple. No need to overcomplicate it. I try to serve humans and respond to life one day at a time. And I learned about my faith and spirituality day by day," he said.

He's a Congregationalist and member of the United Church of Christ (UCC). The philosophy of his church comes from the Protestant Reformation and originates in the United States from the Pilgrims. Congregationalist minister Eleazar Wheelock founded my college, Dartmouth, in 1769, so I'm somewhat familiar with the faith, and I identify with Congregationalist beliefs. The UCC has a liberal view of several social issues like abortion and gay rights. Congregationalists tend to gravitate in the direction of tolerance and forgiveness rather than judgment. Rather than imposing a strict top-down structure, the UCC rests much power and autonomy in each individual church. The motto of the church comes from John 17:21: "That they may all be one," which sounds like our nation's motto, *e pluribus unum,* "out of many, one."

Andy's spirituality was shaped by serious investigation into the beliefs of others. As a boy, he took Christianity for granted and rarely thought seriously about it. While studying in Howard University's college library, he came across Plato's *Apology* and Marcus Aurelius's *Meditations.* He read about the Bahá'í Faith. He sought to learn from the best minds and work out what was meaningful for him.

"I found the spirituality of Sufi Muslims in Pakistan to be similar to New England Quakerism and African mysticism. Whenever I entered the General Assembly at the United Nations, I would walk over to greet the Pakistani ambassador, who was a Sufi, and Rikhi Jaipal, a Hindu. They had such a spiritual presence about them, and so did the Israeli ambassador who invited our family to join his Passover seder," he said. It was as if the General Assembly Hall was just another block in his childhood jam-session neighborhood.

Uncle Andy was a seeker. The UCC creed that he learned in Sunday school was good preparation for life both inside and outside the UN. The creed was simply, "We are united in striving to know the will of God, made known or to be made known unto us." He didn't just memorize the creed, he sought answers elsewhere. By reading about other people's lives and faiths, he absorbed lessons that he could apply to his own life, as he did when he studied Gandhi.

"Gandhi spurred me toward Christ," he said.

"But Gandhi wasn't a Christian," I replied. Gandhi, however, admired Jesus and took to heart the Sermon on the Mount. He once said, "I like your Christ, I don't like your Christians."[4]

"Gandhi took seriously the political implications of Jesus's ministry," Andy explained. "He translated Jesus's idea of nonviolence into a political action program. Then Christianity became relevant to me. Gandhi applied the forgiveness that Jesus taught to the British Empire. Before my readings of Gandhi, I couldn't see what difference Christianity made."

I said, "You found how to make the teachings of Christ relevant to your life as a young person. Not all of us are as curious or compelled to discover how faith affects our lives. Many of my friends don't go to church." One estimate is that only 13.5 percent of 18- to 24-year-olds attend a place of worship at least once a week. Perhaps young religious people grapple with profound questions from an early age and are therefore more comfortable dealing with serious topics.[5]

"Most young people feel like the church betrayed them. The church does not address their primary concerns. They are concerned about the future and the church is teaching them about the past. They are concerned about sex and reproduction, selecting partners and their careers. The church doesn't address those things. They get more information about their lives from secular society," Andy responded.

"What's your advice to young atheists?"

"I think we are all supposed to be atheists at some point in life. Our egos push us to find our own identities and destinies. We think we can do it alone. As the world gets more complicated, however, it is easier to seek and turn toward the experiences and wisdom of others for answers, which lead to faith and spirituality," he explained. "Jesus spoke in parables. That's deliberate. The stories gradually lead you to your own truth. They don't force it upon you like the Ten Commandments."

"Stories leave things open to interpretation," I said. That's probably why he likes stories. They encourage the listeners to infer their own meanings.

"I was secure enough to want to be a seeker. A religious person should be a seeker and not one who is grasping for certainty and reassurance. Young people should interpret and find their own meanings," he said. No matter how good the teacher, it's up to the student to seek his or her truth.

Andy's childhood church tolerated children questioning the Bible. When someone told him at Sunday school that Elijah went to heaven in a flaming chariot, he didn't believe it. "That's baloney and can't be possible," was his exact response. He thinks Sunday school can be unsafe for children if they are taught to blindly accept things: It can turn kids into robots who don't think for themselves. Through questioning you get used to being a constant seeker. Through questions you find deeper meaning. Eventually you discover how to make faith relevant to your own life.

Andy used the gospels of Matthew, Mark, Luke and John to explain his point. Each tells a different story about Jesus. A seeker needs to determine what passages are meaningful and relevant to his or her life. Andy contemporized his gospel example by suggesting that I think about an automobile accident with four witnesses each standing on a different corner. They all have different points of view, and they are all true.

"I don't quite follow," I complained.

"The beauty of faith is that you get to work out what is true and what has meaning for you. The beauty of seeking is that you get answers to your personal questions," he said.

Dr. King, Andy and other civil rights leaders came out of the same social-liberal Protestant tradition. The civil rights leaders took to heart the value of seeking answers to their personal questions. Andy says they didn't take the Bible literally. They saw the Bible as poetic metaphor (a literal reading of "the Lord is my shepherd" implies that I am a lamb). They tried to ascertain the meaning of the scripture and not look only at the words. Their interpretive understanding of the Bible was grounded in historical facts: The Bible went through many translations from Hebrew to Aramaic, which was like a street language, to Greek, Latin and eventually English and other European languages.

"Because of the many translations and penchant for humans to err, it's hard to know what God actually meant. It was difficult to take words literally but we took them spiritually," he explained.

"There are four gospels and hundreds of stories about other gods. Are you saying that other religions are true? Is a little Muslim boy going to hell because he doesn't believe in Christ?" I asked.

"No. God is bigger than any of our understandings or interpretations. Seeking will teach you that there is room for conversation and discussion."

I've internalized Andy's maxim "seek and struggle." I'm still trying to determine what I learned in my college library. Most of the time I was goofing around on computer terminals, but I remember coming across the Gnostic gospel of Thomas, a fifth corner observer of the automobile accident. Its message has always stuck with me. I asked, "Are you familiar with the message of Thomas that heaven and hell are here on earth?"

"Yes. There is some truth to its message. When I look at people who are selfish, self-centered and unable to give or love, I see a certain hell in their lives. You can find a certain type of hell in the Middle East where some people weaponize their faiths," he elucidated.

"And heaven?"

"Love, kindness, generosity. When you give, you get back so much more. That's heaven."

When he was mayor, Andy's national denomination asked him to be a fundraising chair. He accepted and promised to donate $25,000 over five years. Church leaders wanted him to contribute $50,000. His yearly salary was $50,000, and he was struggling to finance the college tuitions of his children. He voiced his frustration to Jean. Without hesitation she urged him to pledge $50,000. She reasoned that without the church both she and Andy wouldn't be anywhere. The church had played an important role in their lives. Their parents and grandparents were educated by church colleges. He didn't know how he would be able to make ends meet if he agreed to the church's request. He gave reluctantly, but he had faith. The next week Andy was walking through the Atlanta airport when he ran into Sam Moore, the CEO of Thomas Nelson Publishers. The publisher asked Andy whether he would write a spiritual memoir. Andy consented. Three weeks later Andy's agent finalized the terms for the book at $50,000. Andy had found "a way out of no way," which became the title of the book. The story doesn't end there. He joined the board of

Thomas Nelson and received board fees in stock. Years later, the company was sold, and he earned almost $400,000, which he shared with schools, the YMCA and the church.

A similar story only reinforces Andy's comment. Andy joined the international advisory board of a gold mining company because he wanted to learn more about the precious metals industry, and he thought he could help. Several years later, his friend and fellow member of the board Vernon Jordan urged Andy to sell his stock options because they had appreciated. Andy hadn't realized he was receiving options. When he called to inquire about the value of his options, he was surprised to learn they were worth a hefty seven-figure sum. Sometimes it pays to be ignorant. But I suppose the other lesson we can learn is that when you give, you get back so much more. The funds went to helping him form the Andrew Young Foundation, along with the funds Carolyn raised for his seventy-fifth birthday celebration.

Perhaps it's necessary for Andy to have faith when it comes to money. He just hasn't made a lot of it. My papa visited Andy at City Hall during his last week as mayor and asked him what he was going to do after his term in office was complete. Andy shut the door and admitted he didn't have anywhere to work. He had almost no retirement savings and no medical insurance (a city pension requires 14 years of service, and Andy had served only 8; a congressional pension requires 5½ years and he served only 4). My dad hired him to work at his engineering company and arranged almost $1 million in medical insurance for Jean when she fell ill. Andy told me, "I had faith things would work out though. And God put your father in my life. Without your daddy, it would have been tough to care for Jean."

Andy's seeking and reading in other beliefs and faiths helped him immensely during his tenures in elected office. It helped him to see faith not as a flashpoint but as a way to find common ground. In 1973, the morning after Spiro Agnew resigned the vice presidency because of criminal charges, Andy led the prayer for congressional members. He prayed for

Agnew and his family, which shocked many Republican representatives. Andy explained that regardless of whether Agnew had committed a crime, he still was a human being who had a loving family that was greatly distressed by the entire situation.

"My faith and spirituality made me sensitive toward others. It helps me see all of us as God's children, as I learned during the civil rights movement," he said.

Praying for Agnew won Andy support and respect among conservatives who thought most liberals were secular agnostics. Because of this, Andy felt more comfortable approaching a Republican who was trying to remove milk from the school lunch program in order to cut the budget. He explained to the Republican that he had a problem removing the milk: "I can't as an individual meet the needs of all of God's children. That's why I believe in government."

"President Franklin Roosevelt said the role of government is to provide hope," I stated.

"Hope for a small child is milk. For the poor, bread is peace. For the rich who have bread, peace is security," he summarized.

"It is noble to legislate to achieve these things. But isn't it dangerous to see government as a tool to enact religious beliefs? What if fundamentalists tried to do the same thing?"

Andy sees fundamentalism, much like racism, as an output of individual insecurity. When one is insecure, it's easy to grasp at people or ideas that offer certainty. Pushing a fundamentalist agenda is unpalatable to him because of the certitude that many fundamentalists exhibit. There is no room for debate. Fundamentalism is the opposite of seeking. "Does fundamentalism lead to quarrels between people of different faiths?" I asked.

"It certainly seems so. But when people of different religions are forced to listen to each other, they can get along. I visited Hadassah Medical Center in Jerusalem, and there you have Jews, Muslims, and Christians working together because they all want the same thing—health," he said.

"What's your advice to a young fundamentalist?"

"Stick to your beliefs if they bring you peace, but eventually young fundamentalists may realize that fundamentalism is not capable of dealing with complex life as we now know it," he replied.

Andy decries some fundamentalists for misinterpreting the teachings of Christ. Fundamentalists sometimes argue for abstinence from sex, drugs and alcohol. But they too can be very materialistic. He steers clear of harshly condemning the megachurch preachers like Eddie Long, T. D. Jakes and Creflo Dollar and others involved in the "business of God." But he thinks many of these preachers see the size of the congregation as the blessing of God.

"The size of your congregation does not illustrate how successful you are as a preacher. That is not the message of Jesus. These preachers often push a too literal meaning of the Bible, but they certainly are entertaining and I get inspired by their preaching." He whispered to me that he wished that the parishioners of megachurches wouldn't be swept up in the cult of personality of their preacher.

"When I first met Eddie Long, he asked me for investment ideas for his personal account. It wasn't much of a religious experience," I said. Then again, he was probably trying to make polite conversation after seeing my business card.

Andy chuckled, "Exactly." Andy sees that a church with 30,000 members faces several financial issues. Churches, much like universities, use endowments to prepare for tough times or to expand their missions. One church even became a buying co-op and credit union to help its members grow out of poverty.

In 2009, the United Church of Christ church that Andy attended was being renovated, so the congregation moved to a nearby firehouse for services. Andy asked a carpenter friend to build a cross with two old boards. He didn't want new lumber: He wanted a rugged cross with nails and railroad spikes in it so the congregation could remember the real foundation of meaning—to seek and to struggle.

"At least that is what Dr. King taught me," he said.

"How so?" I asked.

"Martin was the ultimate seeker. He sought the opinions of others in order to learn. He struggled to find answers. He didn't just accept what others told him. He didn't accept his faith blindly. He struggled to figure out what to do. But it's through the struggling and seeking that he found himself," he explained.

Andy recalled that Dr. King sought the advice and counsel of Buddhist monk Thich Nhat Hanh from Vietnam after Hanh wrote him a letter in 1965 entitled "Searching for the Enemy of Man." Hanh visited with King and other civil rights leaders and helped them see the Vietnam War from the perspective of the Vietnamese. Hanh's views helped to influence King to come out against the war in a speech at the Riverside Church in New York. King even nominated Hanh for the Nobel Peace Prize in 1967, which in the end was not awarded that year.

A few years before, in 1963, when civil rights leaders were in Birmingham, Dr. King considered whether he should dramatize and escalate the protests by going to jail himself. He had to do something. The movement was running out of funds and several supporters were already in jail. Several respectable lawyers, doctors and businesspeople met with him and advised him not to go to jail. They urged King to admit his failure, pack up and leave town. After listening to the opinions of others, he decided not to listen to them. He decided to listen to himself and tap the knowledge of his heart. He put on his overalls and went to jail.

Several white religious leaders from the Protestant, Catholic and Jewish faiths ran a letter entitled "A Call for Unity" in a local newspaper that decried King for upsetting the social order of Birmingham. These religious leaders urged blacks to fight in courts and not take to the streets. Dr. King was in jail with nothing to do but fume over who was right and who was wrong. Andy believes that it was through this struggle that King became filled with spiritual insight and started to write around the borders of newspapers and toilet tissue as a response to the religious leaders.

It was almost as if King were channeling the prophet Jeremiah who spoke of "a fire being shut up in his bones." King had to let his fire out. First published in *Liberation* in 1963, "Letter from Birmingham Jail" became an emancipatory manifesto for folks struggling and seeking freedom around the world.

"There would not have been a letter if he had listened to the whole crowd," Andy said. "He had to go to jail. He had to suffer that humiliation. He pushed his life to the limits in order to be elevated to another spiritual level."

In brief, Andy believes that there is a spiritual reality that resides deep within everyone's core. When you become aware of this core, you start to see the deeper meaning in things. You start to have faith that there is a purpose to your life. This faith helps you to understand right from wrong. Faith doesn't conflict with education, sports life or love life. It gives meaning to it. Most churches present a conflict between the spirit and the flesh. Andy doesn't see that. The spirit guides the flesh and mind. The spirit within enlightens and inspires and makes you see people in a different way. You see people not by their problems but by their potential. You learn to see people as God sees them. You see them as your brothers and sisters.

"That is basically my faith. In order to arrive at my faith, I struggled and tried to seek answers from others," he said.

I struggled to accept Andy's words about seeking. I believe in Jesus Christ, studied at a Christian school for several years and attend church. As a result of our conversations, I've started to attend church more frequently, and make it a point to visit different churches when I travel. It's because of my religious tourism, my seeking, that I've sat through Pentecostal services in the South, Catholic masses in Lagos and even the Church of John Coltrane in San Francisco affectionately known as the Ministry of Sound. Questioning the faith of your parents or ancestors is useful. You need to work out your faith on your own—it will be more meaningful to you when you need it. If you blindly accept the faith of your parents, Andy thinks you won't have personal experiences from which to draw. The struggle to find faith adds to the glory of eventually finding it. Why outsource your decision to what your parents decided?

He urges me to ponder the motto of his church, "That they may all be one." His answer made me realize that all people are welcome in his broad faith, for he believes in the universal religion of nonviolence, worships at the temple of love and forgiveness, and takes solace in the sanctuary of his soul.

"My fundamental faith is forgiveness. God forgives me, but in order to receive it, I have to pass it on to others," he professed. We also must accept God's forgiveness by forgiving ourselves.

He returned once more to the theme of our conversation. "Through seeking and scrutiny, you will find answers. Your faith will ultimately become stronger," he explained.

Andy's theorem on faith as I understood it is: (1) don't accept your faith blindly, (2) seek and question, (3) ascertain and determine new personal truths that are meaningful to your life. How does questioning your faith make it stronger? Doesn't raising doubts make you see the holes in your beliefs? Perhaps, and I suppose that is why some people change faiths and some people grow in their faiths.

I think Andy's perspective on faith shares similarities with Pascal's wager. The French philosopher Blaise Pascal contended that even though God cannot be proved by reason, one should still believe: One should wager that God exists because there is only an upside and no downside to such a belief. What is the worst that could happen if you believe in God? Some may think that a belief in God can lead to violence in the name of the religion or holy war. But Pascal may have advocated faith because it can serve as a positive cohesive force in a society.

To help me understand, we finished where we started—with my grandfather—or at least with his expertise, science.

"We are getting a nanotech view of the molecule and body, a macro-economic perspective of earth and an interstellar perspective on our planet. The more we go into space and into the atom, there are even more questions. What I finally found is that it makes more room for faith not less," Andy said.

"You are saying that the more complex science has become, there is more room for faith and spirituality. The more answers we find, the more questions we have. Look at the many scientists who are trying to resolve general relativity and quantum mechanics," I said.

"You're no Einstein. But you've got it," he chuckled.

"$E = mc^2$," I joked.

He took my joke and ran with it. He explained that Einstein's theory shows that matter changes into energy. But energy doesn't stop there. Andy thinks we are combinations of matter and energy. If we see ourselves as energy, it is easier to accept death as a transition from one state of existence to another. Andy then lectured me on Newtonian physics, geometry and DNA, before embarking on a weird tangent about alternative medicine and healing. He admits his scientific knowledge is elementary. This time you could call him a slumdog scientist. But I listened and took notes on my yellow legal pad. I didn't accept everything he said.

He would be proud.

6 CUPID LEARNS THE RULE OF 4 Ps

Love must be as much a light as a flame.

—Henry David Thoreau[1]

"You're afraid to ask," Andy said.

He leaned back in the large beige chair. He had just returned home after a postchurch lunch with Carolyn and his mother-in-law at Paschal's, the iconic Atlanta eatery. Andy wore a purple Brooks Brothers dress shirt with a pressed collar and had undone his purple bowtie, so it hung freely around his neck. He rested one leg in the chair and extended his other onto the ottoman.

It was a nippy autumn Sunday, and I had stopped by Uncle Andy's on my way to the airport to catch up with him. I didn't have much time because I was trying to make an early flight back to New York. I could hear Paula, one of Andy's four children, speaking with Carolyn in the kitchen. Because Andy and I talk for hours, often at night, Carolyn likes to joke that Andy and I are in a secret society. If she had listened in on our conversation, she probably would have found some validation for her jokes.

"Afraid to ask what?" I wondered. I was perplexed. I ask Uncle Andy any and every question that comes to mind.

"The question that many young people struggle to ask and answer," he began. "You haven't asked me about love. There could have been no civil rights movement without it. There can't be faith or hope without it too. There can be no positive future without love." His platitudes sounded ominous.

I paused to consider his remark. I mouthed the letters L-O-V-E as I thought, hoping I could manage at least an amusing response. All I could think about was how I didn't want to speak of love. I would have rather asked him about topics more germane to his professional life such as justice, urban planning or foreign policy. Even in our earlier conversation on spirituality and faith, I had tried to develop a theorem to understand his views.

Speaking about personal issues like love really helps you understand someone and what makes them tick. But I'm still working on becoming more comfortable talking about these more personal issues. My parents didn't really discuss relationships and love with me much when I was growing up. Obviously my conversations with Uncle Andy are helping me.

"It's not that I'm afraid. I love learning about other things from you," I said.

"Love really is the central issue you and so many others your age must face and understand," he replied.

I am nearing the age when many people think about getting married. That I am Indian American complicates matters: I come from a long tradition of Indian descendants (as far as I know) and must wrestle with merging my heritage with that of my eventual partner should she not be Indian. For centuries, Indian families planned their marriages. But I grew up in America where I've been encouraged to meet and date a wide variety of women.

"You may be afraid to challenge that tradition," Uncle Andy said.

"I've always thought you should marry for love," I responded. I cringed considering what I had just said. It sounded like the closing scene of an animated Disney movie.

"What is love?" he asked.

"Gandhi said that without truth there is no love, which I believe. I also believe love is passion," I replied. I then remembered the literal meaning of passion: suffering. To love is to suffer? That didn't sound right to me. I floundered for a better answer.

"Love is commitment, trust and communication," he declared as succinctly as a fortune inside a fortune cookie.

Andy should know something about commitment. He was married to Jean for forty years. In marriage, you commit to stand by your partner in the best and worst of times. One of my friends dramatizes this notion by claiming that if your partner is incapacitated, or in his parlance "a vegetable," you must continue to support him or her. Finding someone to whom you want to commit can take some effort. Andy had been ready to commit to Jean surely because of her uniqueness—but her distinctiveness was more apparent because she contrasted with the other girls that Andy dated when he was a teenager. He loved Jean because of who she was and also because of who she wasn't.

"I dated a different girl every week while I was growing up in Louisiana. I wanted to learn as much as I could about all different types of women," he said. He was a lifeguard in the heart of Creole New Orleans, so it was easy to meet women.

"A liberal arts education of women?" I asked.

"Yeah," he said, amused.

Andy relished growing up in New Orleans because he was exposed to women from different cultures. The intermixing of French, Spanish and African cultures, among others, spawned a Creole look that attracted Andy. In his humble opinion, the "beautiful blending" of New Orleans women is rivaled only by the women of the South African cape and Venezuela. He believes the intermarrying of people from several cultures created a unique opportunity to learn from many cultures at once in New Orleans.

"Well, what did you learn from dating all those women?" I asked, trying to nudge him back to the topic of love.

"I learned how to have intimate nonsexual relations with women. I didn't have to go to bed with every pretty woman that I met," he replied.

"Is that possible?" I asked. He was making an important point. You don't need to hook up with every beautiful person that you meet. He cited Tiger Woods, who he thinks has a tough time relating to women. Tiger didn't have a sister so was unable to learn at an early age how to have intimate nonsexual relationships with women. That's one explanation for Tiger's infidelity. The other is that he is a young billionaire with access to almost anything or anyone that he wants.

"It takes work," Andy started. "I learned that I could bare my soul with women in a way that I couldn't with men. Women are better listeners. I've found that most of my relationships with male friends tended to get competitive."

That's not to say that relationships with women can't get competitive. A few of my girlfriends felt the need to compete with me in school or outside of class. Those relationships didn't last long. I was looking for a partner with whom I could grow. I certainly deserve blame for my unsuccessful relationships too.

Andy's dating years were in the era before birth control pills. There was little sexual freedom as a result. Among the several girls that he dated were very strict Protestant and Catholic girls. They would like to "kiss, hug and dance close on the dance floor," as he puts it. But the crowd of which he was a part didn't take things much further. Andy entered high school at the tender age of eleven, so he leaned heavily on other boys to learn about women. On one occasion, when he was twelve, he spent some time with a girl who was fourteen and sexually active. The older boys warned Andy that if the girl were to become pregnant, she could lay the blame on him. Andy's street education taught him to be careful when it came to sex. "In a way, the lack of the pill made everyone more careful about sex," he observed.

Andy also learned on the street that it was okay to reject the class and creed notions of his parents. His parents wanted him to spend time only with others in the black middle class. However, he was the sole middle-class student at his elementary school. The other students came from working-class or poor families, like Lincoln, the fellow Andy rescued years later at the swimming pool. He received an education he never forgot on poverty and its problems. Drugs were never adventurous or exciting to him: He associated them with poverty and sickness because even in fourth grade he knew several students who were smoking pot and trying to sell it. When it came to girls later in life, he disliked the stodgy elitism of both men and women at Howard University. He married Jean, who was, as he called her, "a country bumpkin." One of the first times that he met her she was milking a cow. It was difficult for Jean to adapt to the bright lights of New York. She grew up in a small town of only a few thousand residents in Alabama and went to Manchester College, which is located in a small town in Indiana. She had never been inside a big department store or on an escalator.

"You came from an urban, black, middle-class family. Was Jean your opposite?" I asked.

"Oh no, we were very much the same. I didn't know I wanted to be a minister but I did want to follow wherever God led me. I needed to find a woman of faith, a woman who was willing to launch out on a spiritual journey. I didn't find that in college or university. I found that in Marion, Alabama. It just happened that she was a basketball player and a swimmer like me," he explained. He didn't know many black women who could swim. While he was visiting her house, he noticed the Bible on her coffee table in which she had underlined several passages. Clearly they had a lot in common.

His proposal to her was a bit odd and very unromantic though. He visited her in Marion over Christmas. He put her ring in his bag and told her that her Christmas present was in it, and that she should look for it in the bag. She consented to marry him but said he would first have to ask her father, which he did.

"You married for love?" I asked.

"Yes, but now that I think of it, parts of it were maybe arranged."

On further thought, he believes his mother played a crucial role in finding Jean. His mom didn't want him staying in New York, so she called her church conference superintendent and asked whether he could find a job for Andy in the South. Jean's mother was a friend of the superintendent and frequently reminded him that she had three daughters and wanted a young minister to come to Marion and marry one of them. The superintendent invited Andy to Marion. The rest is history. Coincidentally, Jean Young, Coretta Scott King and Juanita Abernathy (the wife of Ralph David Abernathy) were all from Perry County. Small world? No. Andy explains, "God's world."

"I think that there is a real value in arranged marriages and not being left on your own. I'm not saying you need to marry who your parents choose, but you should listen to them and meet the people whom they introduce you to," he said. "Isn't Internet dating like arranged marriages?" He's got a point. Internet dating removes the opportunity of a romantic chance encounter. You are arranging and targeting your mates and destiny.

I can relate to Andy's comment about arranged marriages. My mother has recently started to talk about marriage with my sister and me. She keeps her ears open to hear whether there are young people who would be good matches for us. My sister and I used to push back fiercely. Now we just laugh it off.

My mom is much more relaxed than some Indian parents. One of my Indian friends went on a date with an Indian guy who was introduced to her by her mother. At the end of the date, she invited him back to her house. When they arrived, they could see her mother through the window on her knees praying (ostensibly for a successful date). My friend was horrified. When they went inside, her mom offered him coffee. She spent twenty minutes preparing a huge spread of almost everything in the refrigerator for him—again to my friend's embarrassment.

Welcome to the house of a first-generation Indian in America. *Namaste.*

Uncle Andy has tried to play matchmaker for me. He visited a marble distributor in South Atlanta to pick out marble for his coffee table (which is shaped like the continent of Africa). He met a young Indian American girl who worked at the company but had just finished up medical school. She wasn't wearing makeup and reminded him of Jean when he first met her milking a cow. "I bet she would be a knockout if she wore a sari," he said to me as he herded me into the car and drove to the distributor.

"Um, uh . . . so your family is from India?" I asked the girl. I didn't have any game. I still don't. The girl really was very sweet. She can probably count her fifteen minutes with me as community service.

Arguably the most important lesson Andy gleaned from his frequent dates in New Orleans was that love shouldn't be confused with physical attraction. He would date attractive women and woo them with his large vocabulary and personal charm. (Being a sesquipedalian has never worked for me.)

"I couldn't make a woman want to understand me," he said. "That's why Jean and I got along. She wanted to understand me. And I wanted to understand her." She was still one of the most competitive people that he had ever known. In her final days, she told Andy that she wanted her epitaph to say "Jean Childs Young 1931–1994: Now That Was a Woman." The Atlanta Public Schools system honored her by naming a middle school after her.

Andy points to the Androgynes from Greek myth, whom the gods split out of envy into two halves, one male and one female. We were once whole but now must search for our soul-mate to be complete. He saw Jean as his other half. She completed him like a verb in a sentence. Not only was Andy physically attracted to Jean but he was drawn by her intellect. They were like minds. There were also some practical considerations in choosing Jean. Both wanted to live in the South. Andy had dated another girl in college but the deal-breaker was that she wouldn't move to the South. He dated several white girls while in seminary but it was usually group dates. He admitted to me that it was impossible to return to the segregated South with a white girl, and he was sure his calling was there. "Frankly, you could say I played it safe or was chicken," Andy said. "I married someone from the same church denomination and commitment to nonviolence."

Jean and Andy understood each other and tried to challenge each other to stay true to their innermost beliefs. In 1956, when they were living in Thomasville, Georgia, Andy learned that the KKK was going to demonstrate against a voter registration drive that he was organizing. He thought he and his family would be prime targets. He instructed Jean that if the Klan visited their house, he would walk outside and talk to them while she stayed inside with the family rifle trained on the leader's head. Jean wanted no part of the plan and urged Andy to remember his sermons and to believe that God would look after them. Andy joked that he thought he had married a religious nut. But Jean had taken the time to understand Andy and his values, and made an effort to keep him true to them.

After Dr. King's assassination, Harvard University inquired whether Andy would be interested in leading its urban affairs institute in a tenure-track professorship. The institute eventually became the African American Studies program. Jean wouldn't even consider moving to Massachusetts and insisted that Andy not even interview for the job. His calling, she reminded him, was in the South.

Coretta Scott King was no different. She was much more committed to nonviolence and desegregation in the South than Dr. King. "There would be no Martin Luther King without Coretta," said Andy. Both Andy and King were intellectually committed to fighting racism. They knew it was wrong. Both Jean and Coretta, who also hailed from Marion, Alabama, had watched their families virtually destroyed by southern racism. Coretta's father Obadiah "Obie" Scott had a store and sawmill that were burned down by whites. Even though Obie toiled relentlessly to make a decent living for his family, his white neighbors still caused him pain and suffering. After King was assassinated, it was Coretta who largely stepped in to help lead the cause. She aggressively pushed to educate and train people in nonviolence. Her strong will and desire to play an active role in the movement drew criticism from other civil rights leaders who wanted her to help raise money but not meddle in creating policies or be engaged in the governance or strategy of the movement.

Jean's great-great-grandfather was a postmaster during Reconstruction. He worked hard to purchase one block of property in the town square in Marion, Alabama. Whites swindled Jean's grandfather out of it while she was in high school. Jean's grandfather subsequently committed suicide, and her father became an alcoholic. Her mother was fired from her teaching job because she resisted the advances of the white superintendent. Her mother had to work at another school that was hours away, which just made a bad situation even worse. Jean was truly bitter and angry about racism and segregation. She disliked walking past Marion Military Institute because white boys would harass her. Though she was angered by the hateful acts of white racists, Jean embraced nonviolence and internalized the teachings of Gandhi. Everyone knew her to be a generous and loving lady.

In contrast, Dr. King and Andy, while familiar with Gandhi's teachings, also read the works of Christian theologians Dietrich Bonhoeffer, Paul Tillich and Reinhold Niebuhr. These theologians blamed Christian pacifism for the rise of Nazism in Germany and across Europe in the 1930s. Niebuhr authored *Christianity and Power Politics* and built on the doctrine of "the just war" which originated in medieval Europe. Though both King and Andy explored nonviolence with their minds, their wives were the lantern lights that helped to show them the way.

"We married women who understood us. You end up with a woman with strong convictions with whom you have to battle the rest of your life. Jean always said every issue has a male and female perspective. I learned to seek the female opinion," he said.

"What happens if you don't seek a woman who challenges you?" I asked.

"You end up with a bad deal," Andy replied.

He was referring to a friend and fellow civil rights activist. A rising star with a bright mind, he got a girl pregnant when she was eighteen and married her. It's true that he did well for himself, but Andy speculates that getting married and having children at such a young age may have deprived the nation of a truly great leader and retarded his friend's intellectual development and ability to contribute to the movement. Andy thinks his friend and colleague may have achieved national office twenty years ago. "Before he awoke, he had a number of children. Just like T.I. the rapper, who has several kids from different women. For my friend, though, it was probably the first girl he dated or slept with. You have to be so careful these days. Finding real love can be a challenge. We often confuse love with infatuation. Can you commit to an infatuation?" he asked.

"Probably not. But also I don't think women or men are to blame for wanting to find a partner. That's only natural," I said. Life can be very lonely for young people, and each day there is a new challenge. It's the process of growing up. Searching for a partner is one way to quench your loneliness.

"Sure. But you really must take your time in picking a partner. My friend didn't take his time. He is lazier than me," Andy laughed.

Andy told me about how some of his friends attended Howard University exclusively to find a partner. When he was a student, Howard produced a third of the African American doctors and half of the lawyers. Girls were sent to Howard to find black soon-to-be professionals. It goes both ways. Boys and girls are looking for their mates.

"Young people just need to be careful not to marry too young," he observed.

"Gandhi was married as a teenager," I countered.

"Yes, and that was one of his weaknesses. He never really learned how to understand women," he replied. "I tend to think it's probably better for a man to marry a younger girl so she grows up feeling somewhat obligated to serve you. Those are the marriages that seem to be more successful, especially as you get older."

"With all respect, I think that's nonsense and sexist," I protested.

He didn't back down. "Well, it is what it is. I am who I am. It wouldn't be the first time I've been considered sexist. I just look at marriage from a man's point of view. But, you're right, men also have an obligation to protect and provide emotional and spiritual security," he explained. I realized that Uncle Andy was speaking to me, a young male. You could chalk up his comment to just boys bantering but that doesn't excuse it. I moved on.

"How do you balance that view?" I asked.

"I balance my view by looking at things from the perspective of what would be best for my daughters and granddaughters, and you should look at how things can be best for your sister or my granddaughter. Like Jean said—there is a male and female view," he clarified. But his clarification didn't change my opinion about his earlier comment. Sometimes I think Uncle Andy likes to spread his feathers like a macho peacock; his controversial remarks trick me into paying attention.

I tried to even out his sexist remark. "Do you see how some women think men are just sex-craving horny robots?" I asked.

"Oh sure," he said. "Most men can be selfish pricks seeking their own satisfaction or sexual fulfillment. Everyone has a view on love and relationships. I can only give you my perspective," he said.

Andy expanded on a rule that he thinks young people should consider before settling down. He calls it the Rule of Four Ps: person, profession, partner and parent. First, you should know yourself, your personal beliefs and convictions. Once you do, you can choose your profession. Only then, find a partner, someone who is compatible with your personal beliefs and profession. Finally, be a parent. Preachy dictates perhaps, but I see it as Andy's attempt to provide a decent framework for an otherwise difficult-to-navigate part of life.

It sounds like an old-fashioned approach. He grew up in an age when people had one job for thirty years. They lived in one place and there was little instability. Now people juggle several jobs, commuting long distances. People are nimbler, and communities are more transient than before. I like Zygmunt Bauman's term "liquid modernity" as a fitting description of the transitory nature of our society. Finding a profession before you find a partner can be difficult.

"You've got to find a partner who will grow with you. Jean married me as a country preacher and stayed with me as I rose to become UN ambassador. If I had gone back to being a country preacher, she would have been fine. And Carolyn . . ." he trailed off.

"And Carolyn what?" I prompted him.

"I'm not so sure she would have married me if I wasn't at the top of my game," he said. That's Andy being a rascal again. But in all seriousness, Carolyn and Andy have had an enduring relationship in which they are able to speak and joke freely with each other.

"That's frank," I said.

"You should know the truth. They say it will set you free. But it sometimes makes some people mad," he chuckled. "No truth without controversy."

"Carolyn is a different generation from my first wife. She was not rich, but she was raised like a princess. I love her but can't see her using an outdoor toilet and living the rural life as I did when I pastored my first churches. Now it's a different time and a different life. She's a perfect partner, friendly and unselfish, sensitive to others and, maybe most important, she's secure enough not to get jealous."

The phone rang, and he reached for it.

The phone call interruption of our conversation helped me gather my nerve. If Uncle Andy was going to say that I'm afraid to ask him about love, I would, as they say in baseball, reach back and put some more mustard on my fastballs. I would ask more personal and uncomfortable questions.

"You were married to Jean for a long time. What were the threats or strains to your marriage?" I asked.

"The stress of moving to New York pushed our marriage to the limits," he responded.

In 1957, Andy and Jean lived in Queens, almost an hour-and-forty-five-minute commute to work in Manhattan. He was one of only two black church executives with the National Council of the Churches of Christ USA. He was new to the city and trying to make friends. About half of the guys with whom he worked were gay, so Andy would stop at the gay bars on his way home to Queens. Young women would often come alone to Andy's office with their problems. Andy talked and listened to everyone, which took significant time. He left 200th Street in Jamaica, Queens, every morning at six o'clock and returned at eight or nine o'clock at night. When he returned home, Andy was ready for a drink and his cozy bed. Jean was keen to discuss matters of consequence and engage in intelligent discussion.

"That period in my life was a crisis to my marriage because I didn't take the time to strengthen our relationship," he said. He was too busy trying to establish himself in a large religious organization.

"That's no different from the hours many people work. I'm happy that I'm not in mergers and acquisitions because those bankers sometimes work until two o'clock in the morning," I said.

"I know, but it's still a problem," he replied. "That's why I say you need to find yourself and your calling before you find your partner. You want to make sure your partner understands you and what's important to you. I also had faith that things would get easier for us," he said.

Andy has made mention on several occasions of an invisible hand that somehow intervenes in his life and steers him and those around him in the right direction. This invisible hand or guardian angel helped to guide Jean in those early moments in New York. Jean was only twenty-three when they moved there. They first lived in a quaint hotel at 23rd Street and Eighth Avenue where folks affiliated with the church stayed because it was cheap. Jean's sister lived in Harlem, so she would take the subway to visit with her two babies. The A and E train both stopped at the same subway station and on the same track. If she had ever taken the wrong train, the E, she would have ended up in Queens. But she always took the A train up to Harlem, even though, Andy found out much later, she didn't realize that there were two trains, and she always got on the first train that stopped.

"God takes care of fools and babies. She was running around New York, a fool with my babies," said Andy. "I was also too big a fool to help her much."

"But how did you try to make your marriage work despite your busy schedule? I struggle with balancing relationships with an intense work schedule," I said.

"A good partner works with you and not against you," he began. "Jean never complained about my not having time for the kids. She really understood what I was going through. That's the beauty of finding some-one who understands you. But you've still got to work to make things better for your partner," he commented.

"Like schedule a date night with your girlfriend?" I asked.

"That's a good start," he replied.

The strain on Andy's family was apparent in those early years. Not only did Andy work long hours, he traveled extensively to Europe and Latin America, and was sometimes gone for weeks at a time. Once he re-turned home and picked up his daughter Lisa, who cried loudly for her mother. Jean filled up her life to match his. She pursued a master's degree in education at Queens College. She was eager to maintain her career as a schoolteacher, taking after both Andy's and her mother, who worked while raising children.

Andy took an active interest in Jean's career as a teacher. When they were living in Hartford in 1955, Jean was a third-grade teacher while Andy was still in seminary. One third-grader pulled another boy out of the chair and almost stabbed him with scissors. Jean was alarmed because she had never encountered such a bully in one of her classes. Andy was more familiar with the rough tactics of some children because of his experiences as a kid. Andy went to Jean's school and spoke with the principal. He picked up the bully and took him home with him for the afternoon and evening. The boy helped Jean correct school papers, and Andy played catch with the boy. Jean, Andy and the boy had dinner together, and they didn't fuss at him. This little extra amount of recognition and attention convinced the boy not to create any more trouble in class. Actually, the boy made sure that no other student would challenge or threaten Jean.

Andy endeavored to do little things to make the marriage work and to keep the romance alive. When he traveled he would call her regularly. Whenever he got on a plane or train to go home after a business trip, he thought about what he could do to make her life more interesting. He helped in the kitchen with the cooking and with things she didn't like to do, like taking out the garbage. He wrote love notes and poems, and would bring special records home for her. They tried to make their love-making unusual and creative, and even read *The Kama Sutra* together for ideas. I know, I know—too much information.

A college pal of mine reminds me whenever we talk that he will never get married. "It's impossible to have a monogamous relationship. There are just too many hot chicks in the world," he says. His comment reminds me of Ari, the hotshot Hollywood agent in the television show *Entourage*, who says to his wife that they agreed to suffer through monogamy ensemble.

"Y'all are still going through your player years. You'll outgrow it," said Andy.

"Is monogamy difficult? Have you always been faithful?" I asked.

Before I realized what I'd asked, he answered without flinching.

"Yes, by my definition."

"What's your definition?"

"I was never untrue to our marriage," he replied.

"Love and truth come together. What does that mean?" I asked.

"That I was never untrue to our marriage," he explained. "I never let anyone believe I didn't love my wife. I never let anyone believe that any time or interest I had in them was more than a friendship."

"That's an interpretive view of marriage," I commented.

"You marry for better or for worse. If you are only going to love each other during the good times or for some idea of perfection, then you will be sorely disappointed."

Had Uncle Andy just sent me a coded message that he had been unfaithful? Or was he talking about something else? He once explained to me that Jean and he promised always to trust each other and never to lie. Before they were married, they went to Austria to work in separate refugee camps. She had several close but nonintimate relationships with men. Andy couldn't complain. He made friends with girls from Denmark, Sweden and Germany because, he explains, they all spoke English. He was never alone with them since he had realized at a young age the addictive and possessive aspects of sexual relationships.

If he had been involved sexually with the refugees or his coworkers, he wouldn't have been able to trust and understand Jean and her friendships. The trip laid the foundation for a forty-year marriage that took them "through many dangers, toils and snares." Indeed, when Jean made friends with a daring Croatian exile who had sailed to freedom in a kayak, it made Andy jealous. But she pointed out to Andy that he also had close relationships with women in his camp and had friendships with Dolly Adams, now the wife of a Methodist bishop, and with Sybil Morial, who was dean of Xavier University and wife of New Orleans mayor Dutch Morial (and mother of a later New Orleans mayor Marc Morial). They had to accept each other and recognize their individuality if their marriage was going to work. Andy found meaning in Kahlil Gibran's writing, "For the pillars of the temple stand apart / And the oak tree and the cypress grow not in each other's shadow."[2] For a relationship to work, Andy believes, you need to create space for your partner so you both can grow independently and freely.

"In today's world, as you travel for business, you will come into contact with attractive and independent women. You need to have an understanding with your partner, even a theoretical understanding, that you can trust each other," he summed up. "You trust insofar as you are trustworthy."

At times Jean too struggled with jealousy. A female neighbor used to come over to Jean and Andy's home in Atlanta. The neighbor's husband worked longer hours than Andy, and she would use Andy as an intellectual sounding board. Andy, Jean and the neighbor would sit at the kitchen table and talk for hours. There was nothing physical or emotional between Andy and the neighbor, but Jean was infuriated because the neighbor took time out of their life that should have been time for just her and Andy.

That Andy and Jean understood the importance of giving each other space and of trusting each other at the outset of their marriage would prove invaluable during the tumultuous years of the civil rights movement, a virtual obstacle course for several civil rights leaders and their partners. Andy remembers that Dr. King and the other leaders had to be careful because they were continually under surveillance by the FBI and others. In January 1964, Dr. King received an anonymous package. King's assistant Dora McDonald forwarded the package to Coretta, who opened it and discovered a threatening blackmail note. The author claimed to have damaging material that would defame Dr. King if made public, and Andy believes there is no doubt the author was urging King to kill himself. An audiotape was included in the package. Andy, Coretta, King and King's father gathered at the King home to listen to the recording. The tape was of a party at a hotel after the Washington march in August 1963, when King gave his "I Have a Dream" speech. Dr. King was heard teasing fellow civil rights leader Ralph David Abernathy because he hadn't been allowed to speak at the march. One had to be a leader of a civil rights organization, explained Dr. King, and the only organization that Ralph could lead was the "National Association for the Advancement of Eating Chicken." But that wasn't the damaging material. After the teasing and jokes, the tape cut to sounds of a couple engaged in sex, but the male voice on the tape, according to Andy, was surely not Dr. King's. Even Coretta thought it was a low-down effort to defame her husband. In all the years Andy knew her and long after Dr. King's death, she never questioned his love and commitment to her and their marriage.

Andy and others blamed the FBI for creating the tape because they were one of the few organizations at the time that had the capacity to bug a hotel room. I'm fond of another bugging story that Andy likes to tell about one occasion when Ralph David Abernathy was preaching at Brown Chapel in Selma. While he was giving his sermon, Ralph found a small microphone, which he called "a little doohickey," underneath the pulpit. He picked it up and showed it to the congregation. He started preaching to the bug, "I don't know who you belong to. . . . But I want you to tell them for me, without static or interference . . . that the black people in Selma are on their way to freedom and nobody is going to stop them!"[3]

"Just the other day [summer 2009] we found a bug on our telephone system," said Andy.

"Who was bugging you?" I asked.

"Well, we installed a gate on my front door, and the church electrician who installed the gate said he found five telephone lines. One of them was the Internet line that you installed, one was the fax and the other two are for the telephone. The last line we traced to a house down the street to the end of the block," he explained.

"Who lives there?" I asked.

"There is a schoolteacher who lives there now who is good friends with Carolyn. But when we moved here in the 1960s, the neighborhood was occupied by mostly whites, many of whom we didn't know. We only knew the people who had children and dogs. I bet the bug was left over from years ago," he explained. The bug is one of those odd cobwebs from the civil rights movement that Andy discovers from time to time.

There were rumors and gossip about several civil rights leaders— enough to put the marital relationships of these leaders to the test. And if the gossip and rumors weren't enough, Dr. King created situations that could lead to such gossip. In 1967, King and other civil rights leaders went to Cleveland to campaign for Carl Stokes, who was running for the second time to become the first black mayor of a large American city. One morning, King was driving with his colleagues down Euclid Avenue in Cleveland. Several prostitutes recognized him at a red light and harassed him by calling him an Uncle Tom. Dr. King ordered the driver to turn the car around. He went up to the prostitutes and said, "If you'll allow me the opportunity, I'll tell you why I'm here." He invited the three women to meet him that afternoon back at the Sheraton Cleveland Hotel. When Dr. King, Andy and others returned to the hotel, the lobby was crowded with more than a dozen hookers. The women had informed the hotel management that they were there to meet with Dr. King. Now you can see how easily rumors got started. Quickly Andy secured a conference room and requested the hotel to provide tea and cookies. When the hotel manager realized the purpose of the meeting, he didn't bill Andy and the other leaders for the food. Cleveland had been wracked by rioting and the local businesspeople were pleased that civil rights leaders were in town discussing nonviolence and democracy. Dr. King exhorted the ladies to register to vote. If they wanted a better life, they could do something about it. King saw love as a powerful, cohesive force, and he worked to diminish hatred and promote love and understanding in all quarters. Love, believes Andy, conquers hatred.

"Remember, we were older. The students in the 1960s had a slogan of free love and nickel vodka. It was assumed there was a lot of casual sex among the younger folks. But we were extremely careful," explained Andy.

After Jean died, Andy realized he needed support. He had been married for forty years and his needs had changed. He was past the Rule of Four Ps. He had already found himself, his profession, a partner and was a parent (and grandparent). Andy was looking for someone to love and be a partner with in his older years, and someone who would care deeply about his grandchildren. Because Andy still travels extensively, he sought a partner who could be his anchor in Atlanta. Carolyn was a schoolteacher like Jean, a Sunday schoolteacher as well, and a resident of Atlanta. A divorcée, she had what she described as a "complacent marriage, . . . I never really grew into it, I grew out of it." A marvelous teacher, she was given the Teacher of the Year award in 1993 when she was at the E. Rivers School.

"Was your family accepting of Carolyn?" I asked.

"She gets along well with everyone now, but it was the most difficult to realize that I wasn't trying to replace their mother," he commented.

Almost everyone among his friends and children had a suggestion for whom Andy should remarry. They knew that after forty years of comfortable dependence on Jean, he couldn't make it alone. Unfortunately, they all wanted to fulfill their fantasies of wealth and fame through him.

Andy's sister-in-law suggested Shirley Franklin, the former mayor of Atlanta. "That would have never worked. I worked with Shirley for eight years and knew her in a professional capacity. Plus, I always thought Shirley liked younger men," he joked.

While in Sun City, South Africa, and after Andy had married Carolyn, one of Andy's friends introduced him to a young woman who got to the final stages of the Miss Universe competition. The woman went up to Carolyn and said, "I wanted to spend more time with your husband before you met him." Now that is cold. Carolyn took it in stride and was actually flattered by the remark—a retired schoolteacher had won a competition with a finalist for Miss Universe.

"That is the problem with high-profile men like me," said Andy. "There are always young, beautiful, intelligent and ambitious women around. But you can't take advantage of their vulnerabilities. You must focus on their strength of spirit, not their sexy bodies. I'm not being pious or hypocritical. Just as old men collect trophies, women do too. It's success by association."

One of Andy's daughters urged him to consider Alexis Herman, who served as the secretary of labor and as a political advisor under President Clinton. Others thought Andy should marry someone who was wealthy, like Ingrid Saunders Jones, a senior executive at Coca-Cola. Andy has nothing but respect for these phenomenally successful women. He wasn't looking for someone with money or fame. He simply wanted someone with whom he could partner and someone who would help him look after his grandchildren.

Andy resisted these suggestions because he knew that marriage was much more about inner compatibility. It's not easy to share life, culture, values and emotional needs, he said. Sometimes when you marry someone, you are really marrying their family, which often comes with the burden of several generations—you may be looking for the emotional support of your mother and your partner may be looking for her father. That's been the most difficult challenge for Carolyn and him. She never knew her father. He went into the army right out of college. He disappeared, leaving her mother to raise her and her older brother (who, sadly, died in an automobile accident as a young man).

Andy knew that in marrying Carolyn, he was going to have to be her father, brother, lover, friend and husband. At sixty-four, he was up to the task. She, on the other hand, had to join a family. Jean's family welcomed and supported them completely, in part because Jean's mother's first husband was killed in a complicated racial incident involving the Klan in the 1920s. Jean's mother remarried Norman Childs, and together they had Jean. All of Andy's children were grown, married or about to be, so he came to Carolyn with a small army of emotional dependents. Then there was the battalion of Andy's friends from the civil rights movement, political campaigns and church. Andy's life could have been a heavy burden for a partner. After thirty years in Atlanta's public schools and always being assigned the "bad boys," Carolyn was more than capable of handling the complexities.

Andy is smitten with Carolyn. She is very beautiful, which brings envy, jealousy and prejudice. It's assumed by virtually everyone that she has it all and she really doesn't need anything. Andy thanks God for giving him a devoted saint in her because Andy's globe-trotting is enough to make even a saint cuss and cry.

"I was sure Carolyn would be right with me. I tried not to listen to other people," Andy said. "Bo was only twenty and in his player years. It was his adolescent rebellion to want someone with money because nobody in our family made much. We followed the early Puritan interpretation of Christianity to pursue sacrifice and service. He thought that the reason we were poor was because we didn't respect the value of money."

"Does marrying for money make things easier?" I asked.

"It can and it can't. I've always followed my heart. If I follow my heart and use my mind, the money will always be there. Even Bo came around on this," he explained.

As a young boy, Andy's son wanted to marry someone wealthy, but he grew up and eventually followed the Four P's. He conquered and was true to himself. He found his profession. He eventually married a beautiful lady from Venezuela, whom he admired because she ran her own business at twenty-five. And they have a daughter named Abigail, after Abigail Adams, one of America's founding mothers.

"Bo outgrew his player years. He really grew up and recognized his wife as a partner and confidante with whom he can talk and listen. I've been thinking a lot about Abigail Adams. She had a continuous correspondence with Thomas Jefferson and tried to at least understand those who opposed her husband," Andy commented.

"Abigail Adams was well traveled and educated. She could go toe to toe with Jefferson," I responded.

"You could say the same about Sally Hemings, Jefferson's mistress with whom he fathered a family," replied Andy. He believes Hemings was the second most educated woman (after Abigail Adams) in the colonies because she took Jefferson's daughter to class and attended with her. She traveled to London and Paris to care for her. At the time of their visit, Paris was a hotbed of intellectual turmoil which didn't recognize slavery. "I've gotten into trouble for saying this," he explained, "but anyone who has slept with a black woman over a period of time knows that he is going to get an opinion whether he wants it or not. I wouldn't be surprised if Jefferson saw Hemings as an intelligent and expressive lady, and she probably gave him an earful. They may have been soul mates."

He pointed out that black women have had a strong, shaping influence on the country since they nursed and cared for the children of all of America's leading southern families. Howell Raines, who used to write for the *New York Times,* wrote a tribute to the young black housekeeper who helped to rear him and helped him to avoid the temptations of racism—a false sense of superiority is a dangerous addiction.

"Are you saying to look for a partner with whom you can become best friends?" I asked.

"That's a good start. Isn't that what you look for?" he parried.

"I look for friends with whom I can have stimulating and exciting conversations. Passionate discussion breathes life into relationships," I replied.

Andy chuckled, realizing that his pupil would need more time to introspect. "You're doing all right. You aren't rushing into anything. Relationships are built on conversations. Sex can last sixty minutes, so that means you have to be communicating for twenty-three hours of the day. For some people, it lasts only three minutes, which means you have to communicate even longer. That can be a good thing. I advise all young people to take their time. Learn something from Ray Charles."

John Coltrane was known for playing as fast as he could. He drowned audiences with his waterfall of notes. Ray Charles, on the other hand, wanted to see how slowly he could play. He wanted to groove slowly and let the audience hear the silence between the notes. He wouldn't rush the tempo or plow into a chord change. Andy's point is that when you slow things down, it's easier to understand the situation in which you find yourself.

"I've heard some jazz musicians complain about 'teenage soloing disease.' A young person wants to rush his or her solos. They push technique over melody," I said.

"Exactly. You don't have to rush it. Once you find yourself and your profession, you'll have built a solid foundation to find a partner. Or if you can't get it in that order, find a partner who can grow with you. Take your time," he emphasized. He quoted famed basketball coach John Wooden, "Be quick—but don't hurry."

But time is what I didn't have.

"Kabir, you are going to miss your flight," interjected Carolyn from the other room. I packed up my notepad and hurried out the door. I flew from Georgia to New York, this time with love on my mind.

7

THE CASE FOR CONTRARY COUNSEL (AND THE MAN WHO SHOULDN'T BE PRESIDENT—AT LEAST NOT YET!)

Dissent is the highest form of patriotism.

—Howard Zinn, historian[1]

I wonder whether Uncle Andy has a foot fetish. He must enjoy the taste of toes because he is used to putting his foot his mouth. I'm somewhat used to him sharing his blunt and personal thoughts in private. When he shares his frank opinions in front of a camera and during an intense presidential election, you really wonder what his motivations are. He's almost eighty years old and has been bruised and bullied along the way. He fought for the freedom of speech, and nothing is going to silence him now. That makes him more entertaining. I must admit that I pay more attention because I can never guess what the next outrageous thing out of his mouth will be. And by paying attention, I actually pick up some useful ideas.

Andy helped me to see President Barack Obama and presidential leadership in a new light. Above all, he made the case for why contrarian perspectives are needed not only in the Oval Office but in our daily lives. He made the case for why everyone should seek the counsel of contrarians: because they help us see a range of perspectives, which ultimately can help us make better-informed decisions.

In 2007 Andy was invited to speak at a comedy club in downtown Atlanta on the civil rights movement. The club invited speakers to address the audience on serious matters for two hours before the comedy routines began. He told the audience that he wasn't a supporter of Barack Obama in the 2008 presidential election. At the time, he preferred Hillary Clinton. The moderator asked whether Andy's decision not to support Obama was because he wasn't black enough. Andy thought about the question. What does it mean to be black anyway?

Nobel Prize–winning author Toni Morrison, a friend who helped Andy edit his second book, described President Bill Clinton as "our first black president." Andy sees some truth to this description. The story was told of black leaders who went with President Clinton to Nelson Mandela's inauguration as president of South Africa in 1994. At Mandela's postinaugural party, a soul train line formed. "The so-called Negroes that Bill had brought with him from America all stood around and clapped their hands. The only people who knew what to do on a soul train line were Bill, Hillary, Alexis Herman. Bill was teaching Rodney Slater [Clinton's secretary of transportation] how to moonwalk," Andy said to me. "So you never know what is black."

He joked with the audience at the club about what it means to be black, which stirred up headlines during a presidential campaign, and which he now regrets. He explained his remark to me, "You can tell Obama wasn't a player. He wasn't chasing women when he was young," he said.

"Why does that matter?" I asked.

"Obama lived a simple and scholarly life. There's nothing wrong with that. It's just not stereotypically black. Young black people aren't stereotyped as those who sit in the library. Hopefully Obama is changing that."

He pressed on, trying to make another point. "It doesn't matter what color you are, every young person who wants to go into public office needs to be careful. With the rise of Facebook, there is a lack of privacy. What you do today may come back and bite you."

"If you live your life like you are one day going to hold elected office, you'll probably live a boring life. I think it's stupid and calculating to live thinking about political implications ten years down the road," I said.

"I like that. You must live life without regrets," he said.

"Why didn't you support Obama for the 2008 presidential election?" I asked, moving on.

"I always said I supported Obama for president—but in 2016. I didn't think he was ready for the top post. I still have my doubts. He is too inexperienced. He didn't know or understand the Southern struggle," he explained. Entrusting the legacy of the civil rights movement to a small cadre of Chicago politicos made Andy feel uneasy. Presidents Johnson, Carter and Clinton were born in the South and were more familiar with race and racism in the South.

I think that's pretty contrarian: a respected civil rights icon that didn't support an extremely viable African American candidate. Andy has had a long history of giving and taking contrary advice.

"In 1984 and 1988, Jesse Jackson ran for president on a thin resume," I commented.

Andy explained that Jesse Jackson really believed that by running, he would be able to register black voters and help liberal politicians around America. Andy didn't agree with Jackson's strategy: It's difficult to run for a higher office when you don't have an existing constituency that can help you mobilize. Andy launched his career in public service by running for

Congress (reluctantly, after John Lewis and Harry Belafonte urged him). Obama already had served several years in elected office before running for the presidency. So what's the real story? Does Andy really have an issue with Obama's inexperience?

"I thought I knew how the movie ends," said Andy. "I've seen several young politicians receive lots of attention and then flare out." He remembers how the Democratic Party made an overnight celebrity of Julian Bond. At the 1968 Democratic National Convention in Chicago, though he was only twenty-eight, he became the first African American nominated by a significant political party as a candidate for the vice presidency. Bond declined the nomination, saying he had to adhere to the constitutional requirement that presidential and vice presidential candidates be at least thirty-five years old. He had been elected a representative of the Georgia Assembly in 1965, but the body wouldn't seat him because of his sympathy to draft dodgers and his vocal criticism of the Vietnam War. The Supreme Court decided in favor of Bond, and the Assembly was required to seat him.

"Julian was never surrounded by the financial support apparatus that could nurture him. He was out there with his fifteen minutes of fame. He didn't recover. Everyone expected him to succeed but he had no platform on which he could build. I didn't want the same thing to happen to Barack. That's why I say I supported him for 2016," said Andy.

"What kind of support group did Mr. Bond need?" I asked.

"I think almost everyone needs to surround themselves with believers who see what you can become and contrarians, devil's advocates, who will take the other side of things. They will help you see what is bullshit and what isn't. Julian could have benefited from getting such advice and so could Obama," he explained.

"A black man being judged on his merits and character: Isn't Obama Dr. King's dream personified?" I asked.

"No," he said simply. It's hard to think Dr. King wouldn't be proud though.

"John Lewis said, 'Obama is what comes at the end of the bridge in Selma.' Do you agree with that?"

"No, John is just going for a rhetorical flourish there," he answered.

He explained that Dr. King's dream was about feeding the hungry, healing the sick and clothing the naked, and that King was more concerned with helping the poor than with any individual becoming president. Andy believes King would not have cared about Andy becoming mayor or Obama becoming president unless they could use their positions to help the poor and to pave the Jericho Road. It wasn't the goal of civil rights leaders to elect a black president. King said he wanted to elect people of good will, regardless of their color.

King himself rejected the idea of running for office. He felt that elected office, especially the presidency, was binding—a president had to represent the majority, whereas he wanted to be a voice for the voiceless. There were certainly those who urged him to run for office. Vietnam War critic Dr. Benjamin Spock, the noted pediatrician, sat next to Dr. King on a flight and for two straight hours urged him to run for office. He wanted King to run for the presidency as a way to stop the Vietnam War. Spock said he would run as the vice presidential candidate and promised to raise the money, but King wasn't having it. It just wasn't the role that was right for him. King consulted with his inner circle, even those who vehemently disagreed with him, to make his decision not to run for elected office.

By electing a black president, many Americans believe that they have moved past the issue of race into a postracial America. But Andy thinks that this is a shallow view. When you peel away the scab of race in America, what's left is the cancer of poverty: "Electing a black president is a Band-Aid on race in America," he said. During the last year of Dr. King's life, Andy started to see poverty and not race as the most important issue in America. He still feels that there is much work to be done in regard to poverty: "We've made almost no progress. We've slipped backwards."

"If you want to quell racism or poverty, isn't the best way to change the political situation by using the political system? That was Madison's brilliance. He wrote the Constitution to allow men to go through the political system instead of around it or by toppling the government," I explained. Before the Constitution, disaffected citizens could only resort to violence to bring about their desired demands. Shays's Rebellion is an illustrative example—Daniel Shays and his armed band of poor farmer cohorts rioted in Massachusetts in 1786. The lack of coordinated response on the part of the government showed the weakness of the Articles of Confederation. The Constitution allows rebellious citizens to bring about change in nonviolent ways—petitions, rallies and the freedom of speech, to name a few.

"We were involved in political campaigns but we needed to be outside the political system to bring about the Voting Rights Act of 1965," Andy commented. Though the Civil Rights Act had been signed into law in July 1964, there was still discrimination against blacks at polling stations. Civil rights leaders had worked behind the scenes in Carl Stokes's mayoral campaign in Cleveland. They worked on the front lines of Lyndon Johnson's 1964 presidential campaign. But instead of running for office themselves, civil rights leaders understood that change didn't come from Washington but to it. They had to change the tide of public opinion. President Lyndon Johnson had said in December 1964 that he didn't have the votes to pass the Voting Rights Act. He had barely passed the Civil Rights Act, and it was politically untenable to introduce more legislation. So civil rights leaders went down to Selma, Alabama, and changed the minds of Americans and the course of history.

"We couldn't march for every issue. We needed equal voting rights. Our march for the Voting Rights Act was, in a way, our last march," analyzed Andy. "The brutality of Selma convinced millions of Americans why we needed a voting rights act." Civil rights leaders had to dramatize the need for the Voting Rights Act because President Johnson and his circle of advisors weren't gung-ho about it. Johnson watched the Selma brutality on television and it strengthened his resolve to push through the act. The civil rights leaders had to break through Johnson's realpolitik and the cautious counsel of his advisors to show them the right way. They had to be his devil's advocates.

"Did the struggle of the civil rights movement make you a tougher political candidate?"

"Yes. And that is another reason why I didn't support Obama against Clinton. I didn't think he was tough enough," Andy explained. For the record, he supported Obama against McCain, and so did I.

"Would Colin Powell have been a better choice as the first black president?" I asked.

"I'm not sure he would have been a better president. I just know he is a brilliant, tough and wise man. And all those years in the military strengthens someone's spine," he answered.

Andy looked at the 2008 election through the prism of the 2002 and 2004 elections, when Karl Rove and his mandarins arguably used character assassination to win. Senator Max Cleland of Georgia, a triple amputee Vietnam veteran, was attacked as being weak on defense and unpatriotic. John Kerry's service in Vietnam was distorted too. Surely, Republicans would go after Barack Obama in a similar way, he thought. But Obama's secret weapon was similar to Andy's and Dr. King's—his wife, Michelle. Like Jean and Coretta, Michelle and her family had experienced the hardship of segregation firsthand. They knew what it meant to struggle.

"I felt that Michelle, because of her family background ... well ... was in a way, much tougher than he was," Andy explained. "She came from Chicago's South Side, and her family descended from slaves in South Carolina."

"So if you knew that he had a wife like yours, why not support him?" I asked.

The truth came out: "Well, I have had a strong relationship with the Clintons for thirty years, and I know what they've been through."

The feeling is mutual. A friend and I were at a Jazz at Lincoln Center performance in New York, and I saw a secret service agent walk by me in a hurried manner. I tried to get the agent's attention to see what was up. Luckily a petite blond-haired woman holding a clipboard who seemed more approachable followed the agent. She explained that President Clinton would be going backstage to exit the theater complex.

"How are you doin'?" asked a familiar raspy voice. President Clinton was waving at the technical support staff. Avoiding sudden movements around nearby secret service guards who didn't look too friendly, I slowly stuck out my hand as Clinton walked by.

"President Clinton. I'm wondering whether you know my godfather Andrew Young," I said.

"Andy Young? Ohhh. I adore that man. I really do. I adore that man. He has been such a good friend. I adore that man," he gushed.

Andy has known about Hillary Clinton since her college years. While a student at Wellesley College, Hillary roomed with Janet McDonald Hill, the mother of Grant Hill, the star professional basketball player. Janet's father owned the dental laboratory to which Andy's father sent his work. Andy's mother was Janet Hill's godmother. Small world.

Mr. McDonald had excitedly told Andy about a young girl who exhibited grace under fire at Janet's graduation, where an African American, Senator Edward Brooke of Massachusetts, gave the commencement address. Brooke was a supporter of the Vietnam War and was out of step with the left-leaning student body. The first-ever student speaker at a Wellesley commencement, Hillary Rodham followed Brooke and delivered an improvised rebuttal of Brooke and his conservative policies. She received a standing ovation from her peers and attracted the attention of some in the national media.

Hillary later worked alongside Marian Wright Edelman at the Children's Defense Fund with Jean. Bill and Andy met each other then. For almost ten years, Jean, Hillary and Marian worked together on children's issues. Their enduring commitment to children's issues is evident. When Andy was at the UN, Jean served as the chairwoman for the International Year of the Child in 1979.

Andy considers Bill and Hillary Clinton friends and reached out to them during the 1990s when they were embroiled in the Whitewater and Monica Lewinsky controversies. He wrote a letter to Bill Clinton in which he said that all men and women sin and fall short of the glory of God, that Christianity is a religion of forgiveness. It absorbs, understands and deals with one's weaknesses, and God knows and loves you even as you are. Clinton didn't write back, but the next time they met, he told Andy he appreciated his letter.

None of us, including Bill Clinton, is a perfect human being. Andy thought Hillary's decision to forgive Bill was not personal: it was of national and international significance. Bill Clinton could have never become president without her love, support and understanding, and he could not have kept the presidency without her forgiveness.

The details of Andy's relationship with the Clintons are important because they give insight into their leadership abilities. Andy sees substantial differences between President Obama and President Clinton. Bill Clinton is a more fiery and passionate intellectual than Obama, a cool thinker who is fazed by almost nothing. That's part of the difference between growing up black and white in America, according to Andy. For a black person to lose his temper growing up could cost him his life. One of Andy's earliest lessons as a boy was to keep control of his emotions. Andy broke his arm when he was about five years old. His father took him to the segregated hospital where he wasn't offered anesthetic and said "you can either scream or bite on this towel and take it like a man." Andy bit down.

He said Obama had to grow up realizing that he could not let his emotions get out of control. Many successful black Americans—Jackie

Robinson, Vernon Jordan and Dr. King among them—have had to internalize this lesson. When you lose your temper, you lose the fight.

"It's very hard to be a minority anywhere. Black Americans are taught to be a minority. You can't do what everyone else does. The smallest thing can get you into trouble. Obama had to learn this lesson. Rich white boys can get in trouble and their daddies will get them out of it," said Andy.

Obama's distinctive cool style masks his intense and disciplined work ethic. I think President George W. Bush's bumbling and anti-intellectual image is also deceptive. After his presidency, Bill Clinton visited Prime Minister Tony Blair in London. Clinton gave Blair two pieces of advice. First, don't screw up the upcoming election like Al Gore. Instead of running on the issues such as a healthy economy, Gore ran away from Bill Clinton and his administration's strong record of accomplishment. The second piece of advice was not to underestimate George W. Bush. Clinton said that Bush was one of the most ruthless politicians he had seen in a generation.

"Don't get me wrong. I like Obama. I really do. Did you read his book *Audacity of Hope?*" Andy asked.

"Yes, I think that was the boring one. He talks about two sides to every issue and then explains his views. That book is more of a policy template. *Dreams from My Father* talks about his upbringing and what shaped his global perspective," I replied. I too like him.

"I made the mistake of not reading that book for two years. It just sat on my desk," he said. But after reading *Dreams from My Father,* Andy recognized the strength of Obama's mother. She was a seminal and stabilizing influence on young Obama. As Obama's family moved cities and countries, she was a constant.

"When you consider that Obama's mother went to Asia and married a man of Indonesian descent, I thought God was playing a cruel joke on us Americans," Andy began. "He created a president that would force us to confront our two principal fears: Asia and the Islamic world.[2] Obama seems to be uniquely qualified to lead us to face these two issues. There is a sense of destiny about him. Martin was never a terrific basketball player. But whenever we'd play a group of youngsters, almost everything we threw in the direction of the net seemed to drop. When I saw Barack drain a left-handed shot from behind the three point line on the evening news, I thought God must be with him."

"To be honest, Uncle Andy, I still feel like you are uneasy about President Obama," I said.

"Well, it's more accurate to say that I'm uneasy with his advisors," he responded.

"The buck stops with the president," I replied.

"But sometimes it doesn't get to the president," he began. "Look at John F. Kennedy. He was done in by his Harvard-educated advisors." He was making an obscure reference to the botched Bay of Pigs invasion in 1961 and the escalation of American military force in Vietnam. "There is something insidious and arrogant about that university. It graduates smart people, sure. But many are only capable of just giving you an average smart opinion. When you are in a leadership position, it's critical to get a contrarian perspective," he said.

"Contrarian investing has a strong following on Wall Street. There is a real financial reward for effective contrarian thinking. I like the approach. It requires you to think for yourself," I commented.

"How so?" he asked.

Usually there is a consensus about a certain investment idea or theme, I explained. For instance, say the US government injects massive amounts of capital to stimulate the American economy. A consensus view may form that, as a result of the capital injections, hyperinflation will occur. Thus, gold, which is an inflation hedge, is one of the best things to buy. All the top investment banks may put a "buy" on gold and gold-related instruments.

"So what's the contrarian view?" he asked.

I pointed out that a contrarian might think that the massive injection of capital was actually not helping the broader economy. A contrarian might think that the economy was not seeing massive inflation but entering a deflationary environment, in which case you might buy other assets instead of gold. If you are first to an idea and it turns out to be correct, you can make a lot of money. If you're wrong, you could lose a lot of money. Being a successful contrarian, as one of my colleagues puts it, "not only takes the vision to see something, but the balls to do something about it."

"I like that. In the markets, you can test a contrarian hypothesis almost immediately. In politics, it's tough to measure the validity of advice; it's murkier," Andy said.

"In some cases, politics is more challenging than business. You need 51 percent market share to win," I commented.

"I just don't think Obama has contrarian advisors. His administration has a bunch of elitists who weren't practitioners," Andy remarked. "They went to fancy schools and have chicken shit experience in the business world."

"What about Obama's claim that he hired a team of rivals?"

"What rivals? There is little policy difference between Hillary Clinton and Barack Obama. He needs to include people who can truly oppose him."

His remark may be inflammatory, but I've heard many on Wall Street echo similar sentiments. I remarked that Obama appointed many with little experience in the private sector to help rescue America from the 2008–2009 credit crisis—consulting professors, academics and government wonks.

But is it any surprise, Andy mused, that those with significant private sector experience feel reluctant to take public office or join the administration? In politics, he says, there seems to be less acceptance for someone's previous mistakes. A venture capitalist knows that an entrepreneur who has failed a couple of times is more seasoned than a first-time one. In politics, the press seems to take pride in destroying anyone who isn't perfect.

"I think that is a cop-out," I responded. "The president chooses his advisors. You think George W. Bush didn't know what Karl Rove was doing? Yet many blame Rove for doing the dirty work."

"The presidency is an isolated office, as strange as that sounds. The only information he gets is fed to him through the bureaucracy. How does he get minority military opinions? How does he get any contrarian opinion?" Andy asked.

"He reads the newspapers."

"What newspaper? There's nobody who writes for newspapers that knows what they are writing anymore. Newspapers are the shallowest they have ever been in my lifetime. The writers are very doctrinaire. Have you seen the local newspapers lately?" he said.

I asked Uncle Andy to explain his invectives, so he pointed out that many of Obama's advisors are bureaucrats who served in previous administrations and attended Ivy League schools. He also echoed what I had remarked on earlier, that there are few with hands-on business experience in the administration.

"Okay, so what contrarian creative ideas would you give him?" I asked.

He ticked off three: (1) In 2007, George W. Bush created AFRICOM, the central command for US military operations in Africa, which is based in Stuttgart, Germany. A top Pentagon official informed Andy that military brass doesn't want the center in Germany. If President Obama moved AFRICOM to the South, it would create jobs and help him win political support in red states. (2) Late Louisiana Governor Huey Long refused to award drilling rights in New Orleans, so almost all the gas under Orleans Parish and Lake Pontchartrain has been untouched. Perhaps the region could generate billions by selling municipal bonds guaranteed by the monetized value of the gas and oil. The federal government could create a public-private partnership, a Mississippi Valley Authority, and the funds could go toward infrastructure projects throughout the region. (3) There is a housing shortage in Kuwait. He would like for American officials to reprise conversations that occurred in the early 1990s with Kuwaiti officials to create a first-class twenty-first-century city. Build the best houses and roads and deploy fiber optic cable throughout the country. Use Kuwaiti money from the Kuwait Fund for the Future to pay American construction and engineering companies to build the city.

We talked for hours about each idea.

"Aren't those crazy ideas?" I asked.

"It was a crazy idea to go down to Selma to convince LBJ we needed a civil rights movement. Nobody had heard of Selma. It was a crazy idea for Atlanta to pursue the Olympics—we didn't create any debt for taxpayers and created thousands of jobs," he said. "Obama just needs to look to unusual places for unusual ideas, not the same people every single time."

"You mentioned you think Obama's advisors are elitists. What administration hasn't been elitist?" I asked.

"Carter's," he said.

Of course. I chalked up his remark to his being nostalgic for an administration of which he was a part. He continued, "Carter grew up in the middle of an 80 percent black district, and the whole county was below the poverty line. Lyndon Johnson grew up as a schoolteacher in Texas. Clinton was a poor boy made good. People made such a fuss that he betrayed American citizens. He didn't betray us; he was acting like a kid from Arkansas. He betrayed Arkansas by going to Georgetown and getting a Rhodes Scholarship," he said.

Maybe Andy was just trying to be provocative. It wouldn't be the first time. He sees the importance of contrarian thinking because of the role he played during the civil rights movement. Andy was the devil's advocate in Dr. King's inner circle. He asked commonsense questions and represented the conservative positions, which led others to label him the "Uncle Tom of the SCLC." Eventually Andy grew weary of always being the contrarian. During one staff meeting, he started to agree with the viewpoints of such civil rights activists as Hosea Williams and James Bevel, who usually advocated more liberal and radical ideas. Dr. King and others were surprised with Andy's comments. Dr. King stopped the meeting, pretending to take a bathroom break. He took Andy into a back office and got very angry. Andy said, "Listen, Martin, I'm sick of being the bad guy," which angered King even more. "Martin told me, 'Andy, if you decide you are going to start playing games, I don't see why I need you. I need you to take as conservative a position as possible, then I can have plenty of room to come down in the middle where I want to.'" From that point on, Andy didn't back down from his steely contrarian views. His perspective sometimes leads him to say contrary, unconventional but provocative things.

"A good leader is able to listen to all opinions and all contrarians and keep cool under pressure. Mr. McDonald, Janet's father, taught me that."

"I used to talk politics with Janet's daddy and argue with him like you and I do," explained Andy. "He urged me to have self-control." Janet's father was a Republican and served in World War II. He claimed that the training he underwent to survive segregated Louisiana was more horrifying than going to war. He told Andy of the time he fell asleep and felt a snake crawling up his leg. He knew that if he panicked the snake would bite him, so he slowly unbuttoned his pants so it could crawl out. Janet's father emphasized the importance of being cool under fire.

Listening to a contrarian view is one thing, following such counsel is another. During his time in the Carter administration, Andy took actions that were out of step with those of his colleagues. He wasn't exactly a rogue ambassador acting on his own accord, but he sure did listen to his own drummer, this time to a fault—which resulted in his having to step down from his post as US ambassador to the UN.

Andy was very close to President Jimmy Carter. He supported Carter's run for the presidency when he was a relatively unknown southern governor. Most of Andy's colleagues in Congress supported other candidates, and they questioned Andy's decision. The Congressional Black Caucus had

invited several of the presidential candidates to meet with them. Each candidate was asked how many black people were on his campaign staff. One
candidate said he had one whereas another candidate said he was looking
for one. When it came Carter's turn, he said he didn't know. Luckily,
Carter's staff member responded: twenty-seven. Andy's decision to support
the little-known Carter soon didn't seem quite so contrarian.

Andy once told me that it took one hundred years to understand
Thomas Jefferson's presidency, and it will take at least fifty to understand
President Carter's. In the early days of Jefferson's presidency, the New England elite—John Adams and others—were very critical of the Louisiana
Purchase. It wasn't clear whether the president had the constitutional authority to make such a decision. Very few understood the significance of
the Lewis and Clark expedition that Jefferson supported. Jefferson was
very familiar with France and knew that if France controlled Canada and
Louisiana, they might eventually send troops down the Mississippi River,
and everything west of it would become French.

"Jefferson was ahead of his times. So was Jimmy Carter. Obama may
be too if he can govern with a long-term perspective," said Andy.

"How was Carter ahead of his times?" I asked. Another contrarian
view. I like Andy's verbosity. It makes for great material, but I was hoping
for a concise answer, especially because my hand ached from taking so
many notes. No luck though. Andy gave me a panoramic view on his
work with Carter and the lessons he learned.

Many thought Carter gave away the Panama Canal in 1977 to the
Panamanians and that he was appeasing the Soviets, Andy said. Many
didn't understand why he was interested in Africa and devoted so much
time to efforts there. Even today, there is little appreciation for Carter's
actions on energy. He installed solar panels at the White House and
pushed through a schedule for automobiles to be more fuel efficient.
Over nearly ten years, American automobiles' mileage efficiency grew
from 13.5 miles per gallon to 27.5. President Ronald Reagan repealed
Carter's efforts and cut the budget of his Solar Energy Research Institute.

General Motors had to be bailed out in 2009 partly because of its lack of fuel-efficient cars.

"There still is a love of Reagan and rejection of Carter. It's also amazing how much of the Jewish community hates him. He's the only one who has given Israel any possibility of peace," Andy said, observing that no Egyptian has killed an Israeli since 1978, and no Israeli has killed an Egyptian thanks to the Camp David Accords.

"That's funny. With all respect, I told someone that I was working with you on this book, and he responded, 'oh that is the anti-Semitic ambassador.' Why were you attacked as anti-Semitic?" I asked.

"Yeah, I got that a lot," said Andy with a tinge of sadness. He was exposed to anti-Semitism in his neighborhood as a boy, and he always detested it. Uncle Andy still feels badly about the criticism he received while at the UN. But he was able to get over much of it following the advice he learned from his father as a kid: Don't get even, get smart.

Andy didn't want to accept the UN position initially. He sought the counsel of advisors and contrarians. His closest advisors urged him to keep his congressional seat because he could count on being reelected. His seat gave him the platform from which he could voice his independent opinions and follow his conscience. Coretta King even pleaded with him not to accept the appointment. Working at the UN meant that Andy would have to become a mouthpiece for the administration. Adlai Stevenson, the ambassador to the UN appointed by President John Kennedy, was a brilliant man, but he held the post for only two years.

President Carter appealed to Andy's heart. Carter said that he wanted to make human rights a strong part of the geopolitical dialogue. By appointing an acolyte of Dr. King to the UN, Carter could ensure that. Andy had a moral authority because of his involvement in the civil rights movement. Andy contended that Representative Barbara Jordan of Texas would have been a much better UN ambassador. Jordan delivered the keynote address at the 1976 Democratic National Convention.

She supported the impeachment of Richard Nixon and served on the House Judiciary Committee, and I tripped over her statue once at the airport in Austin. Carter agreed that she would be an exceptional ambassador and had no doubts about her abilities, but he needed Andy because his name was linked to Dr. King's around the world.

"Allow me to interrupt. With all respect, you undoubtedly earned a halo with your involvement in the civil rights movement. Do you find people give you a pass because of your halo? People may see your opinions as out of step or even crazy, but it's apparently okay because you marched with Dr. King," I said.

"No question it gets tiring. I hope that the content of my character was consistent. But my opinions aren't crazy. They're true." he explained. "People like to see me as Carter did, as a stand-in for Dr. King. I try hard to reflect Martin's views."

When Andy was sworn in, Carter gave him a note that instructed him to travel to Africa and ask African leaders what they expected from the new US administration. Carter underlined the word "ask." Henry Kissinger had traveled to South Africa just a year earlier and was planning to stop in Nigeria, but the Nigerians wouldn't let his plane land. The Nigerians said he wasn't welcome because the Americans couldn't lecture Africans on human rights and tolerate apartheid at the same time.

It wasn't Andy's maiden voyage to Africa. He had traveled to South Africa in 1974 with tennis champion Arthur Ashe. Andy was seated in a government box during a match, and a South African diplomat asked him whether he wanted to meet a group of liberals. Andy declined. He wanted to meet the Afrikaners who upheld apartheid laws. He wanted to hear their contrarian perspective. He wanted to listen. Andy's friends and liberal colleagues were irate with him. (Years later, his liberal friends criticized him for his unusual friendliness toward George W. Bush and Condoleezza Rice.)

When he traveled to Nigeria as a UN ambassador in the late 1970s, the Nigerians didn't stop him from landing, but a major newspaper ran

the headline "Send a nigger to catch a nigger."[3] The article was clear: By
sending a black man to Nigeria, Americans shouldn't expect Nigerians to
change their view on apartheid in South Africa. The article did say, however, that since Andrew Young was a close associate of Dr. King, Nigerians should welcome and listen to him to determine whether he had a new
US position to represent, which he did. It wasn't until 1986 that Congress passed the Anti-Apartheid Act that sanctioned South Africa. President Reagan vetoed the bill, but Congress overrode it. Reagan even
initially opposed the creation of a national King Holiday. But at the signing ceremony for the holiday, "Reagan gave one of the best speeches I've
ever heard about Dr. King," said Andy.

His work at the UN was largely successful. Every resolution that he offered to the Security Council was passed without a single veto. But
Andy's civil rights halo didn't shield him from criticism.

One night in the spring of 1979, Harry Belafonte invited Andy to
dinner at his apartment with former Israeli prime minister Shimon Peres.
They talked for four hours in what was largely an attempt to get Andy to
focus some attention on the issue of Palestine. Andy was consumed by
events in Africa and Panama. He figured that Secretary of State Cyrus
Vance and President Carter would deal with the Middle East.

Several weeks later, Israeli Foreign Minister Moshe Dayan invited
him to breakfast to discuss Palestine. Andy told him that he was in favor
of enlisting the support of Jews who lived in Ethiopia and Sudan to help
develop the Nile Valley into a food production center much like the Mississippi Valley. Israeli irrigation experience could go a long way in Africa.
The Saudis were willing to fund the multibillion-dollar project. Andy believed that getting people to cooperate outside the Middle East would
lead to cooperation within the region.

Unfortunately the planning for the project was interrupted. The
Arab Group of UN ambassadors decided to delay their Report of the
Committee on Palestinian Rights.

With the delay, the report's release would fall during Andy's tenure as the president of the Security Council (which rotates monthly). The current president called to warn Andy that he would have to deal with the report. Andy was trying hard to avoid the Middle East drama, but it was doing its best to find him.

At first glance, he thought the report's proposed resolution was good. It called for PLO acceptance of all UN resolutions since 1948, which the Americans were still trying to negotiate. The resolution was supposedly written by Arafat himself. There were several huge problems, however. There were no defined borders. It ignored Jerusalem and the Golan Heights, and didn't address the status of citizens who wanted to return to the region. The timing of the PLO resolution couldn't have come at a worse time politically. President Carter was in the midst of a cabinet shuffle and an economic crisis; Andy couldn't even get on the president's agenda.

Andy realized he had to veto the bill even though the veto would probably strengthen militants within the PLO who didn't want a rational political settlement in the first place. Andy and State Department officials met with the Arab Group and learned that only Zehdi Terzi, the PLO representative, could postpone the report and resolution. Terzi was a tenured university professor at Columbia who taught English and was a Christian. "They don't have many more people like that in the PLO. The intellectual leadership of the Palestinians has been killed off," explained Andy.

Andy immediately reported the situation to Yehudi Blum (the Israeli ambassador) and proceeded to meet with Terzi at the home of Ambassador Bishara of Kuwait. Andy took his six-year-old son to Ambassador Bishara's residency and told him, "For good or ill, this is an important day in our lives. You may not understand it. But you'll know that you were here." Andy realized that meeting with a PLO member was controversial and could end his career as ambassador.

He met with PLO members because he wanted to explain that the United States was not prepared to agree to a two-state solution, a position that the PLO members advocated at that time and is now seen as mainstream. The meeting was a contrarian action, not in accordance with the US State Department policy. Andy explained to them that he would have to veto a resolution because that was the position of the administration. Andy is adamant that it wasn't a secret meeting. He notified the US State Department and reported the meeting to the Israeli ambassador as soon as it was over.

Though he can't prove it, he thinks the State Department leaked word of the meeting to the press. He was asked to meet with twenty-two presidents of Jewish organizations at the Waldorf Astoria hotel in New York. They wanted to make sure that Andy understood the official Jewish position when it came to resolving the Middle East peace crisis. Andy grew uneasy with how events started to unfold. He had read Marvin Kalb and Ted Koppel's *In the National Interest* and knew things could spiral out of control. In the book, a US secretary of state (who was obviously Henry Kissinger) wanted to meet with the Palestinians and set up a secret meeting with Yasser Arafat in a public restaurant in Jerusalem. Arafat was disguised in the uniform of an American colonel. They had dinner in full view of others at the restaurant. Onlookers knew that the secretary of state was meeting with a military man, but when they realized it was Arafat, a series of protests started in New York. When the sun came up the next day, there was one Jew protesting in front of the US Mission to the UN. By nine o'-clock in the morning the protester was joined by others. By ten o'clock, the students from Yeshiva University joined the protesters. By afternoon there were hundreds of thousands protesting the meeting in front of the UN.

In 1979, Andy could see the same scenario unfolding. While he was UN ambassador, Andy spoke at black churches in Harlem and at Columbia University and other schools. He was a fairly popular and visible person. He campaigned with David Dinkins, a former classmate at Howard University and fellow fraternity brother (and pledge master) at Alpha Phi Alpha who would later become mayor of New York. Andy was afraid that if there was a Jewish protest, there would be a black counterprotest. He wrote his resignation that night and gave it to Vance. He felt that if he stayed any longer at the UN, there might be race riots throughout New York.

Andy sees himself as a contrarian in Carter's foreign policy team. "I was one of the few liberals in the administration who liked to argue. Mondale didn't like to argue and wussed out. I was one of the few that enjoyed arguing with [Zbigniew] Brzezinski [Carter's national security advisor] into the late hours."

He liked to argue with the generals and even presented his views formally to several security officials who dismissed Andy as someone who could understand only race relations. Dr. King encountered the same criticism when he wanted to write op-ed articles that were critical of the Vietnam War. What do civil rights icons know about foreign policy? But the feedback didn't deter Uncle Andy. He wanted to present President Carter a range of options just as he had done with Dr. King.

"Do you blame President Carter for not keeping you on as ambassador?" I asked.

"Not really. I just felt it was time for me to leave. I had thought about leaving to help get started on Carter's reelection campaign anyway. Knowing when you've outstayed your welcome is important. You don't take it personally. You just move on."

Andy was closer to Carter than almost anyone else when it came to foreign policy issues. There was a real fear among those in the State Department that Andy might be appointed secretary of state. By Andy's own admission, he had sometimes disrespected the State Department partly because he rejected the bureaucracy. It took seventeen clearances to get one word changed in a UN resolution.

"There were all these bureaucrats too scared to make a decision. They didn't care about the US or the world. They only cared about their jobs. The way you protect your job in the State Department is by not rocking the boat. I call that 'cover-your-own-ass diplomacy.' I bypassed the bureaucrats and went straight to Carter and Vance. If they agreed, I left the State Department alone," said Andy.

He thinks the pathway to peace in the Middle East should be paved with salt—or the lack of salt. He proposes building a desalination plant in which people of all faiths would work together to ease the water resource problems for the region.

"I can't get anyone to listen to me. I just don't think you can get a peace in the Middle East that is built on forgiveness and reconciliation. We need to start with a five-year truce and get people working together on nonpolitical issues like water plants."

"Why not strive for a peace plan?"

"There are not really strong traditions of forgiveness in Islam and Judaism, at least not toward each other. We need to understand this and work with it." In hindsight, I should have brought up Yom Kippur, the Jewish day of atonement.

Andy returned to Atlanta broke and unemployed. He had to start from scratch with no savings. His daughter Andrea was in law school, his daughter Lisa was in engineering school and his daughter Paula had just started at Duke University. Luckily, Jean got a job in education at IBM.

"Were you bitter?" I asked.

"Honestly, being mad was the last thing on my mind when I got home," he answered. "I decided to jump back into politics and run for mayor." The idea to run for mayor was not his own. Andy went to a meeting of city leaders to discuss possible candidates. An eighty-year-old lady stood up in the meeting and pointed her cane at Andy. "Look here, boy," she said, "when you came to Atlanta you wasn't nuthin' and we took you and made you somebody. . . . You've been to Congress, the UN and all over the world. If you can't help us now, we wasted our time on you." She turned around and limped out of the room, shaking her head in disgust. Andy had no choice. He threw his hat in the ring.

I brought us back to the politician we had talked about at the beginning of our conversation. "How can Obama benefit from contrarian advice?" I asked.

"As a country, we are so far from Carter's foreign policy, a policy based on human rights. I think Obama needs to get people around him who can challenge the military's bomb-first, ask-questions-later perspective at the Pentagon. I really think he should base his foreign policy on human rights. Assume the moral leadership of the world and of the country on global economic issues," he said.

"Well, he did win the Nobel Peace Prize, which I think was ridiculous because he wasn't even in office for a year," I observed.

"Be careful to see the prize for what it is. The Nobel Committee is a bunch of old intellectuals," he began. "But they made a preemptive strike. Obama hasn't defined his place in the world. I don't know whether they are extremely Machiavellian. They saw Obama as a potential peacemaker for the free world, and they knew the political and economic pressures in America that push many presidents to war. I think they gave him the peace prize to try to save him," he explained.

"You're saying the Norwegian Nobel Committee is full of moral and intellectual opportunists?" I asked.

"Yes. They claimed a bright young leader for the right side. They also made a contrary and perhaps unpopular choice that may turn out to be the right one in the long run," he said.

"Was the Nobel Committee as realpolitik when Dr. King received the award?" I asked. Obama's Nobel lecture seemed very realpolitik as well, as if he were paraphrasing military historian Carl von Clausewitz's adage, "War is a mere continuation of policy by other means."[4]

"Oh yes," he replied. "Not only can Obama learn from contrarian advisors, he can learn from how Dr. King handled the Nobel Prize. Dr. King almost wanted to give away the prize."

In 1964, Dr. King checked into an Atlanta hospital because of physical exhaustion. Andy kept Dr. King company while he was sleeping. Coretta Scott King called and informed Dr. King that he had won the Nobel Peace Prize. He said "uh, huh" and went back to sleep. He woke up and called her just a few minutes later and asked, "Did you just call me? Or was I dreaming?"

The other civil rights leaders were happy for Dr. King, save Ralph David Abernathy, who was jealous like a sibling because he wasn't awarded the prize with Dr. King. Dr. King's critics, like J. Edgar Hoover, also grew envious and tried to dig up more dirt on the civil rights leader. Dr. King initially knew this prize was the movement's, not just his personally. When he decided to divide the award money among six civil rights organizations, Republican Governor Nelson Rockefeller of New York doubled the award prize of $54,000.

After Dr. King won the Nobel Peace Prize, a Roman Catholic bishop asked him if he could pray for the new Nobel laureate. After the bishop bestowed his blessings on Dr. King, the bishop kneeled and asked for King's prayers. Andy recognized the irony of the moment—a Catholic bishop asking a black preacher named Martin Luther to pray for him. On his way to Norway, King stopped to preach at London's St. Paul's Cathedral, the first time a reverend not of Anglican denomination preached there. While in Europe, King was greeted by heads of state and top diplomats, not one of whom was American.

Dr. King was only thirty-five when he won the prize. There were all kinds of rumors over whether he could make nonviolence work. Critics said he was close to turning toward violence as another means to bring about civil rights. The press was giving Malcolm X and the Black Panthers equal billing, which was not an accurate reflection of the size of either the Panthers or the nonviolent civil rights movement. Andy used to joke that there were more people in four black churches in Chicago who were committed to nonviolence than in the whole Black Muslim movement in America. The Nobel Prize legitimized Dr. King and the nonviolent movement. After he delivered his Nobel lecture at the University of Oslo, hundreds of students greeted him outside by singing "We Shall Overcome." A movement that started in the segregated South had turned into a global cry for freedom.

"That's what I want Obama to understand. As president of the United States, he has the ability not only to improve the condition of Americans but to help those around the world," he said. "But I think he is starting to realize that. You've traveled with Obama. What's your take?"

"I like and admire him. I'm just not that upbeat on politicians over-all," I responded.

To me, politicians as a group are not an inspiring bunch. Many politicians are lawyers. Lawyers don't strike me as the most innovative or creative bunch. Maybe I'm prejudiced. My papa always told me as a kid, don't become a lawyer, hire one. But because our political ranks are filled with lawyers, we end up with conservative and stale ideas in the national political dialogue. Almost all our politicians are conservative when it comes to fresh ideas. Besides the actual biography of the president, what would be the real policy differences if Hillary Clinton had been elected instead? Or if Bill Clinton was serving a third term?

"It seems like you are about to ask me, 'What's the change that has come to Washington other than a black man being president?'" he said.

"You kind of already answered that. Change must come from outside Washington," I said.

"But before that happens, it needs to happen on an individual level."

Not everyone goes to work in the West Wing or commands the US military. But all of us face daily personal dilemmas, from whether to propose to your girlfriend to whether you should take her to Red Lobster or Chili's for the proposal (an easy decision if she loves popcorn shrimp). In order to help us make better decisions, it's critical to get a broad range of perspectives, especially from those who disagree with us. Indeed, it's not easy to listen to those who disagree or to offer dissent yourself. But if you feel a certain way, as Andy says, "You gotta share them views."

8 FOLLOWING YOUR PEOPLE: CHANGING THE WORLD ONE LOIN CLOTH AT A TIME

To keep a lamp burning, we have to keep putting oil in it.

—Mother Teresa[1]

I was in Mrs. Roberts's third-grade class. She was a soft-spoken, southern lady who encouraged me and my classmates to read voraciously. She urged our parents to sign us up for the Pizza Hut book program in which we would receive a free personal pan pizza if we read a handful of books. In the back of the classroom was a large picture of a football field, and each student had his or her name written on a football. The more books we read, the farther we advanced along the field. I don't remember what the prize was for scoring a touchdown. Maybe it was another pizza. I bit off more than I could chew—I wanted to score a touchdown by reading two or three books, not fifteen. Instead of reading *Encyclopedia Brown*, *The Boxcar Children* or other children's novels, I tried to read larger tomes like Daniel Defoe's *Robinson Crusoe* and Herman Melville's *Moby-Dick*. A third-grader reading *Moby-Dick* is like an ant trying to understand the Internet. There was one so-called advanced book, however, that I was able to partly grasp.

My papa couldn't make Parents Day because he was traveling abroad, so Uncle Andy pinch hit. Not only did all the third-graders pack into

Mrs. Roberts's classroom, but several other parents and teachers came to listen as well. He gave a rollicking speech about his tenure as mayor that made us laugh. Garbage workers dared Andy to collect trash, so he showed up and they put him on the back of a garbage truck. He had a ball operating a jackhammer with a construction crew. He poured asphalt into potholes and drove a steamroller over them.

"I realized how insignificant the mayor really was if he didn't have a good team. I went around and thanked the city workers and promised them raises if we could figure out ways to save money," he said.

One of my pals, Daniel, knew that Andy Young was famous but didn't quite understand for what, so he asked the former mayor an innocent question: "Are you a millionaire?"

Mrs. Roberts shot Daniel a disapproving look.

"Naw, not me," Andy replied to chuckles from the crowd, but that still didn't shake Mrs. Roberts's frown.

"Well, what kind of car do you drive?" Daniel asked.

"Oh, just a little old Ford. I think it has a few dents in it too," Andy responded to more laughter. When he left the mayor's office, the Chamber of Commerce gave him a Cadillac and a Lincoln. He traded in the Cadillac for a blue minivan. That wouldn't have been my choice. At Parents Day he paused and said with a serious tone, "But you don't need to drive a fast car or make a lot of money to change the world or make a difference. Gandhi changed the world while wearing only underwear, slippers and spectacles. I encourage all of you to read his autobiography some day."

I do as I'm told. I started Mahatma Gandhi's *The Story of My Experiments with Truth*. And then I did what most third-graders would do. I stopped. The book sat unread on my desk for years and collected dust. I eventually lost it. I'm unsure why I stopped reading it. I probably got caught up in more interesting things, like Mario Brothers or being a bothersome brother to my big sister, Kashi. I remember the gist of Gandhi's message: Nonviolence is the preferred tool for bringing about social change. I always felt badly for not finishing it, as if I wasn't being true to my Indian heritage. Most of what I knew about Gandhi came from the 1982 film starring Ben Kingsley. The irony of an Anglo-Indian actor teaching me about India's most famous figure stung.

Fast-forward almost fifteen years. I was home visiting my parents in Atlanta for the Fourth of July. My mom peered into the kitchen cupboard for some Darjeeling tea leaves from India. She turned to me, "Kabir, I picked you up something from the store." I looked at the kitchen counter. There it was. Gandhi's glowing ochre face on the book cover stared at me as if he were beckoning me to finish it—and this time the whole thing, all 528 pages.

Sometimes God gives you reminders. I launched into the book with heart and speed, hoping to understand Gandhi in his own words. I was familiar with much of Gandhi's philosophy of nonviolence. Like *Moby-Dick* and *Robinson Crusoe,* Gandhi's autobiography reads like an epic journey. It's the journey of a lawyer-turned-martyr, a boy who questions his surroundings and develops a powerful personal mantra for changing the world: "Be the change you want to see in the world," he famously said.[2]

I admire Gandhi for his unswerving honesty. While an elementary school student, for instance, he misspelled the word "kettle." The teacher urged Gandhi to copy the spelling from the student sitting next to him— peculiar rote memorization at best, cheating at worst. Young Gandhi resisted. Despite his inherently strong moral compass, he wasn't born with a crystallized vision of nonviolence. He struggled and evolved to develop his beliefs and philosophy. He learned immensely from his experiences.

I struggled too. Not just in developing my own beliefs and personal philosophy, but with the relevancy of Gandhi's message. The more I read, the more troubled I became. Yes, Gandhi's philosophy helped to emancipate India from the British Empire and to desegregate the American South, tremendous testaments to the power of his message. But that was then. In the twenty-first century, in an age of ghastly Islamic terrorism, what is the role of nonviolence? How do we deal practically with coteries of cloaked terrorists? Will Osama bin Laden acquiesce in the face of non-violence? I believe that sometimes it's right to fight fire with fire. I'm not advocating a strict neoconservative foreign policy, nor am I saying the US should coercively push the ideals of President Woodrow Wilson. Defensive fighting to me is common sense.

My many questions after reading the book went beyond the geo-political application of nonviolence to Gandhi's interpretation of nonviolence on a personal level, the renunciation of things that we most desire. Is it necessary to give up meat, lust and sexual intercourse per Gandhi's example to achieve *moksha,* the Hindi term for spiritual liberation? I really enjoy a succulent strip steak dinner (or steak and eggs for breakfast and bacon dipped in chocolate for dessert). Moreover, was complete devotion to one's parents truly necessary? I had many questions about the philosophy of a spiritual and pious man, so I turned to another spiritual and pious man with a familiar voice.

"You've stumbled onto Gandhi," whispered Andy. "That's not a bad place to be. He changed the world while wearing..."

I cut him off, "Wearing underwear and spectacles." He was amused. He likes it when I remember things that he says. It's flattering. "Am I missing something? Why is Gandhi relevant today? Nonviolence seems antiquated and obsolete."

"Oh no, I think that's the wrong view. His wisdom is timeless. Non-violence was relevant to those in the civil rights movement and even more so today," he opined.

Gandhi's teachings of nonviolence inspired legions of African Americans. Martin Luther King referred to him as a "guiding light" during the civil rights demonstrations. Early civil rights leaders invited Gandhi to come to America, but he declined, saying that his work in India was unfinished. He urged African Americans to stay true to nonviolent ideals and show the world the power of nonviolent methods to bring about social change. In 1959, approximately eleven years after Gandhi was assassinated, Dr. King and Coretta Scott King visited India at the invitation of Prime Minister Nehru, who was a close associate of Gandhi. King was keen to see the impact of Gandhi's teachings firsthand. While in India, he drew comparisons between the untouchable caste in India and African Americans in the segregated South. After his trip, he wrote, "As a result of my visit to India, my understanding of nonviolence became greater and my commitment deeper."[3] And President Barack Obama said, "The America of today has its roots in the India of Mahatma Gandhi and the nonviolent social action movement for Indian independence which he led."[4]

The philosophy of nonviolence didn't start with Gandhi. Andy cites ancient Egyptian civilization's inclusion of nonviolent ideals. Christianity, Buddhism, Jainism and Hinduism incorporate nonviolent tenets in their belief systems. In the Sermon on the Mount, Jesus takes on the "eye for an eye" philosophy of the Old Testament by urging one to turn the other cheek: "And if someone wants to sue you and take your tunic, let him have your cloak as well." Gandhi compared the Sermon on the Mount to the *Bhagavad Gita* and Edwin Arnold's *The Light of Asia,* a long poem that details the life of Gautama Siddhartha Buddha.

Andy credits Gandhi for turning the philosophy of nonviolence, touched upon by Leo Tolstoy and such transcendentalists as Henry David Thoreau and Ralph Waldo Emerson, into a political action program. He established a tactical playbook on how to apply nonviolence to bring about social and political change. Gandhi first used and experienced the power of nonviolence after he was removed by force from a train in South Africa because of his brown skin.

"He decided to establish a demonstration. He deliberately waited until a reporter from the *New York Times* was there before he staged a considered dramatization against injustice," said Andy. Later, when Gandhi returned to South Africa after going to India, he was greeted by a mob that threw stones and rotten eggs at him because he had reportedly spoken out against white South Africans while in India. Gandhi did not want to prosecute any of the assailants. He shamed the assailants, and he forgave them.

"He had a good sense for timing, to wait for a news reporter," I observed.

"It wasn't just a sense of timing. He realized that private acts of protest didn't have much effect. The key to success was exposing the injustice on a world stage," Andy remarked. I recalled Andy's story of how the television networks ran stories of the brutality in Selma, one of which interrupted the broadcast of the film *Judgment at Nuremberg:* a symbolic juxtaposition. He continued, "Gandhi took nonviolence from the theoretical and idealistic to the practical and political realm."

"Wouldn't it have been easier for the civil rights movement to use Jesus Christ as a model instead of some skinny brown guy in India?" I asked.

"Not really. The skinny brown guy was confronting the British Empire, and Jesus never really confronted the Roman Empire. Jesus sacrificed himself and had a greater impact on the world than Gandhi. But such sacrifice wasn't attractive to us. From Gandhi we learned that you can change the world with limited sacrifice, but it didn't require complete death," he explained.

"In a way, Gandhianism requires a psychological death," I said.

Gandhi took the philosophy of nonviolence and added his own twist: personal renunciation was paramount. We must detach ourselves from that which we most desire—money, fame, sex—in order to achieve spiritual enlightenment or nirvana. When we quench our fear and desire, we will free ourselves from the *maya,* the illusion of the physical world. He canceled his life insurance policy, which would have benefited his wife, because he wanted to give his money to the entire community, and he didn't allow the doctor to give her beef tea when she was very ill because of his and her devout vegetarianism. I have difficulty with Gandhi's call for renunciation, and I'm not the only one. Sure, he went on a twenty-one-day fast against caste prejudice in India. But he had some weird idiosyncrasies, like sleeping in the same bed with young women to test his celibacy.

"Gandhi was a self-righteous, arrogant prick. I know that's strong." Andy explained, "He was a bit of a nutcase. I get unnerved because Gandhi required personal sacrifice and renunciation of life in order to be part of the Indian movement. It doesn't have to be that way. Instead of worrying about his own piety, he should have worked with Nehru to think through the social condition of Indians and pointed the country in a sustainable economic direction."

Had Gandhi done so, Andy believes that Nehru wouldn't have adopted a policy of total socialism or what Nehru called the "third way." And that Nehru's daughter, Prime Minister Indira Gandhi, and his grandson, Prime Minister Rajiv Gandhi, would have changed their entire approach and possibly found a solution to the violence in Kashmir much earlier. Andy is not entirely correct about the differences between Gandhi's and Nehru's approaches to the economy. Gandhi made his own loin cloth and urged others to make their own clothes in order to be economically self-reliant. He suggested that India add a *charkha* or spinning wheel to its national flag. He knew that the success of the Indian economy was critical to its everlasting success.

Then again, maybe Andy has a point. I came across a white paper that contended that the cost of delayed economic reform in India was huge. Almost 15 million children would have lived had India moved away from socialism earlier. Over 100 million people would have moved out of poverty, and 250 million would be literate.[5] Clearly, there is no way of knowing for sure what may have happened if India hadn't gone down the path of socialism, and you can hardly blame Gandhi for all of India's socioeconomic problems. But a turn to capitalism and an effective nonviolent way to improve the economic conditions of poor people would have been a boon to India. Andy and I would return to the idea of capitalism as nonviolence later in our conversation.

We agreed, though, that we should give Gandhi the benefit of the doubt. Personal renunciation may have been necessary in India in the 1930s and 1940s because almost everyone was poor and didn't have many material possessions. Perhaps renunciation was just an opiate for the masses. Gandhi learned to economize out of necessity as a youth. He wasn't a wealthy man, and he learned to place almost no value on material possessions.

It's also worth mentioning that Andy disagrees with Gandhi over whether children should be totally devoted to their parents. Gandhi made a vow to his mother that he wouldn't eat meat, and for the most part stuck to it. He told a friend, "A vow is a vow. It cannot be broken." He even joined the Vegetarian Society of England. Andy thinks children should certainly respect their parents, but it is okay to break from them. At a young age he read Kahlil Gibran's *The Prophet* and internalized the passage about children: "Your children are not your children.... They come through you but not from you.... You may give them your love but not your thoughts.... For they have their own thoughts. You may house their bodies but not their souls." Andy regularly recited these words to his parents. It was a personal declaration of independence. Jesus also left his mother at a young age to go about his father's business. The United Church of Christ, of which Andy is a member, gives kids around twelve years old an opportunity to confirm their faith and accept Jesus Christ.

"You reject Gandhi's view on total devotion to parents and on personal renunciation?" I asked for clarity.

"Yes, and we in the movement completely rejected personal renunciation because it's not required by Christianity," he summarized. "But we integrated his call for nonviolence. We took what we liked and ignored the rest."

That's where Andy's acceptance of Jesus and Gandhi parts. In Christianity, it's not required to give up worldly possessions. Jesus says that in the judgment you will be asked whether you clothed the naked, fed the hungry and healed the sick. There is an understanding that God loves you even though you don't live up to the ideal. We are all sinners. Jesus dies to take on our sins. Dr. King even said to African Americans that they couldn't totally absolve themselves from sin and guilt because they participated and cooperated with the evil of segregation: Blacks were partly to blame for their situation because they bent over and let whites ride them, submitting to their oppression.

"Noncooperation with evil is as important as cooperation with good. The Montgomery bus boycott was noncooperation with segregation," explained Andy.

"Nonviolence doesn't mean being passive," I responded.

"Exactly. Civil disobedience means standing up for what's right in a nonviolent way," he said. "What propelled us to engage in civil disobedience was the *soul* force of Gandhianism."

Gandhi and his followers relied on the power of their souls, which gave a spiritual and moral authority to the freedom movement in India. Gandhi called this "soul force." The black community related to the "soul force" of the Indian movement because they, too, didn't have many financial resources. They simply had a conviction for equality and justice. This was enough to mobilize thousands to engage in civil disobedience. But if they had engaged in violence, they would have lost their spiritual and moral authority. They would have lost the upper hand. Andy and other civil rights leaders purposefully spoke in religious terms to appeal to the conscience of not only African Americans but all Americans. He saw "soul force" as a spiritual and cultural power that could bring about social change in the segregated South.

"Soul force is the key to Gandhi's leadership approach. Gandhi instilled in his people such a powerful message that they almost didn't need him to lead them," Andy said. "That's what young leaders today should learn. It's not about getting up on a platform and making flashy speeches. You must instill in your people a strong soul force so they want to carry on your mission."

In 1963, Andy led a march in Birmingham en route to the jail in which Dr. King was imprisoned. The Birmingham sheriff, Bull Connor, accompanied by police and firefighters, yelled at the nearly five thousand marchers to turn back. Andy didn't want to turn around but didn't want to lead the marchers into a violent situation, so he knelt on the ground and prayed. Following his direction, the other protesters knelt and prayed. They sang too. Andy explained to Bull Connor that they simply wanted to march to the jail and sing a few songs. Before he could finish explaining, Reverend Charles Billups stood up and urged the protesters to march, to the surprise of Bull Connor who instructed the policemen to stop the marchers. But the police officers didn't move. The once-barking dogs sat quietly. Andy remembers seeing a fireman with tears in his eyes while the marchers were singing "I Want Jesus to Walk with Me." One lady shouted, "Great God Almighty done parted the Red Sea one mo' time!" Andy and the others had nonviolently parted the Red Sea of violence, racism and ignorance with soul force. They shamed the white police officers and firefighters into seeing the cruelty of their ways. There was a strong moral authority to the nonviolent means of the civil rights movement.

Andy, however, was not initially convinced that nonviolence could work in the South. Gandhi and his fellow Indians were a majority trying to deal effectively with the minority British population. African Americans were a minority in America. In fact, in the early years of the civil rights movement, several observers including Andy mentioned this very point as a reason why nonviolence would fail. Andy first thoroughly read Gandhi's works with Eduardo Mondlane, who became the president of the FRELIMO movement in Mozambique. Mondlane was working toward a doctorate in sociology at Northwestern University and met Andy at a church conference in 1951. They were the only two blacks at the conference. They both read passages written by Nehru on Gandhi. Mondlane was convinced that nonviolence would work in Mozambique, and Andy felt that it wouldn't work in the South.

It turned out just the opposite. When Mondlane helped to launch the nonviolent movement in Mozambique in 1962, the Portuguese army fired at protesters with machine guns, killing many of them. The protesters turned to violence. Many of the protesters were high school and university students. These student freedom fighters raided Portuguese armories in the middle of the night for weapons. A firefight ensued, and they captured several Portuguese troops. The freedom fighters gave blood transfusions to the troops. They also discovered that several of the Portuguese soldiers were illiterate. The freedom fighters set up classes to teach them how to read and write. Many of the Portuguese troops switched sides and joined the freedom fighters.

"I know it's a hypothetical, but what would have happened if Bull Connor and the police had started to machine gun civil rights demonstrators? Would you have rejected nonviolence in favor of violence?" I asked.

"I really don't know. I wasn't yet religiously committed to nonviolence. I was committed to it because it was a practical solution," he responded.

This wasn't the first time Andy had thought about my question. In fact, he had several heated and unresolved debates with Dr. King over whether nonviolence would have worked against Hitler. Andy came down on the side of Dietrich Bonhoeffer: There are times when evil must be restrained. There are differences among aggressive violence, retaliatory violence and defensive violence. Andy felt that a certain amount of defensive violence was necessary to stop Hitler who was aggressively destroying other nations and people. Fortunately, the civil rights movement didn't morph into a violent struggle that might have become America's second Civil War.

"Nonviolence is practical only if the so-called enemy responds in the right way, a compassionate way. But if the enemy doesn't respond to nonviolence..." I said.

He interrupted, "It depends on how you approach it. We were careful with what we said and what we targeted. We didn't attack the American government. We chose our battlegrounds very carefully."

Civil rights leaders could have chosen to confront whites over jobs. In those days, workers were often killed for trying to organize into labor unions. Andy stressed, as he had before, that there was almost no planning that went into how and where to start the civil rights movement. Nobody strategized for Rosa Parks. She made a decision based on a systematic discourtesy that she, Claudette Colvin and others had experienced. Then the movement's leaders turned their attention to the student sit-in movement. Some of the students were military veterans. They had fought for freedom around the world and returned to an America in which they couldn't eat at a lunch counter. The students decided to challenge the systematic discourtesy, and the sit-in movement began. Civil rights leaders responded to small and practical concerns. In Birmingham, for instance, blacks wouldn't shop where they couldn't work or get a drink of water without being segregated.

"We dramatized the small battles that weren't worth killing for. Machine gunning someone at a lunch counter or in a bus wouldn't have been good public relations," declared Andy.

Civil rights leaders took the nonviolent playbook that Gandhi had created and developed it further. For instance, they instituted a policy that loved ones could not take part in the same demonstration. It put too much stress and pressure on someone to see loved ones getting injured. Civil rights leaders refined the tactics so that they could be put toward a movement that would work not only for blacks in the segregated South but for freedom fighters in Polish shipyards and elsewhere around the world. By protesting systematic discourtesies and finding small battlefields, they were able to magnify and dramatize injustices without risking lives.

The commitment to nonviolence of civil rights demonstrators was frequently tested. The violence in St. Augustine, the oldest continuously inhabited city in the United States, was bubbling over in 1963. The Ku Klux Klan kidnapped Dr. Robert Hayling, a black dentist, who was later rescued by the sheriff. Dr. Hayling wrote President Lyndon Johnson requesting federal marshals to protect blacks in St. Augustine, especially since the administration had already sent funds to celebrate the upcoming four-hundredth anniversary of the city's founding—an event that was primarily for whites. Dr. Hayling also appealed to Dr. King for assistance.

Andy, ever the contrarian, was against committing resources to St. Augustine because of the unstable and explosive situation there. Dr. King agreed with him, but sent Andy to the city to stop the demonstrations. He went to St. Augustine to personally observe the situation, and eventually helped to lead a march, only to make sure it did not become violent. When the marchers approached the old slave market, Andy noticed that there were no police officers, only a gang of white hoodlums. He thought about turning the protesters around, but it was their first march and they wouldn't turn back. "Hoss" Manucy, the leader of the white gang, had once boasted, "I'm a good Christian. I don't smoke. I don't drink. I just beat niggers."[6] Andy approached the gang, understanding that he was walking through the valley of the shadow of death, and started to reason with them. He was greeted with a fist in his face and a blackjack across his head. Andy doesn't remember much after that. But after a few moments, before he could feel the pain and in a state of semiconsciousness, Andy went up to the gang again, hoping to negotiate with them. Again he was slugged. He was kicked in the groin. He shrugged off both blows and didn't go down. When the gang saw that he wouldn't back down, somebody stepped in and said, "Let him through." After the marches, Andy cried. He was furious and upset. But he was not deterred. He was convinced of the need for a major nonviolent campaign in St. Augustine. He admitted later though that he wished he could have met his assailants alone in a dark alley away from the civil rights movement. "A part of me wanted to mess them up."

Gandhi and Dr. King were cut from the same cloth, long-lost brothers from different mothers. You (or Malcolm Gladwell) may argue that both were in the right place at the right time: Gandhi's influence rose while the British Empire was already in decline. The cry for self-rule might have occurred without Gandhi in India. Similarly, the push for desegregation might have happened without the leadership of King. But both leaders were similar in the way they led, instilling soul force in their followers and leading from behind. They responded to a greater calling. They didn't set out to be martyrs. They listened and gave voice to a movement that was well on its way.

Indians revered Dr. King too. In 1971, Prime Minister Indira Gandhi posthumously awarded India's highest honor to Dr. King: "He's not with us. . . . We admire Dr. King and felt his loss as our own. The tragedy rekindled the memories of the great martyrs of all time."[7] Andy traveled to India with Coretta Scott King, who accepted the award, and he remembers the occasion with much pride.

"We were in the land of Gandhi, and Dr. King was being feted by the people of Gandhi. It was full circle."

In 2009, it was full circle all over again. Dr. King's son, Martin Luther King III, led a State Department–backed delegation with Congressman John Lewis to India in honor of the fiftieth anniversary of his father's pilgrimage to India. Andy and Carolyn were part of the delegation, as was jazz pianist Herbie Hancock, Congressman Jim McDermott of Washington and former US Senator Harris Wofford of Pennsylvania, who also served as special assistant on civil rights to President John Kennedy. Wofford, who came from a wealthy family, had traveled to India when he was a boy. He was fortunate to see Gandhi walking on the streets. In the 1940s, he helped to raise the money to invite black college presidents to the Indian independence ceremony. The black college presidents were excited about Gandhianism and taught it as a relevant way to fight injustice in America. Andy created a documentary of the trip, *In the Footsteps of Gandhi*, a short flick spliced with video footage of Dr. King and the voice of Maya Angelou reading Gandhi quotes.

"Didn't your daddy meet Gandhi?" Andy asked.

My papa was just a boy sitting with his father at the prayer grounds in Delhi where Gandhi was worshiping. As Gandhi left the prayer grounds, everyone bowed their heads out of respect, but my father stood up, which upset some onlookers. Fortunately it was too late to do anything about it. As Gandhi walked by, he put his hand on my father's head. I used to rub my papa's head for good luck.

"We should've interviewed him for the documentary. How'd you like the film?" he asked me.

I didn't see the point of the congressional trip. I didn't like that my tax money was footing the bill for a hokey commemoration. I voiced my concern, and he countered that India is a critical ally for America in the twenty-first century, a view with which I agree. Without a firm relationship with India, America won't be able to achieve success in Afghanistan or Pakistan.

Andy took issue with my comment: "I believe in congressional visits. The worst sin of Congress is that half the congressmen brag that they don't have passports. Here are people who make decisions that impact the world who don't know anything about the world."

I still wasn't satisfied with Andy's explanation of how Gandhi is relevant today and I said I was disappointed with Martin Luther King III who was the star of the trip and documentary. Man, I'm a tough critic.

"It's true," Andy responded. "He's not as eloquent of a speaker as his father or as impressive a man. A leader is not just a speaker. Martin III has led peace and reconciliation missions to Bosnia, South Africa, Israel and Jordan. He's joined with the children of several leaders like Caesar Chavez, Yitzhak Rabin, and Desmond Tutu who regularly engage in group reconciliation efforts. I was frustrated, however, because I kept on urging him to commend Indians for responding to the recent Mumbai terrorist attacks in a manner that was much more intelligent than America's reaction to September 11."

I suppose the film was more than just a retrospective on Dr. King's visit. It highlighted the relevancy of Gandhi's nonviolence today. The documentary flashed video clips of the abhorrent terrorist attacks at the Mumbai Taj Mahal Hotel in November 2008, part of a series of ten coordinated attacks across the city. The gunmen set sail from Karachi, Pakistan, across the Arabian Sea, and killed over one hundred people and injured over two hundred more. The story made headlines around the world. Instead of reacting violently to the attack by members of a Pakistani militant organization by launching an attack against Pakistan, India responded in an arguably nonviolent and measured way that yielded results.

"The Indians actually got much of what they wanted. Pakistani officials have cooperated in the investigation," I observed.

"Yes, India actually strengthened its relationship with Pakistan," he added.

A part of me, however, was uncomfortable with the Indian response. I think it would have been appropriate for India to engage in defensive or retaliatory violence: "Are you saying that Indians should deal with these terrorists nonviolently?" I asked.

"Yes," he put it clearly.

"But they killed hundreds of innocent civilians. I'm not saying India should enter into a full-scale war with Pakistan. But maybe they should consider a surgical strike with the help of the Americans," I commented.

"If India were to bomb Pakistan, wouldn't that just enflame the situation? The only thing that can really defeat terrorism is nonviolence," he said.

"What about the wars in Iraq and Afghanistan? Are you saying our participation in these wars is misguided?" I asked with alarm.

"The American war strategy has been screwed since the beginning. I really think our civilian leaders need to see terrorism for what it is—a battle of ideas and ideologies," he said, leaning forward as our talk intensified.

I responded with a question: "Can you forgive the suicide bombers of September 11?"

"Yes, easily, and I know that sounds un-American," he said. I was surprised with his answer. It made me mad. How could anyone forgive those sick and savage terrorists? He continued, "Our anger is relative. We embrace the royal family of Saudi Arabia even though that regime is engaged in all sorts of shady behavior. We even sell them weapons. It's not enough to just demonize al-Qaeda. By forgiving, we clear our minds. We act rationally. We can then try to understand the terrorists. By understanding them, we can defeat them. Have you seen *Charlie Wilson's War?*"

I had. I have a crush on Julia Roberts and try to see all movies starring her. Congressman Charlie Wilson tried to help the Afghans get rid of the Soviets. When the Soviets left Afghanistan, Wilson asked Congress for funds to help build schools that would empower people and engender tremendous good will toward America. Instead, Congress and the defense community rejected Wilson's request. By not helping to develop Afghanistan, Andy believes, America helped sow the seeds for the terrorism America experienced on September 11, 2001.

What's that old saying? If you have a hammer, you see every problem as a nail. That nonviolence worked in one instance doesn't mean it will work in another. At first I thought Uncle Andy was just peddling his panacea of nonviolence. He does have a point, however, about addressing the ideas that fuel terrorism.

In my first book,[8] I contended that the Cold War was won in part by hot jazz. The US State Department hired jazz musicians like Louis Armstrong and Dizzy Gillespie to play in Europe, the Soviet Union and the Middle East in order to trumpet a positive image of American democracy. The jazz band was the first part of American civil society that was integrated, well before Jackie Robinson slid into second base. Nazi Germany and the Soviet Union actually banned the music, but citizens in these countries found ways around the bans. They liked our music. They liked what it stood for—freedom and improvisation. They liked us. They wanted to be like us, or at least, be free like us. In a battle of ideas, America won.

"But there is a difference. The Cold War was cold. There weren't improvised explosive devices and two theaters of active battle," I said.

"There was always an implied threat. If you kill a terrorist, you make another terrorist," he said.

At the end of Steven Spielberg's *Munich,* after many Israelis and Palestinians have been killed throughout the film, the audience is left with a feeling of futility. Despite all the killings, the Israelis and Palestinians still continue to kill each other. It's almost as if they don't know why they are killing each other. To stop the killing in the Middle East and in hotspots around the world, one must go after the underlying philosophy. After all the killing is over, there will always be some people left who will have to learn to live with each other. So the questions remain, What is the root cause of terrorism, and How can one nonviolently address it?

"Martin and I always agreed with Gandhi who said, 'Violence is the worst form of poverty,'" Andy responded. "When you are poor, you panic and resort to irrational means to change your situation or change the situation of others."

"You're changing the world as a young banker," Andy began. "You're actually a foot soldier in the nonviolent capitalist revolution that has swept the world. I mean that. Capitalism can be the nonviolence movement of today. It must be humanitarian capitalism that produces goods and services for humans as well as profits. Profits without productivity is just greed. Greed without goods can destroy an entire economy." Andy is no Gordon Gekko.

There is no better shining example of this belief than Gandhi's homeland of India. Consider the Mumbai terrorists who came from Pakistan, which is a very poor country. India is also a poor country. Several of my friends and colleagues traveled to India after reading Thomas Friedman's *The World Is Flat* and expected to see an industrious, clean and efficient India. But when they arrived, they saw hordes of animals and people crammed into shantytowns. Millions live in huts that are made from animal dung. Clean water is scarce. Millions are exposed to toxic indoor air pollution. Poor roads, bridges and tunnels hinder economic development. Bureaucracy and inefficiency plague government and business institutions.

But India is different from Pakistan. It is a place where centuries coexist. Some villages may not have clean drinking water, but they have wireless Internet access and advanced mobile phones. I've seen elephants adorned with advertisements to buy laptops, mobile phones and other electronics. Above all, the mind-set of India has changed. Ask almost any taxi driver and he will say that the future belongs to India. There is a hustle to Indians. When you pull up to a red light, vendors try to sell you copies of *Harvard Business Review* or *The World Is Flat*. It's common to see clusters of teenagers huddling on the street reading books and studying for an upcoming examination. As a top Silicon Valley venture capitalist of Indian descent once explained to me, "Education is sexy in India. The first time I got laid was when my hometown newspaper ran a story saying that I was accepted to one of the top universities in India." The educational services market is booming. Studying is in. Procrastination is out.

Success in India is not limited to just Hindus. India has a pluralistic society in which several minority groups have excelled. Most notably, there is a clear pathway to success for Muslims. Billionaire Azim Premji, the chairman and CEO of Wipro, a large software company in India, is a Muslim. Bollywood actor Shahrukh Khan, also a Muslim, is one of the biggest stars in India. Another Muslim, Dr. Abdul Kalam, served as the eleventh president of India. The third president of India, Dr. Zakir Hussain, was a Muslim. A young Muslim child growing up in India can see models for success in almost every profession and field.

In Pakistan this is not so. As Tom Friedman points out, young Muslim children in Pakistan may end up going to an Islamic school, also known as a *madrasa,* where they may learn that the root of all evil is India or America—places that are more economically successful.[9] Friedman neatly ties several loose geopolitical issues together. Because America gives subsidies to its farmers, Pakistani farmers may not be able to sell their crops in the world marketplace and are therefore kept in poverty. Perhaps that's too great a leap. But what is not that difficult to understand is that commerce and trade have helped to stabilize ethnic violence in India.

If there were a war between India and Pakistan, global investors and asset managers would be less likely to invest in the region. Political uncertainty usually leads to economic uncertainty, so foreign direct investment

would dry up. IBM, Microsoft, Accenture and GE might think twice before opening additional facilities in India. Peace on the subcontinent is
sponsored by GE: imagination at work.

The contagion of the killings in Mumbai was contained. It did not
lead to violent ethnic conflict in Kashmir, a typical flashpoint for Pakistan
and India. The higher-ups in India's political and economic establishment
clearly understand that business and commerce is good for India. Anything that threatens the peace on the Indian subcontinent jeopardizes investment in India which, in turn, hinders the future of India.

The global supply chain compels countries, companies and citizens
to work together. It forces people to look past ethnic and religious differences and to find common ground. If one cog in the greater system
breaks down, it threatens the viability of the entire supply chain, so it's of
vital importance that all parts are working soundly together. Viewed from
this perspective, trade, commerce and multinationals are nonviolent and,
as Andy said, "Peace on the Indian subcontinent is brought about by
nonviolent means."

"Let me get this straight. Are you saying that business and commerce
is the nonviolent movement of today?" I asked. Andy's message wasn't too
different from what we had talked about before—that the civil rights
movement should be seen through a macroeconomic lens.

"It's not just of today. Remember the boycotts of the civil rights movement. I've always seen the importance of the business community and economic development. So did Gandhi, to some extent," he explained.

"I'm in accord that business can bring about positive social change,"
I said. "I just find it odd that you compare it to Gandhianism. The civil
rights movement was shaped by religious and spiritual ideas. That's what
gave it a moral authority. Does the nonviolent business movement have a
similar moral authority?" I asked.

He didn't answer immediately. I think I stumped him momentarily.

"Nobody has really assumed the mantle, but there is a moral authority to business. I always used to tell people when I worked for your daddy

that preaching and engineering aren't so different. Both require clean water, roads, buildings and dams in order to fulfill the message of Jesus to feed the hungry, clothe the naked and heal the sick. You need engineers and financiers to take care of the world's poor too," Andy explained.

"You're preaching to the choir. I don't think boycotts work well today because of the large number of consumers around the world. It's not terribly difficult to find another market or group of consumers ready to buy your product."

"If boycotts are targeted to specific injustices they almost always work. But you shouldn't boycott before you attempt to communicate. The nonviolence mantra is investigation, negotiation, demonstration (boycotts or marches) and finally reconciliation. You have to do all four to make it work." he said.

"So the Gandhianism of today is compassionate capitalism?" I asked.

"Well, I still don't think we've had what Martin talked about—a revolution in values. So many businesses don't recognize the greater role they play in the world. They worship profit as a god. I'm still looking for us as a society to focus on what Jesus talked about—feeding the poor and so on. I'm looking for us to have a revolution in values," he explained.

"I think we'll be waiting a long time. That sounds so utopian. It is wishful thinking," I countered.

"How do you figure?" he asked.

In *The End of History and the Last Man,* Francis Fukuyama famously made the case that humans struggle for recognition. There is a deep-seated urge in humans to seek recognition, pride, esteem and dignity. We often value ourselves on what other people think of us. Nietzsche described humans as "the beast with red cheeks."[10] The French Revolution and liberal democratic theory, however, convinced many that human equality was paramount. Nietzsche detested liberal democracies and felt that they created "men without chests." Democracy has ostensibly taught us to value reason and intelligence. But the ever-present, intense desire among humans to be recognized took the form of imperialism in the nineteenth and twentieth centuries, when one group of people asserted their dominance over other groups. It was in Germany, the most advanced and industrial country in the 1930s, that the Nazis came to power wanting to assert dominance over other European countries and Jews.

Humans spend much of their lives trying to be unequal. In modern times, the struggle for recognition can be a catalyst for suicide bombers: The ability to go against instinctual self-preservation, as sick as it sounds, is celebrated in some quarters. Segregation gave status and recognition to poor whites in the South. It's preferable to direct man's struggle for recognition into a capitalist system. Making more money than someone else is very much part of the human struggle for recognition. To try to reduce the profits man makes in business is to dampen his pride and struggle for recognition. It's asking man to go against his desires. It's asking man to be inhuman.

"You raise a good point and have hit upon the tension between capitalism and democracy," Andy acknowledged.

"Fukuyama mentions the fanatical desire to create equality as a threat to democracy because it goes against man's nature. That's why I admire the brilliance of the Madisonian system. James Madison let people struggle for recognition by engaging the democratic system and not going around it. Gandhi even wanted to work with the British government to bring about change and not topple it outright. But we arguably need capitalism so people can strive to be unequal," I observed.

"I have no problem with profit. To make profit without creating value is a crime," Andy asserted. Andy blamed those on Wall Street for seeking profit without creating substantial value or productivity. Trading commercial paper, buying credit default swaps and engaging in risk arbitrage doesn't produce food for the hungry or shelter for the homeless.

I didn't want to get into an argument with Andy, so I looked for common ground. We found it in municipal bonds, another form of high finance, which is a tax haven for investors. It's one of the financial instruments that Andy would deem public-purpose capitalism. Atlanta is basically run on municipal bonds. They helped to fund the airport, create a sewer system and build roads. These bonds attract money for projects that support the public good.

"I have a problem with capitalism that is devoid of the public good," he concluded.

Having reached a concluding note on capitalism, I still wanted to hear Andy's commentary on foreign policy. Nonviolence is just not part of the dialogue of international relations.

Andy leaned back and sighed, "You've put your finger on something I've had trouble explaining to others. We still are locked into a kind of Kissinger-power-politics vision of the world. There is no respect for spiritual power or moral power. It wasn't always this way."

He believes that President Jimmy Carter was the intellectual heir to the nonviolent philosophies of Gandhi and Dr. King. When he assumed the presidency, Carter started out by showing respect for his enemies. He sent emissaries to talk and listen to America's so-called enemies. These simple acts of courtesy, Andy believes, had enough moral power to keep America out of war during Carter's presidency. The Carter administration even showed respect for the Russians, Chinese and Vietnamese, not by making concessions to them but by simply welcoming them back to the United Nations.

Critics dismissed Carter's actions as weak and naïve, but Andy celebrates Carter's actions as wise: Nobody lost their life and it didn't take much money. America could have easily gone to war if Carter had mishandled the Panama Canal or the situation in the Middle East. Critics panned Carter's handling of the Iranian hostage situation. Even though Andy was no longer part of the administration at the time, Carter asked him for help. Andy traveled to Algeria to help negotiate the release of the hostages into that country. It's impossible to prove, yet Andy believes that George Bush and others at the CIA cut a backroom deal with Khomeini not to release the hostages until Carter was out of office.

Andy instead focuses on Carter's diplomatic successes with the Soviets. There were cultural exchanges and sports contests between the Russians and Americans. There was an exchange of military generals and scientists too. At one point, many oncologists traveled to Moscow to learn from the Russians, who were supposedly superior in cancer therapy. Russians understood that Americans were superior in food production and agriculture. Dwayne Andreas, then CEO of food processing giant ADM, traveled to Russia and gave books about Franklin Roosevelt and the New Deal to Mikhail Gorbachev, who was serving in a top position in the Agricultural Secretariat. Andreas made the point that someone would have to reform communism just as Roosevelt reformed capitalism because clearly communism wasn't working. He helped to plant the seed of reform in the mind of a young, bright and ambitious bureaucrat.

"What Reagan did was absolutely stupid—to come into office and designate some countries as part of an empire of evil and launch a policy of confrontation. If we hadn't softened the stage with Russia and China, he might not have gotten away with that," Andy said. It's easy to pan Andy as having sour grapes over Reagan's win. But it's just Andy being Andy, contrarian to a fault.

"Why is it so difficult to include nonviolence in the dialogue of international and foreign relations?" I asked.

"Because when you get down to it, nonviolence is tough. It's all about forgiveness. That's the problem in the Middle East. Neither Judaism nor Islam incorporates dominant ideals of forgiveness, but you do have it in Hinduism and Christianity," he observed.

"Love your enemy?" I asked. That is so contrary to everything I have heard regarding foreign policy over the last decade. Can you imagine Dick Cheney saying that?

"Cheney and Halliburton effectively colonized Iraq. Many Iraqis who had jobs became terrorists and killed young, innocent Americans. You can't say Cheney was strong. His greed devalued the wealth that could have generated economic success in the region."

"But you still find space in your heart to forgive him?"

"Um ... yeah. Even Dick. Love conquers evil," he replied.

Forgiveness is a guiding philosophy of Andy's life. It comes from an understanding that hatred and violence are really rooted in fear. People who hate you really fear you. You don't overcome that fear by making them more fearful. You have to do something that is disarming and forgiving. You have to break the cycle of fear, hatred and violence by exhibiting some understanding. You have to deal with them nonviolently.

It took a concentrated effort, but Andy even found the courage and strength to forgive neoconservative Paul Wolfowitz. Andy believes Dick Cheney, Donald Rumsfeld and Paul Wolfowitz met with George W. Bush while he was still a presidential candidate and convinced him of the neocon strategy to democratize the Middle East starting with Iraq.

"It was so naïve. Wolfowitz was the smallest one of the three. I used to say that if I ever saw him in an alley, I'd like to beat the shit out of him for just being so arrogant and stupid," Andy said. In 2005, Wolfowitz moved on to head the World Bank, and he immediately started to reform the bureaucracy that had inhibited the success of the organization. Andy commended Wolfowitz for being the bull in the china shop at the World Bank and bringing about needed changes. Both Wolfowitz and Andy were scheduled to be panelists at an event, so Andy Googled Wolfowitz and was surprised with the findings: Wolfowitz was a math major and had a close relationship with Secretary of State George Shultz. Andy didn't agree with Shultz on everything but held him in high regard and considered him a mentor and teacher, a true compassionate conservative. Andy reasoned that Wolfowitz couldn't be all bad.

At the World Bank, Wolfowitz demonstrated his commitment to Africa, which is of particular importance to Andy. When Wolfowitz found himself in the middle of a scandal that involved a promotion for his girlfriend, Shaha Riza, Andy came to his public defense. Some believe critics of Wolfowitz used the scandal as political retaliation to jettison him from the World Bank because of his role in crafting the American war in Iraq.

When Andy saw Wolfowitz and Riza at an event years later, he gave Riza a big hug. He said, "I was happy to see they were doing all right."

It's hard for me to unconditionally forgive people who have mistreated me or who I don't respect. And I still struggle with Andy's evergreen call for nonviolence. But it's natural to struggle. Andy struggled. Dr. King struggled. Gandhi struggled too. The way to overcome your struggles, Gandhi believed, is to listen closely to your mentor: "true knowledge is impossible without a Guru."[11] Some of the most difficult things to learn in life—forgiveness, compassion, conviction and courage—are better understood when they are whispered from the lips of your guru.

9 THE OUTER VOICE

Let no man in the world live in delusion. Without a Guru none can cross over to the other shore.

—Guru Nanak, religious leader and founder of Sikhism[1]

Andy's house is like a miniature version of Grand Central Station in New York. There are always people coming and going, stopping in to say hello or leaving with a collection of papers, books or some other odd cargo. Sometimes I can't help but feel that I'm just another whistling train pulling into the station, waiting for the master engineer to give me a close inspection. Have I taken the metaphor far enough along the tracks?

Andy and Carolyn welcome and take an interest in almost everyone who makes it to their nook in southwest Atlanta. That's why I was surprised when I saw their new sturdy black gate. My first thought was that Uncle Andy must have seen the irony of a peacemaker installing a gate. But then I considered the practical. Were the Youngs trying to prevent their dogs from venturing into the street? Were they attempting to stop the drip, drip of visitors? Or were they sending me a not-so-subtle message?

"Oh hey, daaarling. You look so handsome!" said Carolyn. I turned around to see if she was speaking to me. She's liberal with her praise. She walked barefoot around the small island in the kitchen toward me. I saw a package of dried seaweed and Scotch tape on the kitchen counter. I was still basking in Carolyn's compliment, so I didn't ask.

"We had to get that gate because of the burglars in our neighborhood. Ain't taking any chances," she explained as we hugged.

I saw Uncle Andy in the den watching a Raisin Bran commercial on mute. He looked serene, wearing dark tapered blue jeans, black socks and a fitted black sweater—like he had recently been to Banana Republic.

"That's Carolyn's reason. My reason is that it gets so busy in here. It's hard to hear myself think. Remember what we first talked about—finding an inner voice? It's hard to hear sometimes," he said from across the den.

Most of us have a voice deep within that shapes and guides our conscience. Some call it their gut. It lets us know when we've erred. Once I watched my toddler nephew throw his plate of pasta. None of the adults realized it was intentional or reprimanded him, and still he went to hide underneath a table. He knew he had done something wrong, even at that young age. The inner voice is with us from the very beginning of our lives until our last breath.

"What are we talking about today, Kabir?" Andy asked as I joined him in the den.

What was there left to talk about? We had covered spirituality, faith and love. We had talked about Andy's time in public office and in private life. We had even alluded to funny video clips on YouTube. I had thought hard on my drive to his house about what I would ask.

"I want to talk about us," I affirmed. He looked at me with interest. I continued, "I'm blessed beyond belief to be able to come to you with my questions and concerns. When I share some of your insights with friends, they ask me a very simple question." His eyes narrowed. I spoke slowly: "They ask me how they too can find a mentor, a sounding board."

The alarm system blared: left main door open. Carolyn greeted the visitor in the kitchen.

"Mentors are much more than a sounding board. They are . . ." said Andy, searching for words.

I interjected, "An outer voice."

"An outer voice," he confirmed. "I like that. Mentors help you see a breadth of perspectives and wise you up."

Mentors played a significant role in the development and education of a young Andrew Young. His father was his first close and dear mentor. But most of Andy's mentors weren't members of his family. Many times we take to heart the words of a stranger even if they say the same thing as a parent. And sometimes a mentor appears when you aren't even looking for one. It wasn't until Andy rescued his classmate Lincoln from the pool that he understood what his father was trying to tell him all along: to take his studies seriously and to complete his college education.

"Mentors don't have to be old and senile like me," he joked. "Sometimes you are mentored by people just a few years older."

Pastor Nicholas Hood was twenty-seven when he came to preach at Andy's church. Andy was nineteen and a senior in college. Hood was a significant presence in Andy's life. Hood had just finished Yale Divinity School, and it was likely his first time in New Orleans. Both Hood and his wife stayed at the Youngs' house in New Orleans. He was the first religious person that Andy had met that he could openly admire. Hood was about something. Andy would return home at three or four o'clock in the morning and the young pastor would already be up reading the Bible and working on his sermons. Andy admired Hood's diligence and discipline for studying. He respected Nick for being deeply committed to a cause at a relatively young age. It didn't hurt that Nick also took a personal interest in Andy, and they developed a genuine friendship.

"I'm familiar with many of your male mentors. Did you have any female mentors?" I asked.

"Oh yes, there are things that a woman can teach you that a man can't. I am obviously familiar with the male perspective, so I paid special attention to the advice of female mentors," he said.

Thelma Deselle Smith was probably Andy's closest female mentor while growing up. She was a contemporary and colleague of Andy's mother. She wouldn't let Andy complete a thought without pushing him to think longer. She provoked and challenged him. Andy received poor marks in tenth grade, so she suggested that he study the details of the Marshall Plan for a class project. She urged him to read the newspaper and Wendell Willkie's *One World,* a thin book on postwar peacekeeping.

I was pleasantly surprised that he mentioned Willkie because I had recently finished Charles Peters's *Five Days in Philadelphia,* a chronicle of the 1940 Republican Convention. A former Democrat and businessman, Willkie was the unlikely winner of the Republican nomination for president. He ran against three isolationist Republicans, including Senator Robert A. Taft who had opposed America's entrance into the war against the Nazis up until the Pearl Harbor attack. An interventionist and internationalist, Willkie supported President Franklin D. Roosevelt's decision to aid the British, a principled position that gave President Roosevelt the political cover to do the right thing. Willkie's book and the Marshall Plan captured the imagination of young Andy and shaped his interventionist and internationalist outlook. He learned how nations could help other nations succeed and thrive.

A small suggestion from a mentor turned Andy on to foreign affairs and diplomacy. As a child, he figured out how other parts of his life could inform his views on international relations. At Sunday school, he internalized one of my favorite hymns (and now my BlackBerry ring tone performed by guitarist Howard Fishman), "Down by the Riverside," which includes the lyrics "Going to lay down my sword and shield . . . I ain't gonna study war no more." These nonviolent lyrics probably convinced Andy to find a peaceful way to prevent the bigger boys from picking on him. His elementary school was nicknamed "bucket of blood" because of the many fights that occurred there and in the surrounding neighborhood. Andy was smaller than most of the other students, so he worked diligently to make friends. He gathered a small group of rascals that would rally to his side if anyone picked on him. Andy and his group didn't like the free cafeteria food of Spam and lima beans, so he convinced his friends to pool their money so they could buy some better food across the street.

"The other day, a Georgia State student asked me how I became an ambassador, and I told her I got to be an ambassador in third grade running around with my group of friends," he said.

Mentors can also be complete strangers. His father taught him to be comfortable conversing with strangers. As a kid, Andy would rush through the living room of his house, which doubled as the waiting room for his father's dental practice. His father would make sure that Andy stopped to speak to every person in the waiting room. After all, his father told him, it was because of these people that Andy would be able to attend college.

"So how do you find a mentor?" I asked.

"I think what you've done. You've been a seeker your entire life. I think most people are like that, but they are discouraged and told to shut up. They are told not to ask questions and never to doubt adults. We had affirming mentors who praised our curiosity," he explained.

At an early age, my dad spoke to me about mentors and the importance of speaking to others outside the immediate family for guidance and support. He believes so strongly in mentorship that he made it the central point of his commencement address at the Georgia Institute of Technology (Georgia Tech) in 1993. He told the graduates that mentors can come from all walks of life. They don't have to be well educated or have fancy degrees. The mentor can be a strange uncle, a teacher or even a neighbor. Probably the best reason to have a mentor is that you can learn what not to do. You can learn from someone else's mistakes which can save you anguish and time. Why reinvent life when you can learn from others and stand on their shoulders? He suggested that the graduates look for mentors for different things. My father's business mentors were Atlanta businessman J.B. Fuqua and architect John Portman. His spiritual mentor was his guru in India.

Finally, my father instructed, when you've had some life experiences, you must give back and mentor those around you. When you receive, you must give back. Pat Crecine, the late president of Georgia Tech, commended my father for his speech. Several students and their parents requested copies of his remarks. I was just a boy in the audience but the speech made a lasting impression on me. I sought out many mentors in various fields. I probably wouldn't ask Uncle Andy about the financial projections related to a new business idea because that's not his area of experience or knowledge. I go to different mentors for different things.

"Who mentored your children?" I asked.

"Lisa turned to her math teacher who said that girls who are good in math should attend engineering school, not just boys. Five girls in her class eventually became engineers. The founder of Habitat for Humanity encouraged Paula to volunteer in Uganda where she taught ninety students under trees. Andrea learned from Secretary of Transportation Bill Coleman about how she should prepare for Georgetown Law School. Carolyn was one of Bo's mentors."

The alarm blared again: left main door open.

"Should I put these ribs in the freezer, Andy?" asked Carolyn from the kitchen.

"Yes ma'am." He looked to me, "Did I tell you that Martin loved ribs? He loved the mess."

The alarm blared once more: left main door open.

"So you find your outer voice the same way you find your inner voice. You start where you are," I said.

"Just open your eyes. You have to be proactive and ask those around you for advice. And you're not only mentored by people but by books like *One World*, music, situations like my group of childhood rascals and life."

In Theological Seminary, Andy's Old Testament and New Testament professors were both Quakers. He didn't know much about Quakerism, but he dove into his studies and came across Kelly's *A Testament of Devotion*, a book that helped him discover his inner voice. He never expected to read a book on Quakerism, but it helped to inform his views on faith and spirituality.

Andy grew up listening to blues and jazz music. He liked the erotic lyrics of some songs, many of which angered his mother. She would scratch his recordings because of their vulgar lyrics. Andy told her she could scratch the records but couldn't erase the words from his head. When he became a preacher at a country church in Georgia, he realized that his congregation didn't want to hear a lecture from their new pastor. They didn't even want him to use notes. They wanted him to speak from his heart and touch their souls. He drew on his love of jazz music and in-fused his sermons with lyrical cadence and improvisatory cadenzas. He soloed around the central theme of the sermon, riffing on an odd story or trumpeting a funny fact. Jazz music had taught Andy how to think on his feet and improvise.

"Everything I ever learned, I learned in a jazz band," I said.

"There is something to that," he said.

"I find that the more I plan, the less things work out. I used to think if I studied A, I could get to B. But it's rarely a linear process. Many times a per-son from one part of my life helps me with another part of my life," I said.

"It rarely works in a linear process. And it shouldn't. I used to like that poem 'Invictus' by William Henley, which says, 'I am the master of my fate: I am the captain of my soul.' What utter bunk. I have a problem with that old English way of thinking that I call Rudyard Kipling colonialism. You are deluded to think you are the only one steering the ship," he said. "I would never have thought that I would get to Congress by going to Marion, Alabama, or pastoring a church in Thomasville, Georgia."

"You are comfortable with 'if,'" I said.

"Life is all about 'if.' When you can start applying the lessons you've learned—whether they're from a mentor or music—then you can handle the ifs of life. Otherwise you end up being naked and screwed," he laughed. Andy likes to say that he knows where he is going but doesn't know how he is getting there. I like his philosophy.

Andy's earlier comment about being mentored by situations reminded
me of an episode in my dad's life. My papa grew up in the northwest part
of India which is now considered Punjab. The chief minister (which is
like a governor in the United States) and the deputy chief minister of
Punjab didn't like each other. In 1953, the chief minister, Colonel
Raghbir Singh, had helped some students who were from his district
gain admission into medical college over some students from the
deputy chief's district. The deputy minister was upset with the prefer-
ential treatment and helped to instigate a large student protest. My father was just a bystander, watching the student protests outside Singh's
house. At the tender age of thirteen, he had a reputation for being
bright and politically astute. He had already helped several local politicians in their local elections.

One of Singh's aides recognized my father at the protest and asked
him if he would come inside to meet Singh. My father was speechless.
He admired Singh and was named after him. Singh felt that the strike
was unjust and wanted my father's help to promote peace among the
students. A few days later, my father helped to resolve the dispute in a
peaceful and nonviolent manner. Singh invited my father and his father
to his home to express his gratitude. My grandfather, a mid-level bureaucrat, was surprised to learn that Singh held my father in such high
regard. Singh said to my grandfather, "I have planned your son's future." He said that he would send my father to America to receive a top
education.

Singh said he would help my father get elected from the district of
Samana and make him the youngest minister in the chief minister's cabinet. My father and his family cried with joy. Six months later, they were
in tears of sadness because Singh died from a heart attack and the deputy
chief minister was promoted to chief minister. He canceled my father's
scholarship. My dad felt that his future was in jeopardy and didn't know
what to do. But he slowly and steadily worked toward the goal of studying in America. My grandmother eventually sold her jewelry to buy a

ticket for my father to travel to England to work in a factory and eventually go to America for education. Singh had planted the idea of studying in America in my father. But it was Singh's death that helped my father toughen up and prepare for the arduous path ahead. The situation that my father found himself in taught him lessons and mentored him for later in life. As you meet the challenges in life, you become stronger and that prepares you to face the next challenge.

"As a kid, I can remember you making me feel uncomfortable with your views," I told Andy. "Even now I'm uncomfortable with your views on marriage. Do mentors need to make their pupils feel uncomfortable?"

"It's not required but I strongly suggest it. Growth comes when you struggle. After the mentor makes you feel uncomfortable, he or she should be affirming and point out the good," Andy said.

While growing up, Andy was absorbed with athletics. He ran track and enjoyed the discipline of the sport. He used to run as fast and far as he could, until he was out of breath and his legs started to cramp. He trained his mind to relax to a point so that he could overlook or minimize the discomfort. Just when he felt he was going to give in to the pain, he was able to push himself to new limits because of his relaxed mind.

"Just like in running, you have to seek out uncomfortable situations in life in order to grow. And that can come from a mentor. At the moment of despair and pain, you learn to let go of your feelings and ego, and you begin to see life from a new perspective. You don't see that new perspective until you realize the inadequacy of your present perspective," he explained.

The house phone rang and Andy picked up. It was Gene Duffy, a Democratic operative who wanted to talk about the mayoral election in Atlanta. Andy made the case to Duffy that white people didn't like then–state senator and mayoral contender Kasim Reed because some folks saw him as an "angry black man that doesn't smile." Andy suggested they splice a campaign commercial with notable whites like former Georgia governor Roy Barnes and blacks like Hank Aaron to bolster Reed's chances. After a seventeen-minute conversation, he turned his attention back to me. Clearly, the metal gate in his driveway wasn't going to eliminate all distractions.

Andy had already made mention of his mentor Secretary of State George Shultz in a previous conversation. He elaborated further this time. In 1973, Shultz invited Andy on a trip to the Caribbean and Africa. Bo had just been born, and Andy didn't want to leave his wife and baby to travel to Jamaica. Schultz told Andy that his wife was a nurse and would love having a baby on the trip, so Bo got to go on a congressional junket when he was three months old. Andy was impressed that Shultz's administrative assistant was an African American PhD student. Shultz's generosity and demeanor ran counter to Andy's intellectual prejudices about conservatives.

"How did Shultz make you feel uncomfortable?" I asked.

"Oh, his mere presence made me uncomfortable. He was a contradiction of everything I thought about Republicans. Until Shultz, I thought all Republicans were rich, white and arrogant. Well there is still some truth to that," he joked.

I grew up thinking all Republicans were rich, white and arrogant, an idea I picked up from my dad. He came to New York on January 2, 1960, aboard the *Queen Elizabeth I* in cabin D136, a four-day trip from Southampton, England. He had spent the previous few years working as a common laborer in a Goodyear tire factory. He took an eighteen-hour Greyhound bus trip from New York to Auburn, Alabama, where he attended university. The bus stopped in Atlanta, and my father needed to go to the restroom at the bus station. There were two restrooms, two options: colored and white. Unfamiliar with segregated society and unsure of where to go, he took the third option—he went behind the bus. He was slow to come to grips with southern segregation.

As a teenager, my father had been active in politics in India and then had helped members of Parliament in the United Kingdom in local elections. In the United States, he admired the entrepreneurial spirit of the Republican Party over the apparent socialism found in the Democratic Party. Socialism in India hadn't worked, so my father was keen to get involved in local Republican politics in Alabama. He went to Birmingham to meet with Republican Congressman John Buchanan to see if there were any opportunities to work with the local Republican Party. Buchanan explained that there was no opportunity for my father because he wasn't white or wealthy. The experience obviously disgusted my father and he signed up with the Democrats. (Andy served with Buchanan in Congress and had a more positive experience than my papa.)

My father stayed a Democrat even after he became the head of a large corporation and had gained a comfortable lifestyle. At the suggestion of Guy Vander Jagt, a Republican who had just retired from Congress, my father decided to make peace with Newt Gingrich, our congressman in Georgia's sixth district. He thought Gingrich was like Buchanan—arrogant, white and stupid. Gingrich and my papa met in the early 1990s, and my father was blown away by his intelligence and personal charm. My dad was so surprised, he asked Gingrich, "Are you really as obnoxious as you appear on television or is that just an act?" They both laughed. Before the meeting concluded, my father said he might support him but still thought he had a lousy hairdo which looked like that of Dennis the Menace. A few days later, Gingrich stopped by my dad's office to show him that he had just gotten a new haircut.

At the school I attended, the Lovett School, almost every student was Republican. Some of the jocks wore big belt buckles with the Confederate battle flag, supposedly to honor the heritage of their ancestors who had fought as part of the Confederacy in the Civil War or, as they called it, the War of Northern Aggression. Many couldn't even name a battle that was part of the Civil War or a commanding general. I grew up thinking Republicans were just as Andy and my father said—rich, white and arrogant.

And then James "Jim" Stuart Castiglione Baehr paddled into my life. I met Jim in college and my first impression was that he was another

Republican. He certainly dressed the part with popped collars on his pink Polo shirts and plaid pants. During the summer term of my sophomore year, which is required attendance at Dartmouth College, there was a celebratory weekend organized by students that was affectionately known as Tubestock. All of the fraternities and sororities band together to build rafts and float down the Connecticut River. Girls get to finally show off their bikinis and guys sport swimming trunks, and hopefully the sun shines in this far corner of northern New England. It's the closest thing Dartmouth has to MTV Spring Break, and in recent years it has made Cancun look altogether tame. I was drinking a Keystone Light on my fraternity raft and spotted a canoe in the distance. As it came closer, I saw Jim Baehr holding an oar and sipping from his water bottle. I wanted to jump in the water, flip his boat over and mess up his neatly combed hair for looking so perfectly pretentious. But I thought better of it and got distracted, probably by one of the bikinis.

A couple of weeks later I ran into Jim in my fraternity basement and we struck up a conversation. I came away totally impressed with his commanding knowledge of political history. He didn't come from an old-money oil family and had a self-effacing humor that made me laugh. He wasn't rich or arrogant, but he was still white. We are still close friends and I've learned a great deal from him. He mentored me on conservative political philosophy and helped me to see the intellectual foundation behind his beliefs. I helped to run his unsuccessful campaign for student assembly president. Jim is a contemporary mentor and my George Shultz.

Having listened to my experiences with perspective changes, Andy asked, "Kabir, do you notice a difference between your college friends and those here in Atlanta?"

Again Andy was taking me somewhere I didn't know. I reflected on his comment. Going to good schools and getting a good job, you surely run into people who are very intelligent. With intelligence often comes cynicism. Sometimes those who are overeducated and overpaid feel like only they know the way to success or why things won't work. It has taken me some time to understand that what I most admire in people like Uncle Andy and my Atlanta friends is that they are wise and hardly cynical.

"Folks here in Atlanta may not be as fancy as the bankers and lawyers up in New York, but there is a calmness to folks here," he stated. "They are wise."

My friends and family in Atlanta have mentored me to realize that while I respect intelligence, I don't envy it. Nor am I as infatuated with it as I once was, especially if it comes with cynicism.

"Politics affords a wonderful opportunity for mentorship," Andy said. "Most of life's problems come at you physically and emotionally. In politics, you can learn from mentors and experience how to respond to these problems intellectually and dispassionately."

"Who mentored you in Congress?" I asked.

"I sought out the intellects. I didn't confuse the congressional leadership with the intellects. Carl Albert, who was the speaker of the House, was a compromise candidate. Nobody thinks Harry Reid is an intellectual or leader. In fact, he's quite the opposite. He is there because of seniority and compromise," he explained.

While a rookie in Congress, Andy was invited to join a group of representatives who met on Wednesday mornings at ten o'clock to discuss legislation, which was a huge honor. The group was founded by Dick Bolling of Missouri and included congressional stalwarts like Lee Hamilton from Indiana, Paul Sarbanes of Maryland and Dave Obey from Wisconsin, among others. The group helped to mentor Andy to understand the inner workings of Congress and how to manage a bill. On one occasion, all the members of the group were intellectually against peanut and farm subsidies. As a Georgia congressman and having been a pastor in a rural community where folks depended on peanut subsidies, Andy recognized the importance of the subsidies. He learned how to respond to an emotional problem that confronted the people of his district in an intelligent and dispassionate manner. Outside of the Wednesday morning groups, Andy found mentors in Senators Ted Kennedy, Herman Talmadge and Ed Brooke, who was a skillful mediator in Conference Committees.

Most importantly, he learned legislative tactics that he used to insert a one-line amendment that wasn't even discussed into a mass transit bill. Everyone voted "aye" without deliberation and his amendment became law. The amendment authorized the transit authority to create a private-public planning committee within a half-mile radius of every transit station, which immensely benefited Atlanta and its mass transit system, MARTA. There used to be a poor African American community called Johnson Town where the MARTA Lenox Station is now located. Because of the planning committees, the poor people were given full value for their properties as well as the future value of their properties when MARTA acquired them to build the station. The planning committees helped to secure the money needed to develop Underground Atlanta, the IBM building and several of the properties around Fourteenth Street in midtown Atlanta.

"It was probably my most meaningful contribution while I was in Congress. It was small. The mentoring group taught me that the small things in a bill can make a world of difference," he explained. "I was very proud of my congressional record and contribution to the civil rights movement and that I made the world a better place. But then I realized I had it all wrong."

"Had what wrong?" I asked the contrarian.

"Why would I want to deny my children all the agony and ecstasy of my life? I want my children and you to be in uncomfortable situations like your father and I experienced. Children grow when they are confronted with challenges that push them. Without these challenges they won't find out who they are," he explained. "I was a privileged middle-class child thrown into a poor school with poor students. I was the only one that had a sense of entitlement and privilege. If I didn't learn how to share my resources, I would have had my ass beaten every day. Sharing became a survival skill."

"So you are wishing pain on your children?" I asked.

"No, just uncomfortable situations. That's why I support public schools. The sooner you encounter the problems of the world—poverty, racism and so on—the more prepared you are to deal with them later in life," he said.

"You don't believe in vouchers then?" I asked. We have a habit of sliding into the topics of politics and public policy, but it's usually instructive.

"I did, until I realized the people who supported vouchers were actually trying to destroy public schools. Just as you diversify your investment portfolio, you should diversify your educational portfolio. If you go to a private school, try a public university. Seek mentors who are your intellectual opposites," he said.

I reflected on his remark. I went to a sheltered private school where boys wore ties and girls wore khaki jumpers and skirts, the same school that denied admission to Martin Luther King's children way back when. Thankfully, the admissions policies have changed. I'm unsure about the belt buckles. Should I blame my parents for not putting me in a public school? No. I can't fault them for wanting me to receive a good education. In fact, I am incredibly thankful and have the utmost gratitude. I also credit my school for trying to expose the students to the problems of the world with a mandatory session in which we worked with poor people in downtown Atlanta, albeit for only three or four days. I also don't think we need to make our society deteriorate or make our children return to a pre–civil rights society.

"I'm kind of hungry. How do you feel about Chinese?" he said. We hopped in the car and drove about a mile to Mu Lan, his neighborhood Chinese restaurant. We walked in and heads turned. A professor at Morehouse College cooed at Andy and introduced herself. Andy shook hands with everyone sitting near the cashier. "I learned that from Maynard Jackson and Jimmy Carter," he whispered to me.

He considers both excellent politicians and indirect mentors. They knew how to work a room, which is something that didn't come naturally to Uncle Andy. He doesn't always look you in the eyes when he shakes your hand. When Jimmy Carter was running for governor of Georgia in the 1970s, Andy ran into him at Paschal's. Carter went around to everyone and shook their hands. Before going into the manager's office to pick up a check, he shook the hands of everyone in the kitchen. Carter made every voter feel important.

Years later, when Andy was campaigning for Congress, he went to Paschal's and shook hands with almost everyone. He asked a friend to save him a seat. Andy sat down with his friend and ordered breakfast. After breakfast, the friend asked whether Andy had a problem with him. Andy couldn't believe it since he had spent an hour eating with his friend and paid for the meal, but then Andy realized he never shook hands with his friend. Everyone wants to be touched.

After the greetings in Mu Lan, we sat down to order. Earlier that day, Andy had been to the dentist, so he didn't want to irritate his teeth. He ordered hot and spicy soup, moo shu vegetables and sweet tea. He asked the waiter for extra hot sauce for me. Even though we had changed locations, our topic didn't.

"What uncomfortable things did your mentors point out about you?" I asked.

"Well, probably that I was slothful. I also have a habit of picking my nose, which I've tried to break for seventy years," he said while opening his darkened palms.

"That isn't so bad," I said.

"That's because I learned to recognize my weaknesses and own up to them. I am disarmingly honest, so I don't catch flack for things that I deserve flack for."

As a six-year-old, Andy demonstrated his commitment to the truth. His Aunt May was visiting from California, and she said something that wasn't true. Andy pointed it out and she turned around and slapped him across the face. She warned Andy not to call her a liar. Andy responded that he wasn't calling her a liar, but what she said wasn't true. She slapped him again.

"I like being uncomfortably honest. It provokes people. You get an honest reaction out of them, whether they can handle the truth," he said. His comment oddly reminded me of the 2008 flick *The Dark Knight,* in which the late Heath Ledger stars as the Joker. In one scene, the Joker says to a victim that he likes to cut people on the face with a knife. He can tell who is a coward and who is courageous. It's a rather sick comparison, I know, but you can certainly learn about people and their characters in uncomfortable situations.

If mentors are supposed to make you feel uncomfortable, I felt there was no better moment to ask, "What are my flaws or vulnerabilities?"

He paused for a moment and said, "Ambition." It wasn't the first time I had heard that. "I don't know any other young person quite like you. You've accomplished so much at a young age, but you must understand the difference between ambition and achievement," he said.

"Ambition sounds self-seeking. It's self-promotional," I responded.

"Yes, that's correct. Our conversations are giving you a broader perspective on achievement. You don't have to be a managing director at an investment bank by the time you are thirty or have started a Fortune 500 company," he said. He pointed out that the head of a nonprofit organization, someone he works with, has had difficulty shedding the crutch of self-promotion.

"It's difficult for him to shake because he is a street hustler and has jostled his way to some success, but he has still done a lot of good. Al Sharpton is another self-promoter who grew up in the shadow of the civil rights movement and never understood a damn thing about the movement. The movement wasn't about shining the light on yourself," he said. It's about finding systematic ways of changing social injustices. "Al is great at focusing on injustice, but we disagree on reconciliation as a path to redemption."

"And what's achievement?" I asked.

"Achievement is selflessness," he replied. "I'm sure you know this be-cause of your deep commitment to service in New Orleans and elsewhere." We had talked about service and humility many times before. His constant reminder to give other people credit is burned into my brain. He thinks Jimmy Williams, the former head of SunTrust Bank, exemplifies selfless and silent leadership. Williams was the power behind the throne in Atlanta for many years, and almost nobody knew his name, yet he was able to bring about many positive changes in the city.

I'm no saint, but I do try to seize service opportunities. Maybe I'm just feeling guilty because I work at an investment bank. My mom, who started and runs a foundation that spotlights university students engaged in community service around the world, taught me that real service, real charity begins at home—take out the trash, be respectful to your parents and siblings, look out for your friends. Andy worked as a junior coun-selor at the YMCA and made sure to make time for the kids who didn't fit in. When you do the small personal acts of service, you understand the true meaning of achievement.

"Achievement is being committed to others and to something that is greater than yourself," Andy explained. "You can never self-promote yourself into any significant position. It happens to you. When you've touched enough people, you will be called to a position of significance."

Andy has been a reluctant warrior his entire life. He didn't aim to work directly with Dr. King. He didn't actively push to be considered for Congress or mayor. He didn't lobby to be appointed United Nations am-bassador. Others came to him and convinced him. At times, Andy admits, perhaps his reluctance to run was cowardice. He was comfortable staying behind the curtain. There was real influence in working behind the scenes with Dr. King and President Carter, and even in courting the members of the International Olympic Committee. He was a very successful number two or alter ego. One could argue that the civil rights halo of working with Dr. King made Andy an automatic candidate for almost any open posi-tion. By thinking of himself as a good number two, others eventually considered him a great number one. I often argue with him that for the rest of us without halos, there is something to be said for hustle and pluck.

Listening to others (even your mentors) doesn't always work out perfectly. After he was mayor and after working for my papa, he decided to run for governor of Georgia in 1990. Andy blames his decision on the fact that he was trying to satisfy other people who were pressuring him to run. My father, however, urged Andy not to run and wrote him a letter on July 19, 1990, in which he paraphrased the Old Testament—without a vision, the people will perish. He felt Andy's campaign was without vision and unity but he supported him nonetheless.

John Ehrlichman, a senior domestic policy advisor to President Richard Nixon (and who went to jail for Watergate) also worked for my father and echoed my dad's sentiments about the gubernatorial campaign: "Andy tends to come across rather bland... what is his great vision for Georgia?"[2] Ehrlichman thought Andy should take a tougher stand against the favorite, Zell Miller, who, he thought, came across as a "prototypical old-time, white southern politician with a Jim Wright/R. Nixon smile, false teeth and a canned speech about 'issues.'" Zell Miller won the race, but Andy's run pressured Miller to commit to allocating the money raised from the proposed Georgia Lottery to education and the HOPE Scholarship.

While in college, I received a call from Sally Rosser, a fiery and intelligent activist in the Democratic Party of Georgia. She informed me that Andy was considering a run for the Senate. I designed his campaign Web site, complete with the requisite red, white and blue color scheme. A few weeks later, however, Uncle Andy held a press conference to announce that he would not run for Senate and wanted to spend time with his family—a textbook reason. After the press conference he told me, "Honestly, I didn't want to be a rookie senator, the lowest member on the totem pole having to please the other ninety-nine egomaniacs." He remembered his experience running for governor and didn't want to run for an office if his heart wasn't in it. He thinks many politicians fall into this trap of listening to what others say. He believes Ted Kennedy probably ran for president against the incumbent Jimmy Carter to please people around him before he was ready.

Your inner voice can also be wrong. A lawyer ran for mayor of a large city and spent almost $200,000 of his own money. He told Uncle Andy that it was God's calling for him to run for mayor.

"I get scared when people say they have a calling from God and no other reasons. That's when you need mentors more than ever. You need to balance God's supposed voice with others," he said. His friend is an Ivy Leaguer and Rhodes Scholar who, Andy thinks, feels a sense of entitlement. "I'm glad you didn't get the Rhodes Scholarship," Andy remarked. It's still a sore spot for me; I reached the final stage but am, alas, a Rhodes reject.

"How do you balance the outer voice and inner voice?" I asked. "After you seek counsel, how do you know what to do?"

"Good leaders know how to balance the two. How did you learn how to solo on the bass?" he replied. I don't like questions as answers but I played along as I do with the game show *Jeopardy.*

In order to develop my soloing technique and ideas, I listened to recordings of several bass players from all genres. From Flea, the bassist with the Red Hot Chili Peppers, I learned how to play punchy phrases. I tried to emulate the bowings of classical bassist Gary Karr and the slapping of Victor Wooten. I admired and learned from bass players Christian McBride, Jaco Pastorius, Avishai Cohen, Ray Brown and Scott LaFaro. I borrowed ideas from other instrumentalists like Miles Davis, Sonny Rollins and Oscar Peterson, among others. I don't sound exactly like any of these masters—far from it. My style was forged by learning from these musicians and blending their ideas, as well as adding my own. I listened to everyone else in order to learn. I sought an outer voice. But when I'm standing on the stage performing for an audience and my turn comes to solo, I'm not thinking about my outer voice. I simply play what comes from within. I play what comes from my heart.

I'm developing my investment style in the same way. I read and study the master money managers like George Soros, Boone Pickens,

Warren Buffett and Julian Robertson, among others. It's still a work in progress and I'm not a natural, but I hope to forge my own unique investing style and approach. From studying and seeking an outer voice, I will gain more confidence in creating an inner voice.

"When it comes down to it, your inner voice triumphs. You can seek all the advice and counsel from mentors, but then you need to evaluate it on its own merit." Growing up, I used to ape Andy's advice. He was my wise ventriloquist. But over the years, I gained my own voice. I formed my own opinions.

"You need to have integrity and stay true to yourself just like John Lewis," he said.

"What about John Lewis?" I asked.

"I don't think he's done that many noteworthy things in Congress, but he gets by on integrity, not intelligence. And that is very respectable. He listens to his inner voice. Everyone respects his moral compass. You could get by on a lot worse," he replied.

"Isn't it tough to say no and disagree with your mentors?"

"It can be. I believe in the 'Holy No.' Learning how to say no can save you headaches down the road. I gave the Holy No when deciding to run for the Senate. Your mentors sometimes see you as the fulfillment of their dreams and images, so you need to say no to them at times."

I said, "There is the Holy No and the Hell Yes. If you are unsure about something, then it's probably a Holy No. But if you feel deep within that you must do something, then it is a Hell Yes."

"You've got it, grasshopper," he laughed.

"Huh?"

"You know those kung fu movies in which they call the pupil the grasshopper?" he asked.

I laughed. Maybe the Chinese food was getting to him.

AFTERWORD

This has been fun! Challenging, risky, dangerous but not harmful. Indeed, as I've said many times before, "there can be no democracy without truth. There can be no truth without controversy, there can be no change without freedom. Without freedom there can be no progress." That's life!

But we've barely scratched the surface. We've largely engaged in "boy talk." This is not the way I'd talk to Kabir's sister, Kashi, or my granddaughters Taylor, Lena, Abigail. My daughters always reminded me that I could not think for them. Both Jean, my wife of forty years, and Carolyn, whom I married fourteen years ago after Jean's passage to Glory, always reminded me that whatever my views of life are in any situation, there is a woman's view that must be heard and respected.

I once expressed to Oprah Winfrey that I wished that my granddaughters could talk with her in the same manner I've tried to share my life with Kabir. Wonderful though that may be, we never have enough time with important people. What we do find all around us is great moments with wonderful people.

Mentors, elders, wise counselors are everywhere. You've just got to open your eyes and your mind to receive their wisdom. They need not be famous or even successful. Many of my mentors have little formal education, power or money. What they possess is the wisdom of survivors.

Most young people are surrounded by folks who truly love them and want to help them develop. But there is a rebellious instinct that makes you resist those closest to you, and I'm not sure that's all bad. The search for one's self is a search for both identity and meaning. It is the root of all spirituality, and you can't find it. It must find you.

"Wait on the Lord and be of good courage" are lyrics from a gospel hymn based on the prophet Isaiah. "They that wait upon the Lord shall renew their strength. They should mount up with wings like eagles. They will run and not get weary. They will walk and not faint. Wait on the Lord" (Isaiah 40:31). I know that sounds passive, but in the faith of Abraham, "go into a land that you know not." For Moses, it's wandering in the wilderness in search of the Promised Land. But Jesus says that the "kingdom of God is within you" or "in the midst of you." So you find your meaning, identity and purpose each day, one day at a time. And the Spirit, Energy and Creator is present in everything you do, every person you meet and everything you create.

Your life is lived, your race run, your achievements crowned. So long as it is a loving, creating and forgiving life, showing great tolerance and forbearance of others who might disagree.

I know this is getting too religious. But it's the religious, spiritual, transcendent Being in you that is seeking existence or a new birth. When you don't reach a certain balance in mind, body and spirit, you get the tormented genius of a Michael Jackson or Tiger Woods.

St. Augustine, one of the church's founding fathers, is quoted as saying in his youth, "Save me, dear lord, but not right now." Later he confessed, "Thou has made us for Thyself. And our hearts are restless until we find our Peace in Thee."

Bill Gates and Bill Clinton learned that "one must lose one's life in order to find it." Billions of dollars and the power of the presidency could not bring the peace that comes from serving the "least of these, my brethren," God's children.

Jimmy Carter is one of the few people I've known who seems to have achieved this balance and discipline early in life. The farm, the church, a loving, free-spirited mother, the Naval Academy and a wonderful wife—

all seemed to conspire to create a man too good to be true, and so we rejected his leadership, as we rejected Thomas Jefferson for almost a century and Abraham Lincoln too.

Franklin Roosevelt's reform of laissez-faire capitalism in the 1930s was rejected by Reaganism (and Milton Friedman's economic theories) in the 1980s. And we're back in the same type of recession that Roosevelt tried to save us from. But this is a political and economic view. Your struggle and mine must be intensely personal. We can't retreat from the world's challenges. We must embrace them.

In 1951, the year of my graduation from Howard University, I was at the lowest point of my existence. My parents were bursting with pride, though I received no special honors. I realize now that their joy was in achieving their goal to give me a college degree and a good education. My despair was that though I received the degree, thereby making them proud, only I knew how much I didn't know and how empty my life really was at that point. Now I know that is exactly why they call it commencement. It's the beginning of one's life and the end of parental responsibility.

Little did I realize that my future was practically defined. In the midst of my anxiety, I overheard Dr. Chester Pierce, at that time a resident in psychiatry, talking to my father: "He has no choice, he will be a leader. In life's pyramid, there are so many people at the bottom end that he will either offer them hope and leadership or they will tear him down to their level or destroy him. Don't worry. You've raised a survivor. And in this world that means Leader."

It may have comforted by parents but it scared the hell out of me. Realistically now, as well as in 1951, the American high school or college graduate is already in the top percentile of the global population pyramid.

Life is a battle of inches. You're not changing the world—revolution is always disruptive—you're growing a new world. When I was at the

United Nations, the seven chiefs of Mohawk Nation in Upstate New York came to visit me. They made only one request, that I realize that my decisions should be made for "seven generations not yet borne." My decisions would affect several generations yet to come. The issues of environmental preservation, ending poverty, feeding the planet, healing the sick, projecting and financing a peaceful and prosperous future are your life-long agenda.

Writing this on New Year's Day 2010, it's hard not to use sports imagery. Life is a team sport: Pick your team carefully, balancing strengths and weaknesses. You won't score on every play, but be prepared to get up quickly after you are knocked down.

The game never ends. Life is struggle. Struggle keeps you strong. Believe that this day's dreams will be tomorrow's reality. So take it one day at a time and always remember that the joy is in the building, financing and getting your dreams to pay off in a dynamic marketplace where dreams and needs combine to create a stable, prosperous and peaceful order.

Peace and Blessings,
Uncle Andy

ACKNOWLEDGMENTS

I sure as heck made a lot of friends while writing this book. By friends I don't mean the type that you add to Facebook and never talk to again. Putting together a manuscript in just over a hundred days means that a lot of things must go right, and it really wouldn't have been possible without the contributions of so many dear friends.

Roll the credits. Our wonderful literary agent, Paul Bresnick, was the alchemist who made this book happen. Andy and I wouldn't have met the wonderful team at Palgrave Macmillan without him. We call them "the Palgravians," a team of top-notch professionals. It's been a joy to work with our editor, Alessandra Bastagli, who is a literary visionary. Thankfully Jake Klisivitch believed in us and didn't laugh when he first saw our work. Thanks, Alan Bradshaw, for being a generous bricklayer, and building this book page by page. I hope I didn't annoy Colleen Lawrie with my dizzying number of emails, but she took it in stride and was a graceful and immense help. Roberta Scheer brilliantly copyedited the work and eradicated typos. We are very grateful to Christine Catarino and Courtney Allison who combined to promote and market the book.

With Andy comes a dedicated group of colleagues, friends and family members who strengthened the work, like Patra Marsden, Layfayette Wilder, Bo Young and especially Uncle Andy's kind, gracious and helpful daughter Andrea. She is an immaculate example of generosity and author of *Life Lessons My Mother Taught Me*. Andy's daughter Paula Young Shelton wrote a superb children's book, *Child of the Civil Rights Movement* (especially the part where she compares the civil rights leaders to musical instruments to describe their personalites). I want to personally thank C.B. Hackworth for challenging me and making this book stronger.

A special thanks to those who read early versions of the work, such as Christian Littlejohn and fountainhead Benjamin Phillips. Allan Carl Jackson III was so helpful I'm thinking about naming my firstborn "the fourth" in his honor. Creative genius Sindhya Valloppillil shared astute and vital comments. Others who contributed to the project include Hannah Russin, Noah Riner, Geoff Schwarten, Katie Clark, John Probst, Chirag Garg, Matt Kibble, Surajit Sen Gupta, Daniel Shin, Xavier Helgesen, David Murphy, Peter Israel, Jeff Hoffman, David Gardner, Gretchen Young (you rock!), Nick Baum, Adam Starr, Ron Grant, Clarine Nardi Riddle, Nadine Hack, Daniel Regenstein, Jerry Dunfey, Todd Smith, Clayton Smith, Christina

Yu, Mollie Petersen, Sabrina Singh, Vivek Sodera, Kristin Brzoznowski, Jon Bishke, Amir Tehrani, Chavonne Hughes, Sally & Paul Rosser, Robin Yang, Grady Hannah, Francisco Drojohowski, Alex Zivic, Dick Parsons, Ron Markham and Dhruv Parekh. Curly haired Ariana Pieper must have read the book a dozen times and never complained. I learned from her earnest comments and wisdom: thank you. My partner in crime Brent Reidy helped me survive fall 2009 with his compassion and support, as did Anthony Defeo. Anthony's talented mother Lisa Miller did the Lord's work and photographed me (I don't want to know if she Photoshopped my face!).

A special thanks to my colleagues who contributed—Aroon Balani, Nick Shevloff, Kevin Sun (who bolstered the chapter on macroeconomics), Emily Portney, Carlos Hernandez, Dominic Myers and especially my dear friend and maven Slavka Glaser. Thank you to Ana Marie Coronel, Amitabh Desai, Joe DeSantis, President Bill Clinton, Amir Dossal, Simon Hammerstein, Tamie Peters, Dr. Joyce Williams (big, big thanks!), Archbishop Desmond Tutu, Vernon Jordan and Jeannie Adashek.

I'm eternally grateful to the great Douglas Brinkley for helping me from the very beginning to the end. Doug, I look up to and admire you. Almost everyone knows you are a mastermind historian, but I want everyone to know what a caring, thoughtful and bighearted person you are (as is your lovely wife Anne). One conversation with Doug makes me think for the next three weeks—he's that good of a teacher.

My deepest and sincerest thanks to the beautiful, elegant and truly spectacular Carolyn Young. She welcomed me into her home, spent time with me, advised and counseled me. I now know why she won the best teacher of the year award while she was a school teacher. Though I was never in Carolyn's class, I am blessed to consider her a teacher.

My family is not your typical family. My parents Raghbir and Surishtha go above and well beyond, making sure my sister Kashi and I are well and thriving. My sister helped by transcribing interviews when I broke my wrist (it still hurts!). Kashi, I am proud to be your annoying little brother. And Mom and Dad, thank you for just being you. Now that I'm making some money, dinner at the Olive Garden on me!

What do you say to someone whom you lionize and call your Godfather and intellectual giant? Well, you write an 80,000-word manuscript in his honor for starters. Uncle Andy, you have helped and shaped me more than you know. It's been a celestial experience working with and learning from you. While the next chapters of our conversations may not be published for the world to read, they will be indelibly etched in my heart and soul.

NOTES

CHAPTER 1

1. Steve Jobs, Commencement Lecture, Stanford University, June 12, 2005.
2. Thomas Kelly, *A Testament of Devotion* (New York: Harper & Bros., 1941), 29.
3. Luke 17:5, King James Bible (Nashville: Thomas Nelson, 1988).
4. Matthew 6:34, King James Bible.
5. Benjamin Mays, *Dr. Benjamin Mays Speaks: Representative Speeches of a Great American Orator,* ed. Freddie Colston (Lanham, MD: University Press of America, 2002), 257.

CHAPTER 2

1. Laurence Chang, *Wisdom for the Soul* (Washington, DC: Gnosophia, 2006), 45.
2. Alyssa Abkowitz, "How LinkedIn's Founder Got Started," August 25, 2009. http://money.cnn.com/2009/08/24/technology/linkedin_reid_hoffman.fortune/index .htm.
3. Fisk was created in 1866, after the Civil War, to educate free blacks. It was a strong center of black education and achievement. Other notable graduates include W.E.B. Du Bois; Colin Powell's wife, Alma; and former Washington, DC, mayor Marion Barry.
4. Charles M. Payne, *I've Got the Light of Freedom: The Organizing Tradition and the Mississippi Freedom Struggle* (Berkeley and Los Angeles: University of California Press, 2007), 180.

CHAPTER 3

1. Marc McCutcheon, *Roget's Super Thesaurus* (Cincinnati: Writer's Digest Books, 2004), 553. Professor Levenstein was a statistician and professor of business administration at Baruch College.
2. Martin Luther King, *A Testament of Hope: The Essential Writings and Speeches of Martin Luther King, Jr.,* ed. James Melvin Washington (New York: HarperCollins, 1991), 217.
3. George Lakoff, *Moral Politics* (Chicago: University of Chicago Press, 2002), 55.
4. The speech inspired *Creative Capitalism,* an edited collection of articles that debate the merits of Gates's views: Michael Kinsley, ed., *Creative Capitalism* (New York: Simon & Schuster, 2008).
5. Thomas Friedman, "Foreign Affairs Big Mac I," *New York Times,* December 8, 1996. http://www.nytimes.com/1996/12/08/opinion/foreign-affairs-big-mac-i.html? pagewanted=1.

CHAPTER 4

1. Abraham Joshua Heschel, *To Grow in Wisdom: An Anthology of Abraham Joshua Heschel,* ed. Jacob Neusner and Noam M.M. Neusner (Lanham, MD: Madison Books, 1990), 166.
2. The actual poem can be found in William Butler Yeats, *The Winding Stair and Other Poems* (Whitefish, MT: Kessinger Publishing, 2004).

3. For further reading, see C. Vann Woodward, *The Strange Career of Jim Crow* (New York: Oxford University Press, 1974).
4. Jim Crow laws came about because of the Compromise of 1877, also known as the Hayes-Tilden Compromise. The 1876 US presidential election between Republican Rutherford B. Hayes and Democrat Samuel Tilden ended in a stalemate. Louisiana, Florida and South Carolina agreed to support Hayes and protect the rights of blacks if he withdrew federal troops from the South, a move that effectively ended Reconstruction and ushered in a new era of beleaguered race relations.
5. Jack Bass and Walter De Vries, *The Transformation of Southern Politics* (Athens: University of Georgia Press, 1995), 47.
6. Andrew Young, *A Way Out of No Way* (Nashville: Thomas Nelson, 1996), 80.
7. Samuel Eagle Forman, *The Life and Writings of Thomas Jefferson* (Brooklyn: Bowen-Merrill, 1900), 302.

CHAPTER 5

1. Elizabeth Basset, *Love Is My Meaning* (Atlanta: John Knox Press, 1974), 263.
2. Kahlil Gibran, *The Kahlil Gibran Reader* (New York: Citadel Press, 2006), 38.
3. M.K. Gandhi, *The Way to God* (Berkeley: Berkeley Hills Books, 1999), 47.
4. Dan Kimball, *They Like Jesus but Not the Church* (Grand Rapids, MI: Zondervan, 2007), 37.
5. Christian Smith with Patricia Snell, *Souls in Transition* (New York: Oxford University Press, 2009), 112.

CHAPTER 6

1. Henry David Thoreau, *Letters to a Spiritual Seeker* (New York: W.W. Norton, 2004), 71.
2. Kahlil Gibran, *The Prophet* (Ware, UK: Wordsworth Editions, 1952), 7.
3. Andrew Young, *An Easy Burden* (New York: HarperCollins, 1996), 351.

CHAPTER 7

1. Sharon Basco, "Dissent in Pursuit of Equality, Life, Liberty and Happiness: An Interview with Historian Howard Zinn," TomPaine.com, July 3, 2002. http://www.tompaine.com/Archive/scontent/5908.html.
2. Indonesia has the world's largest Muslim population.
3. Olujimi Ogunlana, "Conversation with Andrew Young," *Worldview Magazine* 22, no. 11 (November 1979). http://worldview.cceia.org/archive/worldview/1979/11/3293.html/_res/id=sa_File1/v22_i011_a002.pdf.
4. Carl von Clausewitz, *On War* (London: K. Paul, Trench, Trübner & Co., 1908), 23.

CHAPTER 8

1. George Hathaway, *Leadership Secrets from the Executive Office* (New York: MJF Books, 2004), 66.
2. Peter Karoff and Jane Maddox, *The World We Want* (Lanham, MD: Rowman Alta-Mira, 2007), 143.

3. 　Martin Luther King Jr., *The Autobiography of Martin Luther King, Jr.,* ed. Clayborne Carson (New York: Warner Books, 2001), 134.

4. 　Barack Obama, "Statement by President Obama on Mahatma Gandhi's Birth Anniversary," October 1, 2009. http://www.whitehouse.gov/the_press_office/Statement-by-the-President-on-Mahatma-Gandhis-Birth-Anniversary/.

5. 　Swaminathan S. Anklesaria Aiyar, "Socialism Kills: The Human Cost of Delayed Economic Reform in India," Center for Global Liberty & Prosperity, October 21, 2009. http://www.cato.org/pubs/dbp/dbp4.pdf.

6. 　Andrew Young, *A Way Out of No Way* (Nashville: Thomas Nelson, 1994), 93.

7. 　Indira Gandhi, *Indira Gandhi Speaks on Democracy, Socialism, and Third World Non-alignment* (New York: Taplinger Publishing, 1975), 151. Her comments are also footage in the documentary *In the Footsteps of Gandhi,* produced by Andrew Young.

8. 　Kabir Sehgal, *Jazzocracy: Jazz, Democracy and the Creation of a New American Mythology* (Mishawaka, IN: Better World Books, 2008).

9. 　Thomas Friedman, *The NewsHour with Jim Lehrer,* March 9, 2004. http://www.pbs.org/newshour/bb/asia/jan-june04/friedman_03-09.html.

10. 　Francis Fukuyama, *The End of History and the Last Man* (New York: Free Press, 1992), 16.

11. 　Mahatma Gandhi, *Gandhi: An Autobiography* (Boston: Beacon Press, 1957), 89.

CHAPTER 9

1. 　Jashan P. Vaswani, *Short Sketches of Saints Known and Unknown* (New Delhi: Sterling Publishers, 2008), 43.

2. 　John Ehrlichman, private correspondence to R.K. Sehgal.

INDEX